Quantitative Easing and Tightening

Quantitative easing (QE) is a relatively new form of monetary policy whereby a central bank buys up government bonds and other financial assets to stimulate economic activity. It came to prominence in the aftermath of the Global Financial Crisis of 2007–11 when standard monetary policy tools were unavailable to central banks due to low inflation levels. Quantitative tightening (QT) is the opposite, whereby central banks sell off bonds and assets to reduce the size of their balance sheets. The conference 'Quantitative Easing and Tightening', held at the National Institute of Economic and Social Research in September 2024, brought together leading academics and practitioners to assess the legacy of quantitative easing and look at where new quantitative tightening measures may take us. It examined three of the most important actors in the QE/QT story – the Bank of England, the European Central Bank and the US Federal Reserve – to provide an overview of the effectiveness, governance and fiscal costs of quantitative easing and tightening. This volume is based on the work presented at the conference.

FRANCIS BREEDON is a professor of economics in the School of Economics and Finance at Queen Mary University London.

Macroeconomic Policy Making

Series editors:

Professor JAGJIT CHADHA NIESR University of Cambridge

Professor SEAN HOLLY University of Cambridge

The 2007–10 financial crisis has asked some very hard questions of modern macroeconomics. The consensus that grew up during 'the Great Moderation' has proved to be an incomplete explanation of how to conduct monetary policy in the face of financial shocks. This series brings together leading macroeconomic researchers and central bank economists to analyse the tools and methods necessary to meet the challenges of the post-financial crisis world.

Published titles:

Chadha and Holly, *Interest Rates, Prices and Liquidity: Lessons from the Financial Crisis*

Coffman, Leonard and Neal, *Questioning Credible Commitment: Perspectives on the Rise of Financial Capitalism*

Chadha, Durré, Joyce and Sarno, *Developments in Macro-Finance Yield Curve Modelling*

Chadha et al., *The UK Economy in the Long Expansion and Its Aftermath*

Mizen, Rubio and Turner, *Macroprudential Policy and Practice*

Holly, McMahon, Millard and Watson, *Reflections on Monetary Policy after 25 years of the MPC*

Quantitative Easing and Tightening

Lessons after the Financial Crisis

Edited by
FRANCIS BREEDON
Queen Mary University of London

CAMBRIDGE
UNIVERSITY PRESS

CAMBRIDGE
UNIVERSITY PRESS

Shaftesbury Road, Cambridge CB2 8EA, United Kingdom

One Liberty Plaza, 20th Floor, New York, NY 10006, USA

477 Williamstown Road, Port Melbourne, VIC 3207, Australia

314–321, 3rd Floor, Plot 3, Splendor Forum, Jasola District Centre, New Delhi – 110025, India

Cambridge University Press is part of Cambridge University Press & Assessment, a department of the University of Cambridge.

We share the University's mission to contribute to society through the pursuit of education, learning and research at the highest international levels of excellence.

www.cambridge.org
Information on this title: www.cambridge.org/9781009742320

DOI: 10.1017/9781009742306

When citing this work, please include a reference to the DOI 10.1017/9781009742306

First published 2026

A catalogue record for this publication is available from the British Library

A Cataloging-in-Publication data record for this book is available from the Library of Congress

ISBN 978-1-009-74232-0 Hardback

ISBN 978-1-009-74229-0 Paperback

Contents

Figures

Tables

Contributors

William Allen (National Institute of Economic and Social Research)

Richard Barwell (BNP Paribas Asset Management)

Nina Boyarchenko (Federal Reserve Bank of New York)

Francis Breedon (Queen Mary University of London)

Filippo Busetto (Bank of England)

Jagjit Chadha (National Institute of Economic and Social Research)

Matthieu Chavaz (Bank of England)

Maren Froemel (Bank of England)

Michael Joyce (Bank of England)

Iryna Kaminska (Bank of England)

Simon Lloyd (Bank of England and Centre for Macroeconomics)

Jack Meaning (Barclays)

Daniel Ostry (Bank of England and Centre for Macroeconomics)

Or Shachar (Federal Reserve Bank of New York)

Tomasz Wieladek (T. Rowe Price)

Jack Worlidge (Bank of England)

Tim Young (National Institute of Economic and Social Research)

Foreword

THE RT HON. LORD TYRIE

Immediately after the financial crisis, the banking system was largely disabled. Panic had gripped the markets. Quantitative easing (QE) was introduced in 2009 as an emergency response by the Bank of England and other central banks. In the real economy there was cause for grave concern: even good borrowers were unable to get credit. Inventories were slashed and output fell sharply, awaiting a recovery of demand. There was a serious risk of economic depression. Policy options appeared to be limited. Short-term interest rates had already been reduced as far as possible. But further action was essential. Quantitative easing had been used recently in Japan and, after the financial crisis, an international central bank consensus in favour of QE quickly developed.

Prompt action, both in the US and internationally, was greatly facilitated by the chairman of the Federal Reserve, Ben Bernanke. He appreciated the scale of the crisis better than most, partly as a consequence of having studied the Great Crash as an academic.

Did it work well? Only up to a point, Lord Copper. It is generally agreed – by central bankers, politicians, economists and others – that QE made an important contribution to staving off disaster and restoring confidence, and also facilitated the early stages of the economic recovery. But there is much less agreement that the application of QE by the UK authorities later in the 2010s and during the Covid-19 pandemic had beneficial effects. Some of the evidence suggests otherwise. Among other things, large losses to the exchequer have been racked up. Asset price inflation has brought with it unwelcome distributional consequences too. Even to those who thought that further asset purchases were necessary, their scale seemed larger than needed.

The Treasury Select Committee, which I chaired between 2010 and 2017, inquired closely into QE as part of its oversight of the Bank of England. It was apparent at the time that the Bank of England didn't fully grasp its implications. These include the large losses and unwelcome distributional effects mentioned earlier. Rachel Reeves is still grappling with the consequences for fiscal policy. The Committee also pressed the Bank to reveal its thinking about the unwinding of QE. It had to wait a long time for an answer. Arguably, some earlier unwinding would have reduced the financial risks of the programme and might have curtailed the likely eventual losses. Likewise, the adverse distributional consequences would probably have been smaller.

The Committee sought clarity about monetary policy, in particular about the financial risks of QE and the pressures on commercial banks to restrain lending during the recession, both of which were being aggravated by capital and liquidity regulation.

When, after the 2010 election, the Committee was reconstituted, it discussed whether to launch a major inquiry into the conduct of the Bank, prior to and during the handling of the crash. Needless to say, the then governor of the Bank was deeply concerned by such an idea! So was George Osborne, when he learnt of it. They argued that the post-crash rescue operation was still continuing and was complicated by the Eurozone crisis. I was told, and passed on to the Committee their view, that a major parliamentary investigation would deflect the attention of the key people needed to handle those problems, not least the governor and his immediate subordinates. The Committee went ahead with a somewhat smaller inquiry into Bank conduct, leaving itself more room for other urgent work. Had it investigated the Bank's performance in even greater depth, among other things, it would have exposed the hierarchical and centralised nature of Bank decision making at that time ('a monarchy', as someone close to events put it) and probably some poor governance ('we made it up as we went along'). The Bank's working methods left it ill-prepared to respond to the crash. The Committee would, no doubt, have proposed remedies, with better subsequent decision-making on QE, among other things, a plausible consequence.

Be that as it may, looking back over the QE programme as a whole, a number of questions now merit further investigation. For example in 2012, when the QE operations had produced a substantial positive cash flow, it was decided to transfer the surplus cash from the Bank of England to the Treasury. The Chancellor of the Exchequer, George Osborne, promptly spent it. That decision was widely questioned at the time, including by the Treasury Select Committee. As the sceptics feared – and I was one of them – the cash flow has turned negative with a vengeance. The 2012 decision had left no reserves available to soften the blow. Among the objectives of government debt management policy is the containment of risk, including exchequer risk.[1] But when the surplus funds were there, no provisions for these future risks seem to have been considered. Was the objective of risk mitigation simply ignored? What advice was offered to the Chancellor by officials about it? Not much is known about these issues, even at this distance. It should be.

The largest chunk of QE – more than half of the total over the whole period from 2009 – occurred after the outbreak of Covid-19 in March 2020 and the evaporation of liquidity which had made the gilt-edged market dysfunctional. Plainly something had to be done to restore the gilt market to health. But, as action taken in the wake of the Truss–Kwarteng episode in the autumn of 2022 has demonstrated, being a market-maker of last resort in a dysfunctional gilt market can be accomplished with much smaller purchases. The scale of QE in 2020–21 was such that, in effect, the Covid-19 budget deficit was very largely financed by short-term borrowing from commercial banks. But the pandemic was a rare event, for which long-term financing might have been more appropriate. Why was so much QE undertaken? Would a smaller amount have done the job?

Should QE be classified as monetary policy, debt management policy or fiscal policy? Is it a matter for the Treasury or the Bank of England? Has QE altered the public perception, or the reality, of the Bank's independence?

On the first question, it seems blindingly obvious that it is all three; on the second, that it is a matter for both. Yet the Treasury persist in arguing that it is monetary policy, and therefore, a matter for the Bank of England and its Monetary Policy Committee to handle, subject to approval of specific applications of QE by the Chancellor. Maintaining this fiction is in no one's interest. Quantitative easing has drastically shortened the maturity of the public sector's debt. This has had massive implications for debt management, as the Office for Budget Responsibility has frequently explained. The Treasury has indemnified the Bank against losses incurred by QE. These are likely

[1] The Debt Management Office's objective is 'to minimise, over the long term, the cost of meeting the government's financing needs, taking into account risk, while ensuring that debt management policy is consistent with the aims of monetary policy'.

to be very large. Fiscal policy – the Treasury's bread and butter, and the stuff of politics – is therefore manifestly in play.

The Treasury's position on this has been pernicious for a long time. It is not just that the Treasury is articulating a line of argument with a gaping hole in the middle. It is that, by doing so, the Treasury exposes the lack of clarity about the Bank's independence that QE has created.

Powerful reasons can be deployed in favour of the Bank remaining independent in its conduct of monetary policy. It is widely held to assist the maintenance of price stability. And it probably lowers the cost of servicing the debt. But, when it comes to implementing QE, protecting that independence requires far greater transparency about the degree of Treasury involvement in the Bank's decisions than is currently evident. The government has finally published – a full sixteen years after it was agreed – at least a redacted version of the deed of the Treasury's indemnity to the Bank, but only after repeated requests for its publication by me, among many others. That is scarcely transparency in action. It would be helpful to bring into the public domain both the loan agreement between the Bank of England and the Asset Purchase Facility (the subsidiary of the Bank in which the gilts bought in the QE programme are held), and the related clauses of the indemnity which have been redacted. It would also be helpful to bring into the public domain the record of the exchanges – both formal and informal – which must have taken place between the Bank and the Treasury on each occasion the QE was deployed. Perhaps very little remains tucked away from view; all the more reason to bolster the Bank's independence by publishing the relevant exchanges.

The losses made by the QE programme are likely to be colossal. Is there any way in which the burden on taxpayers can be alleviated, without impairing financial stability or damaging the government's credit standing? Some have advocated ending the practice of paying interest on banks' reserve balances, but it is not clear that this could be done without the Treasury breaching the terms of its indemnity to the Bank of England, or the Bank of England breaching the terms of its understanding with the banks about the remuneration of reserve balances. Banks might reasonably consider this a breach of trust. Ending the interest payments would amount to a new and large bank tax. It would carry an enduring price. Neither the banks nor the markets would forget it. They might tread very carefully in their dealings with the Bank – excessively perhaps, from a public policy perspective – in the next crisis. We could all be the losers as a consequence.

The most important and difficult task of all is to identify what lessons could be learnt about the handling of these recent financial and other shocks that can help improve policy in the next emergency. It is certain that there will be another one. What's more, the international political environment will be very different from that of the past several decades, and for the worse. Since the Second World War the US has been willing and powerful enough to stabilise global financial markets in a crisis. President Trump's America can no longer be relied upon to perform that role. The legacy of unreliability is likely to be enduring. Equally concerning, the Trump administration is undermining the conditions for financial stability as I write (in April 2025), thereby heightening the risk of a financial crisis. All the more reason to do the spade work now by way of preparation and contingency planning. I very much hope that this is well under way, both at the Bank and in the Treasury and that high levels of cooperation are facilitating similar work among the central banks of 'the rest of the West'.

This book does policymakers a great service. By taking an understanding of the response to the last crisis a step further, it lays firmer ground for working out what to do next time, a task of all the best political economy.

Acknowledgements

We would like to thank Paula Bejarano Carbo for her help in arranging and preparing for the conference 'Quantitative Easing and Tightening' and Margherita Servente and Neil Lakeland for conference arrangements. We also thank Professor Jagjit Chadha as the guiding intellect behind this whole project, and Professor Sean Holly gave useful insights on how to prepare this book.

Overview[*]

0.1 What Is Quantitative Easing (QE)?

In normal economic circumstances, central banks operate so that the level of reserves they issue is consistent with those required by the banking system to operate normally at the current interest rate – central banks effectively use their position as monopoly suppliers of base money to set interest rates. However, if reserves bear interest (or interest rates are zero) then the central bank can in principle issue reserves significantly in excess of those required by the banking system since these 'excess' reserves will be treated as an asset by the banks and be willingly held even if they are not required for normal liquidity management.

It is this capacity to create 'excess' central bank reserves that is at the heart of the policy of quantitative easing (QE). With the rate of return on reserves effectively equivalent to that on other safe assets the central bank has a choice to either supply just enough reserves to satisfy the core demand for reserves (i.e. the minimum amount of reserves consistent with the normal operation of the financial system) or to supply reserves hugely in excess of that requirement.

In practice, not all operations to create significant amounts of excess reserves are called QE, since excess reserves are often used to stabilise financial markets at a time of stress, most notably in lender of last resort operations when the central bank will often lend out reserves to stop a financial panic. Another, more controversial, reason for creating excess reserves is as a source of finance for the government. Chapter 8 describes such an event in late eighteenth- and early nineteenth-century England. Given the many uses of excess reserves, the term QE generally applies to prolonged periods of excess reserve creation with the objective of avoiding harmful

[*] This book is based on papers presented at the NIESR conference 'Lesson from QE and QT', 13 September 2025.

deflation. It will also only tend to be implemented when interest rates are (close to) zero so QE is seen as a substitute for conventional monetary policy (i.e. a substitute for cutting interest rates when interest rates are at their lower bound). It is also worth noting that although it is the creation of excess reserves that characterises QE, in practice central banks tend to focus on the assets they purchase with those reserves rather than the reserves themselves. Thus, QE operations are often compared with 'twist' operations (where a central bank sells/buys short-term government securities and buys/sells long-term ones in return, with the aim of influencing the yields of the longer-term ones).

0.2 QE and Asset Purchases

An important aspect of the policy of QE is how these excess reserves are created and passed to the private sector. In practice the mechanism is usually an expanded version of how reserves are normally created – through open market operations. In essence, the central bank purchases financial assets (usually government securities) from the private sector in return for newly created reserves. Whilst the asset purchased is normally a government security, it need not be and indeed most central banks have purchased some other form of interest-bearing security, such as mortgage-backed securities (MBS) in the case of the US Federal Reserve.

Some have argued that limiting QE to the purchase of financial assets is unambitious and have proposed instead that the creation of reserves should simply be used to directly fund government expenditure (as in Britain during the Napoleonic era – see Chapter 8). However, this policy – sometimes termed 'helicopter money' – whilst entirely feasible, is arguably the mixture of two separate policies, that is, QE and deficit-financed government spending, and thus is probably best analysed in that way. As discussed in Section 0.6, the creation of reserves is not 'free' money, and governments who fund expenditure through that route are likely to face funding costs not very different to those associated with short-term borrowing (unless the government imposes legal restrictions requiring Banks to hold reserves against their wishes, as discussed in Section 0.7).

0.3 A Brief History of QE Programmes

As noted earlier there have been plenty of occasions in history when central banks have deliberately created excess reserves, but QE as a policy (periods of large-scale excess reserve creation as a substitute for conventional monetary policy) began in Japan in 2001 after the economy entered a period of prolonged deflation despite interest rates being close to zero. As Figure 0.1 indicates, Japan's initial foray into QE was quite tentative and it was not until the aftermath of the global financial crisis in 2007–8 that a number of other central banks started undertaking large-scale QE programmes. Figure 0.1 shows the size of central bank asset holdings since 2000. Whilst it does not precisely measure QE activity, it is clear that the very significant increases in central bank balance sheets over this period were caused by active QE. The six countries shown in Figure 0.1 are not the full set of countries that undertook QE, but these were the most prolonged (for example, countries like Canada and New Zealand only undertook QE during the Covid-19 pandemic).

Of the six countries in Figure 0.1, Switzerland stands out as having the largest QE programme (as a share of GDP), Switzerland's programme was also unusual for being focussed more on the exchange rate, with the Swiss National Bank effectively undertaking unsterilised intervention to weaken the Swiss franc. Given this intervention was ultimately unsuccessful, the losses on this programme were substantial, as discussed in Section 0.6.

0.4 How Does QE Affect the Economy?

Ben Bernanke (former chairman of the Federal Reserve) once observed that 'the problem with QE is it works in practice, but it doesn't work in theory'. In theory supplying excess reserves is a pointless policy as, when interest rates are at zero (or reserves pay interest), banks and other financial institutions will quite willingly hold reserves since they deliver the same return as any comparable short-term liquid asset. However, as the first four chapters of this volume discuss, there are a number of channels through which QE can influence the economy. These are usefully summarised in Chapter 1.

- Portfolio balance channel – If investors have 'preferred habitats' for a certain maturity range of bond, shrinking the supply of that bond (by purchasing it in return for reserves) can raise its price and so lower its rate of return. This lower rate of return may encourage borrowers to borrow using the squeezed maturity, so stimulating the economy.
- Signalling channel – by purchasing bonds with reserves, the central bank is at risk of losing money if the price of those bonds falls (i.e. interest rates rise). So by holding those bonds the central bank is signalling that it is unwilling to raise interest rates in future. That signal encourages economic activity.
- Liquidity channel – regular bond buying by the central bank can make them more liquid and easier to sell, thus encouraging borrowers and reducing any liquidity premia.
- Market functioning channel – rather like lender of last resort operations, buying bonds and supplying liquid reserves can improve market functioning in potential crisis situations.
- Uncertainty channel – simply by visibly acting to stop deflation, the central bank can encourage confidence in economic recovery.
- Bank lending channel – by creating excess liquid and a safe asset in the form of reserves, QE can encourage bank lending.

The next four chapters of this book assess these channels and the overall impact of QE. Chapter 1 and Chapter 2 assess the UK and US evidence respectively and find evidence that QE does have an impact, with the portfolio balance channel being the most strongly evidenced. Chapter 3 takes a closer look at methodological issues, trying the explain the very wide range of estimates of QE effects. It finds that the difference in results is due to different model set-ups rather than differences in the definition of QE itself. Chapter 4 takes a narrative approach assessing public pronouncements on QE from Bank of England officials. It notes how the Bank's confidence in strong QE effects tended to decrease over time. It also notes how the Bank explicitly ruled out using QE to signal future possible interest rates, thus ruling out the signalling channel that many US researchers have emphasised.

0.5 Quantitative Tightening (QT)

Around 2022, countries that undertook QE started raising interest rates to more normal levels in order to offset growing inflationary pressures. This situation also allowed them to start removing excess reserves created during QE from the financial system (see Figure 0.1). This process of reducing the stock of excess reserves is called quantitative tightening (QT) but, unlike QE, QT is not implemented with the aim of influencing the economy but simply as a means of shrinking the central bank's balance sheet. As a result, the central banks' objective is to achieve QT on the q.t. – that is, as quietly as possible – and most central banks have decided to implement passive QT, whereby the stock of central bank assets shrinks simply as bonds mature rather than active sales (the Bank of England is an exception to this). Despite this quiet approach QT has been at least partially associated with some significant market movements, such as the US 'taper tantrum' of 2013 and Repo market disruption of 2019. In the case of the UK, whilst not directly responsible for the liability-driven investment (LDI) crisis of 2022, QT may have contributed to the vulnerability of the UK government bond market to such a shock. Chapter 5 looks at the differential impact of QE and QT and finds

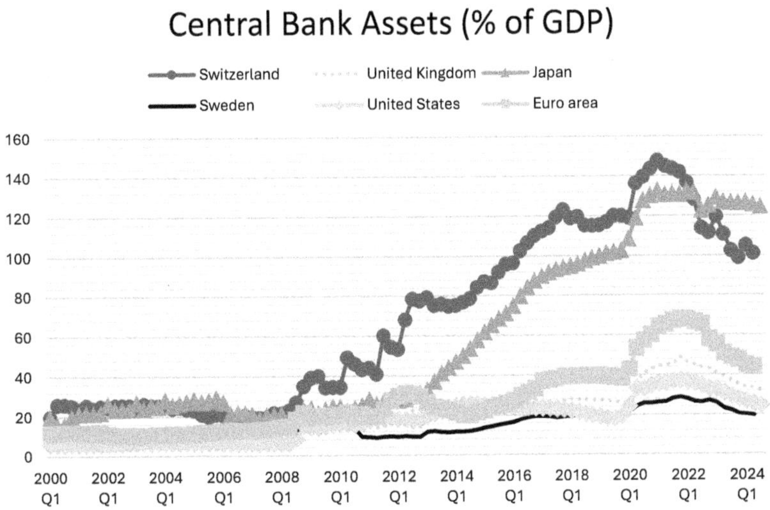

Figure 0.1 Central bank assets (% of GDP).
Source: Bank for International Settlements.

evidence that, although QT announcements have indeed had a smaller impact than QE ones, it may have been more due to the predictable and gradual nature of those announcements rather than a fundamental difference between the impact of QE and QT.

Although the process of QT is well underway, there is an important question that central banks are still working on – what stock of reserves is now appropriate? It is already clear than the financial system has become accustomed to plentiful reserves and would find it hard to operate with the reserve levels that were customary before QE began, but it is not yet clear what 'normal' level of reserves banks need. Most central banks are currently operating a wait-and-see approach and monitor several markets carefully to see if inadequate reserves are causing strains. They have also been asking banks for their preferred minimum range of reserves. When that 'normal' level is determined, central banks will then have to answer the subsequent question – is the new normal level desirable? Some of these issues are discussed in Chapter 6.

0.6 The Fiscal Costs of QE

An important feature of quantitative easing that was not fully appreciated at the beginning of QE was the potential for large losses on the QE portfolio that would have to ultimately be funded by the government.

To see how losses arise it is simplest to think of how the value of the QE assets held by the central bank (mainly government securities) changes since the liability (reserves) created to purchase those assets tends not to be subject to significant capital gains or losses. Thus, during the early days of QE central banks tended to make profits on their QE programmes as the bonds they purchased rose in value as longer-term interest rates steadily fell. However, almost inevitably, by the end of QE when inflation was beginning to rise, longer-term interest rates increased significantly reducing the value of bonds held by the central bank so that the value of the asset held fell well below that of the liability created to purchase them (reserves), thus by the end of QE the bond portfolio held by the central bank was not valuable enough to buy back the excess reserves that had been created to purchase them.

Whilst it is true to say that these losses were not inevitable (with a different profile of QE the gains made at the beginning of the process could have outweighed the losses at the end) they were always likely, so it was surprising how long it took central banks to acknowledge the potential fiscal costs of QE. The starkest example of this was an interchange that took place between Mervyn King (governor of the Bank of England) and Andrea Leadsom (Conservative Member of Parliament and member of the Treasury Select Committee). In her role on the Treasury Select Committee (chaired by Andrew Tyrie), she repeatedly asked the governor about potential losses on the QE programme and he repeatedly stated that, considering the public-sector balance sheet as a whole, there would be no losses. Even reading the letter of explanation that the governor wrote to the committee to clarify his argument, it is hard to understand the point he is trying to make other than to note that government bonds held by the central bank are both an asset and liability of the broad public sector (i.e. an asset of the central bank and a liability of the government).[†] This connection is irrelevant to the costs of QE unless he is trying to imply that, if the Bank had not purchased the bonds, the government would not have issued them in the first place, which is of course incorrect.

Although estimates of the fiscal cost of QE vary over time and approach (and do not typically allow for the potential fiscal benefits of better economic outcomes caused by QE), most recent estimates indicate that all major QE programmes have incurred significant costs. These range from about 1% of GDP in the case of Sweden through to around 3% to 5% of GDP for the USA, Euro area and UK and over 18% of GDP in the case of Switzerland, where the scale of the QE programme was both larger (as a share of GDP) and exposed to significant foreign exchange risk, as foreign exchange reserves increased significantly.

In effect these losses are calculated by comparing the market value of the central banks' QE asset portfolio to the value of the reserves created to purchase that portfolio adjusted for gains or losses already realised. Over time this valuation loss will increasingly be in the form of realised losses incurred because interest on reserves is higher than interest earned on the QE bond portfolio. So, for example, if the central bank decided to simply hold its portfolio of bonds until they matured, they would face many years when the income from the portfolio (i.e. coupons) was less than the interest it paid on excess reserves so it

† www.parliament.uk/globalassets/documents/commons-committees/treasury/11 1124-Governor-to-Chair-RE-AFP.pdf.

would realise losses year-by-year even if no bonds were bought or sold. Eventually, after all the QE portfolio had matured it would find that the revenue from bond maturities would not be enough to buy back all the excess reserves created and so it would either have to find the extra funds from elsewhere (effectively the government) or continue to operate with a higher level of reserves and so pay a higher interest bill in perpetuity. Chapter 7 discusses these fiscal cost effects.

Chapter 7 also discusses how some central banks, such as the US Federal Reserve, generate enough income from other sources to mean that they can bear the costs of QE themselves without actively asking for government funds. Thus, the Federal Reserve plans to keep QE losses on its balance sheet as a 'deferred asset' until income from other sources (e.g. seigniorage) cover the costs. Although this has led some to argue that there are no fiscal costs, that is untrue, as if the Federal Reserve's income was not used to pay off these losses it would be remitted as profit to the government – thus the government is ultimately bearing the cost. For other central banks, such as the Bank of England, which has very little income of its own (e.g. in the UK seigniorage is paid directly to the Treasury), QE losses are borne directly (rather than indirectly) by the Treasury.

0.7 The Interest on Reserves Debate

The fiscal losses described previously have ignited a debate as to whether central bank reserves should continue to bear interest. Paying interest on central bank reserves is a relatively recent innovation and there are still many central banks who do not – relying instead on legally mandated minimum reserve requirements. Therefore, on the face of things, it would seem that a relatively simple way to reduce the fiscal losses on QE would be to simply stop paying interest on reserves.

In practice, of course there would be a number of complications. The most important would be that, if reserves stopped paying interest, they would become loss-making for banks to hold (i.e. reserves would not compensate banks for the cost of raising the funds used to acquire them). This would not only mean that a high, legally imposed, minimum reserve requirement would need to be implemented in order to ensure banks held reserves, but the losses made by banks would have to made up for elsewhere, thereby raising the cost of banking to individuals and creating an incentive for the more wealthy in particular to take their funds out of the domestic banking system (recent advances in fintech would make this far easier than it was in the 1970 and 1980s when the Eurodollar market offered larger US depositors a means to avoid the implicit tax imposed by the Federal Reserve due to unremunerated reserves). Thus, not paying interest on reserves would raise costs to users of banking services and distort incentives in the same way as any tax does.

Chapter 8 highlights how not paying interest on reserves has historically made excess reserve creation an important source of revenue. It discusses the period in the late eighteenth and early nineteenth century, when the Bank of England used excess note issue as a means of financing government debt which had risen to alarming levels.

0.8 Governance Issues in QE

Throughout this book it is clear that QE as a policy has both costs and benefits and that as well as its direct monetary impact it has implications for fiscal policy and financial stability. Chapter 9 argues that, despite this broad-ranging impact, there was limited oversight of the UK quantitative easing policy. Although the Bank of England's monetary policy committee was asked to confirm the scale of excess reserves to be created, the means of doing so was decided entirely by Bank of England executives. Chapter 9 highlights two areas where this lack of oversight arguably leads to poor decision making. First, by purchasing a significant amount of long maturity debt the Bank of England effectively increased the fiscal risks of QE without any clear impact on the efficacy of the policy itself. Second, by effectively refusing to continue purchasing private sector debt (despite being asked to by the Treasury) the Bank both increased the fiscal costs of QE and, arguably, reduced its efficacy as QE could only operate indirectly (i.e. the Bank reduced the stock of government bonds with the hope that this would encourage banks and other institutions to lend to the private sector instead).

I

The Economic Impact of QE and QT

1 *QE at the Bank of England*

FILIPPO BUSETTO, MATTHIEU CHAVAZ, MAREN FROEMEL, MICHAEL JOYCE, IRYNA KAMINSKA AND JACK WORLIDGE

1.1 Introduction

The policy of quantitative easing (QE) as implemented by the Bank of England (Bank) involves the central bank making large-scale purchases of financial assets in the secondary market in exchange for newly created interest-paying reserves, with the aim of boosting aggregate demand and hence inflation.[*] This policy has been used by the Monetary Policy Committee (MPC) of the Bank, as well as by a number of other major central banks, in situations of disinflationary pressure where policy interest rates have already been reduced to their effective lower bound, leaving the central bank to turn to so-called unconventional policies.[1]

Quantitative easing was first used by the Bank in response to the global financial crisis (GFC) in March 2009. It was subsequently used in response to several large economic shocks: the euro area sovereign debt crisis, the aftermath of the EU referendum vote and the onset of the Covid-19 pandemic. At the beginning of 2022, the Bank began to unwind its QE portfolio, a process known as quantitative tightening, which is still in progress at the time of writing.[2]

* This paper draws extensively on our earlier article, 'QE at the Bank of England: A Perspective on Its Functioning and Effectiveness', that appeared in the Bank of England Quarterly Bulletin 2022. Matthieu Chavaz's contribution to this paper was made while working at the Bank of England. The views expressed in this paper are those of the authors and not necessarily those of the Bank of England or its committees or the Bank for International Settlements. We are grateful to a number of Bank colleagues for comments.

1 Other monetary policy tools used by the MPC include forward guidance and credit policies, like the Funding for Lending Scheme and the Term Funding Scheme (see discussion in Section 1.2).

2 This chapter does not discuss the impact or transmission channels of QT. For an initial assessment of this, see Bank of England (2023).

The objective of this chapter is to review the available evidence on the impact of QE in the United Kingdom and draw out implications for monetary policy.[3] While little evidence was available to guide the first QE programmes introduced in 2009, over time a growing number of studies have analysed the impact of QE here and abroad. A particular focus of the chapter is to draw out what has been learnt about the channels through which QE transmits to financial markets and the real economy.

We begin in Section 1.2 by describing the Bank's five QE purchase programmes to date. Section 1.3 goes on to explain some of the main channels thought to explain the impact of QE. Section 1.4 turns to the UK evidence and explains how QE has affected the yield curve. Section 1.5 discusses the evidence on other transmission channels and the broader macroeconomic effects of QE. Section 1.6 offers conclusions.

1.2 The Bank's Five QE Programmes

The Bank's QE programmes have been implemented under a variety of economic and financial conditions, where the MPC judged that *additional* monetary accommodation was warranted to meet its remit, beyond that achievable by setting the Bank Rate at its perceived lower bound.

The large majority of QE purchases have been of longer-maturity conventional UK government bonds ('gilts'), although some sterling-denominated corporate bonds were purchased during the first QE programme[4] and further purchases were made with the start of the Corporate Bond Purchase Scheme (CBPS) in 2016 and in 2020.[5] The Bank bought assets from financial market participants in the secondary market through an auction process.[6] The MPC has at times used QE

[3] Earlier reviews focused on the UK evidence are provided by Haldane et al. (2016) and Bailey et al. (2020), while Bhattarai and Neely (2022) review the international evidence.

[4] Corporate bonds and commercial paper were bought and sold in 2009, with the objective of addressing corporate market illiquidity.

[5] The rest of this chapter focuses on the Bank's purchases of gilts, since they made up the overwhelming share of QE purchases. The stock of corporate bonds held as part of the CBPS reached a peak of £20 billion in October 2020. Sales operations began in September 2022, and the scheme was closed in April 2024, when the last bond matured.

[6] The Bank's purchases were made on behalf of the Asset Purchase Facility (APF), a subsidiary of the Bank indemnified by the Treasury, funded by a loan from the Bank. For further discussion of these accounting arrangements, see appendix D of Busetto et al. (2022).

alongside other policies to provide additional monetary stimulus, including Bank Rate cuts, forward guidance and funding schemes (i.e. the Funding for Lending Scheme (FLS), the Term Funding Scheme (TFS) and the Term Funding Scheme with additional incentives for SMEs (TFSME)).[7]

The first QE programme (QE1) began in March 2009 in the aftermath of the GFC, when, in response to weakening activity and inflation, the MPC cut Bank Rate to 0.5% – believed to be its effective lower bound at the time[8] – and announced a programme of £75 billion of asset purchases financed by newly created reserves.[9] During the first QE programme, the Bank eventually purchased around £200 billion of financial assets, predominantly gilts, over an eleven-month period.

The stock of purchased assets was maintained at £200 billion until October 2011, when the UK inflation outlook again weakened in response to fallout from the Eurozone sovereign debt crisis. With Bank Rate still at its lower bound, the MPC decided to resume gilt purchases. Between October 2011 and May 2012, the Bank purchased a further £125 billion of gilts (QE2), followed by an additional £50 billion between July and November 2012 (QE3).

The next QE programme was launched in August 2016 (QE4), following the referendum vote to leave the EU in June that year, which led to a deterioration in the economic outlook. This consisted of £60 billion of gilt purchases and was also accompanied by a package of other measures, including a Bank Rate cut to 0.25%, a TFS to provide funding for banks at interest rates close to Bank Rate and a £10 billion programme of corporate bond purchases.[10]

The stock of assets remained at £375 billion until February 2020, when the onset of the Covid-19 pandemic led to a sharp deterioration in

7 The importance of using various tools in a package was also emphasised by the Bank for International Settlements (2019).

8 A particular concern on the MPC about cutting Bank Rate further was that it 'could have some adverse impacts on the economy, given its effects on the profits that banks and building societies were able to make through the spread between their deposit and lending rates'. Bank of England (2009).

9 The US Federal Reserve had announced its own asset purchase programme in November 2008, which initially comprised housing agency debt and mortgage-backed securities. In March 2009, the programme was expanded in size and extended to include purchases of Treasuries as well.

10 The August 2016 MPC minutes noted that the Committee now judged the lower bound for Bank Rate to be close to, but a little above zero.

the economic outlook and an increase in economic uncertainty. As in the case of the first QE programme, this deterioration accompanied severe market volatility, although in this case it uniquely reflected a global 'dash for cash' (where investors started selling off even safe assets). In response the MPC announced a further £200 billion of asset purchases, a cut in Bank Rate from 0.25% to 0.1% and an extension of the TFS with additional incentives for SMEs (TFSME). Further QE expansions in June and November of that year resulted in the stock of purchased assets rising to a peak of £895 billion by the end of the QE5 programme in December 2021. The stock of purchases was retained at that level until the MPC voted in February 2022 to begin unwinding its QE purchases, initially by ceasing to reinvest in maturing assets and then by actively selling them. Active sales commenced in November 2022.[11] Figure 1.1 shows how the Bank's holdings of gilts evolved over the various QE programmes.

The Bank also undertook asset purchases between 28 September and 14 October in response to the severe dysfunction in the UK government bond market, associated with forced selling of gilts by liability-driven

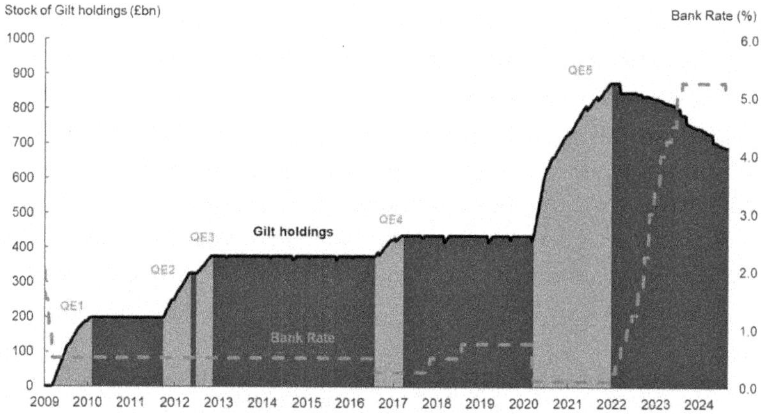

Figure 1.1 Stock of gilts held by the Bank of England's asset purchase facility (£ billions, left scale) and Bank Rate (%, right scale).
Note: Data from March 2009 to August 2024.
Source: Bank of England.

[11] The start of active sales was delayed by the outbreak of the financial crisis related to the LDI strategies of defined-benefit pension funds as discussed in this section.

investment (LDI) funds (see Hauser (2022); Alexander et al. (2023)). But these purchases cannot be regarded as QE. They focused on restoring financial stability by providing a backstop facility and were recommended by the Bank's Financial Policy Committee and not the MPC. The purchases were deliberately targeted and temporary. The Bank only purchased assets that were required by LDI funds to rebuild their resilience (long-maturity conventional gilts initially and then index-linked ones) over a short period which was announced in advance, with all resulting gilt holdings fully unwound within three months.

1.3 QE in Theory

The main objective of QE has been to boost aggregate demand in the economy and hence support inflation, thereby helping the MPC to meet its inflation target.

The main way QE affects the economy is through its impact on the yield curve. Asset purchases should initially lower longer-term gilt yields and other interest rates, thereby reducing borrowing costs for households and corporates, and stimulate spending and investment.

It is helpful conceptually to decompose gilt yields into two components: the expected policy rate over the bond's term to maturity, and a term premium that captures compensation for the investor from interest rate and illiquidity risk and potentially from the impact from demand/supply imbalances. Quantitative easing can affect both components but is likely to have a larger relative impact on term premia than conventional policy. Moreover, to the extent that term premia tend to increase with bond maturity, QE will have a stronger impact on longer-term interest rates.

Policy rate expectations and term premia will be affected through different channels and the relative strength of each transmission channel will likely depend on the state of the economy and financial markets. Therefore, the mix of channels and the total impact of QE may be state dependent – that is, vary across time according to circumstances – implying that different QE programmes may have different effects on asset prices and the real economy.[12]

The primary transmission channels are highlighted in Figure 1.2:

[12] Potential sources of state-contingency include market stress and proximity to the perceived lower bound for yields. See e.g. Haldane et al. (2016).

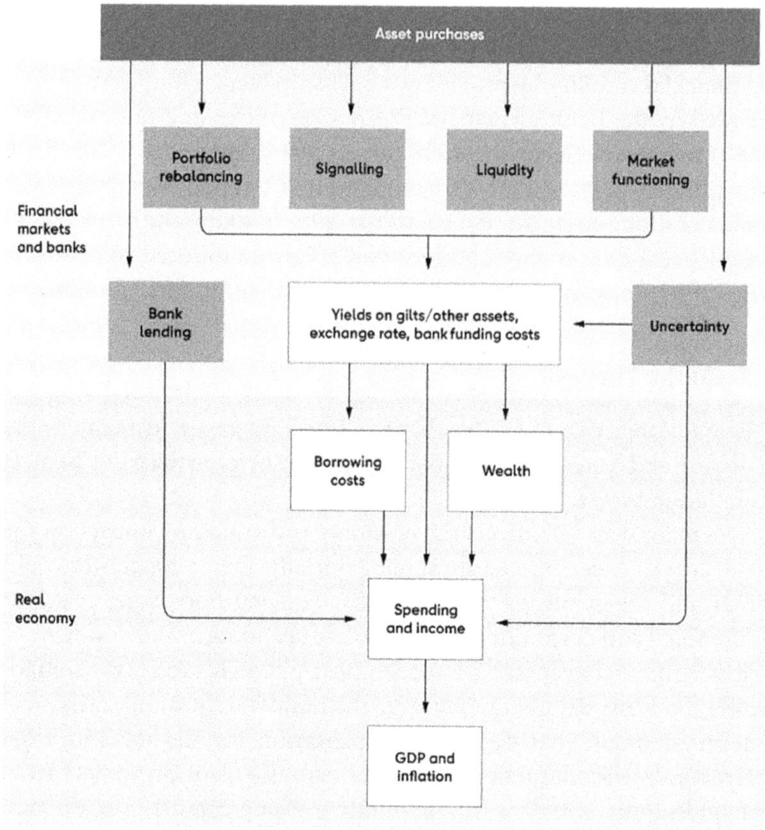

Figure 1.2 Stylised QE transmission mechanism.
Source: Bank of England.

- Portfolio balance channel – QE reduces the 'free-float' of bonds available to financial market participants, which has two main effects. First, by reducing the supply of certain bonds, the central bank can lower the yield on these bonds and their close substitutes ('local supply' channel). This requires that there are investors in the market who have a demand for bonds in specific segments of the yield curve (e.g. have preferred habitats), so that bonds are not regarded as perfect substitutes. Second, to the extent that it shifts investors' portfolios towards shorter-dated assets by buying longer maturity assets, QE reduces the overall amount of duration risk borne by market participants ('duration channel') and therefore decreases the compensation for being exposed to interest rate risk. These two effects – local supply and duration risk – are expected to lower term premia across the yield curve, but for this to be the case a necessary condition is that there is a 'financial friction' of some sort that prevents other investor groups from undoing these effects by exploiting arbitrage opportunities across the yield curve (e.g. investors need to be risk averse).[13]

- Signalling channel – when the central bank engages in QE, markets may infer that the central bank is credibly committing to a period of protracted low policy rates. One reason for this belief could be related to the expectation by market participants that the central bank will not raise policy rates before the end of the QE programme.[14] This would lower short to medium-term maturity yields by lowering the expectation component.
- Liquidity channel – bond yields can also incorporate a liquidity premium to compensate investors for the risk that they might not be able to sell the bond immediately, particularly in times of stress. In this case, purchases of assets by the central bank can lower yields by stimulating trading and therefore improving the liquidity of assets purchased or eligible for purchase.
- Market functioning channel – in exceptionally stressed circumstances – for example, when a negative demand shock for gilts is compounded by a limited ability of dealers to intermediate trades – large-scale asset purchases can act as an ultimate backstop to improve wider market liquidity and mitigate the risk of a broader tightening in financial conditions that might disrupt the monetary transmission mechanism. The strength of this channel therefore depends on the severity of the demand shock, the degree of market dysfunction and the amount of gilts held by dealers. The market functioning channel is expected to mainly work through changes in term premia.
- Uncertainty channel – QE might also help to lower yields – and market volatility more generally – by reducing uncertainty about the economic outlook and the path for the policy rate. Quantitative easing

[13] The key academic reference here is Vayanos and Vila (2021). A related macro literature explores the consequences of incorporating portfolio balance effects into a dynamic stochastic general equilibrium (DSGE) setting; early contributions to this literature include, for example, Andrés, López-Salido and Nelson (2004), Harrison (2012, 2017) and Chen, Ferrero and Curdia (2012).

[14] See Bernanke (2020).

could be seen to lower the probability of the most negative economic outcomes when Bank Rate is close to zero, relative to a situation in which Bank Rate is the only available policy instrument.

In addition to its transmission through the yield curve, some QE transmission channels potentially impact the real economy more directly.

- Quantitative easing's impact through reducing uncertainty may also directly encourage consumption (by reducing the incentives for precautionary saving) and investment (by encouraging risk-taking).
- Bank lending channel – QE may also work through banks. Quantitative easing will mechanically increase the size of investor deposit accounts with commercial banks, to the extent that bonds are bought from non-banks.[15] At the same time, the affected commercial banks' reserves with the central bank will increase by the same amount (all else equal). Under some conditions this may increase the ability and willingness of banks to lend, particularly if greater holdings of liquid assets relax their financial constraints. But whether this is the case in practice depends on regulatory requirements and the financial position and risk appetite of the banking sector. It will also depend on how stable this new source of funding is.

Whereas three of these channels are also part of the transmission mechanism of changes in Bank Rate, the liquidity, market functioning and portfolio balance channels are specific to QE.

1.4 The Impact of QE on the Yield Curve

As already discussed, QE affects the economy initially by reducing interest rates across the yield curve through several channels.

Since financial market participants are forward-looking, the expected impact of asset purchases should in large part be reflected in yields as soon as the central bank announces a change in its purchase target.[16] In

[15] For a summary of how QE affects the balance sheets of the Bank of England (through the APF – see footnote 6), commercial banks and the institutions selling assets, see McLeay, Radia and Thomas (2014).

[16] In principle, asset prices may react to any news that affects the expected path of future purchases. Therefore the impact on yields might reflect not only the announced purchases but also any change in future expected purchases that have yet to be announced.

line with this idea, many studies have estimated the impact of QE by exploring how government bond yields change within a short time interval (window) after each QE announcement, with the length of the window chosen in order to help exclude the influence of other news.[17] Among others, the evidence on the yield impact of QE announcements has been reviewed by Gagnon (2016), Haldane and colleagues (2016) and Rebucci, Hartley and Jimenez (2022).

While based on a limited number of episodes, the UK-specific evidence shows that the main QE announcements have indeed consistently lowered interest rates across the maturity spectrum (Figure 1.3), although the magnitude of these effects has varied significantly across different QE rounds. The largest yield reaction to QE was associated with QE1, with medium to long-term gilt yields estimated to have fallen by about 100 basis points in response to £200 billion of purchases (Joyce, Tong and Woods (2011); Christensen and Rudebusch (2012)).[18] Evidence across all the major subsequent QE episodes also suggests that gilt yields fell across the maturity spectrum after asset purchase announcements, but the magnitude of the effect was smaller than for QE1.[19]

Time variation in the yield curve impact of QE between different programmes (also observed in the US) has led to a debate about how effective QE was outside of crises.[20] One argument is that, in times of stress, the conditions necessary for QE to lower yields via liquidity, market functioning, portfolio balance and uncertainty effects are likely to be met to a larger degree. Applying this argument to the UK, Vlieghe (2021) argues that QE had little impact outside situations of heightened market stress like March 2009 and March 2020.

Another explanation is that subsequent QE rounds were anticipated by the market to a greater extent (Gagnon (2016); Bernanke (2020)). In

17 It needs to be acknowledged that there is a trade-off between capturing the full effects of the announcement, which may extend over a longer period if there are financial frictions, and inadvertently including the impact of confounding factors.

18 See also Joyce and Tong (2012) and McLaren, Banerjee and Latto (2014).

19 In some cases there were other non-QE related events that moved yields intraday. These confounding factors seem particularly important in QE2 and QE3. It should also be noted that news about QE may affect the yield curve even in the absence of an announced programme. In February 2009, for example, following the Bank's Inflation Report press conference there was a large move in the yield curve in the expectation that a future QE programme would be introduced (see e.g. Joyce and Tong (2012)).

20 See, for example, Bernanke (2020) for a review of the arguments and the evidence.

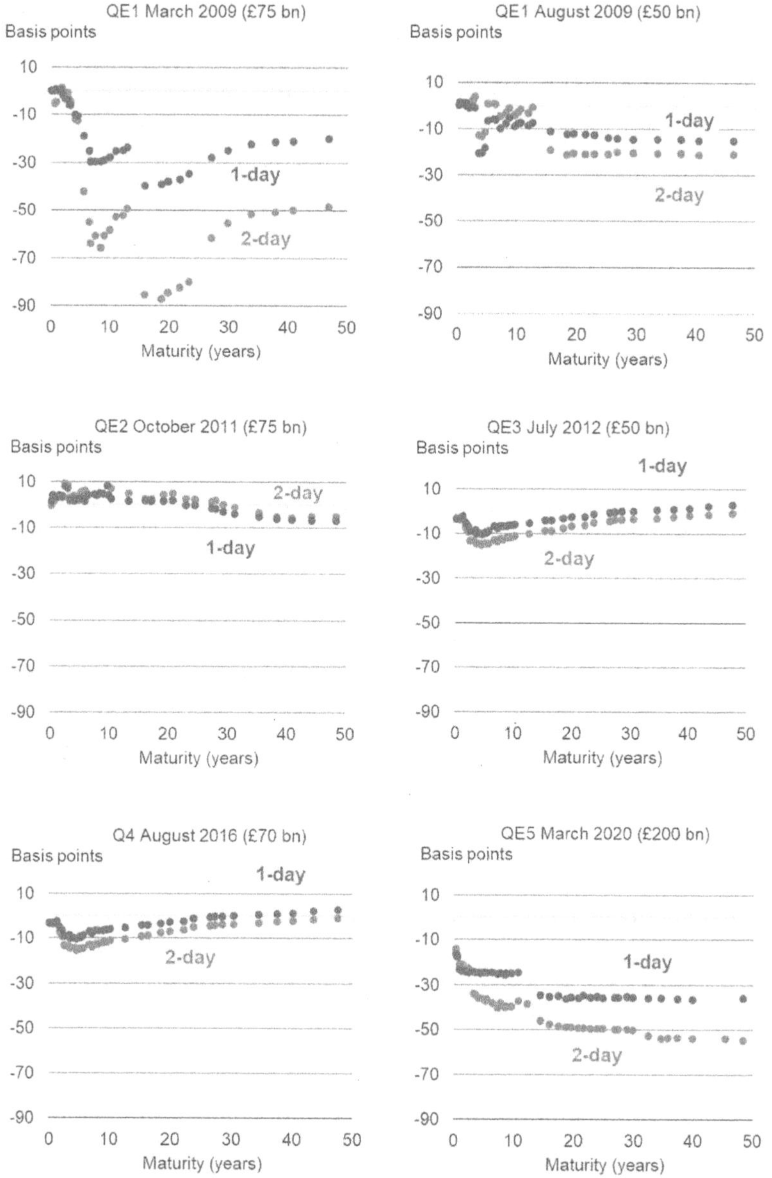

Figure 1.3 Change in gilt yields by maturity after Bank purchase announcements: one-day and two-day windows.

Note: one-day changes are shown as darker circles; two-day changes are shown as lighter circles.

Sources: Tradeweb; Froemel, Joyce and Kaminska (2022).

line with this, survey data for the UK suggest that a majority of MPC QE announcements were expected to a significant degree by financial market participants. This complicates empirical analysis of the impact of QE, but it does not mean QE was necessarily less effective. Instead, it implies that the expected impact of future programmes may have already been incorporated into asset prices ahead of QE announcements.

That said, the impact of QE appears to have varied across programmes, even if one allows for what had been expected beforehand (Figure 1.4). The response to the surprise component of QE – the announced target minus what markets had anticipated – was much greater in March 2009 than at other times. But there was still a material impact of QE surprises on other occasions, even when markets were functioning well.

As discussed in Section 1.3, the impact on the yield curve could reflect a combination of signalling, portfolio balance, liquidity and uncertainty effects. The relatively small number of QE programmes and thus available case studies provides a key challenge to separate the operation of these channels. Although generalising from individual studies is difficult, several common themes emerge across a range of studies.

In particular, the empirical evidence is consistent with different channels operating together, but with variation in their relative strength over time. One key distinction is between channels that work by lowering term premia – including portfolio balance and uncertainty – and those operating by lowering expectations of future policy rates (signalling). Decomposing these effects is difficult because these components are unobserved and must therefore be inferred from models.

Focusing on the UK, Kaminska and Mumtaz (2022) decompose high-frequency changes in the yield curve using a dynamic term structure model over a sample period which includes the first four UK QE programmes. Their decomposition suggests that QE announcements lowered interest rates by affecting both term premia and expectations. Compared to the preceding period in which monetary policy was implemented using changes in Bank Rate, QE announcements had a stronger relative impact on term premia.[21] The decomposition by Kaminska and Mumtaz (2022) nevertheless suggests that signalling has been one of the key QE channels, although its importance was

[21] Kaminska and Mumtaz (2022) demonstrate the existence of a QE-specific channel of monetary policy that works explicitly through term premia and can be linked to local supply.

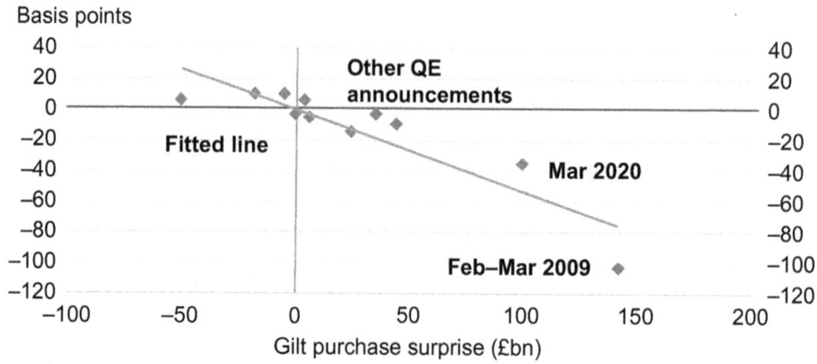

Figure 1.4 Change in ten-year gilt yields after QE announcement and gilt purchase surprise.

Notes: The diamonds in the figure show two-day windows around QE announcements, except when there are confounding events within this window. The changes over two days after the announcement have been suggested as a plausible time frame for markets to absorb news in the context of QE1 (Joyce, Tong and Woods (2011)). October 2011, February 2012 and March 2020 use a narrower window, as MPC announcements coincided with other central bank announcements or major political news. The picture is similar if one uses an average across gilt maturities. Purchase surprise is the change in the expected target stock of QE purchases among market participants surveyed by Reuters (QE1–QE4) and market intelligence (QE5). The purchase surprise for QE1 is the difference in the terminal expectation for asset purchases between April and February 2009, while the surprise in QE5 is estimated using market intelligence obtained shortly before the March 2020 MPC meeting.

Sources: Bloomberg Finance LP, LSEG, Reuters and Bank of England calculations.

relatively less pronounced during the first QE programmes. Similarly, other papers have found that initially the signalling channel played a statistically significant but quantitatively modest role. Using different methods to decompose short-term changes in gilt yields, Christensen and Rudebusch (2012) and Joyce, Tong and Woods (2011) both find that expectations of future Bank Rate fell in response to the announcement of QE1 – in line with a signalling channel. But according to their decompositions, signalling effects across the entire programme explain at most up to a third of the announcement impact of QE on gilt yields.

By comparison, some studies (see e.g. Krishnamurthy and Vissing-Jorgensen (2011); Christensen and Rudebusch (2012); Bauer and Rudebusch (2014); Lloyd (2020)) find that signalling explains a larger share of the impact of the announcement of the Fed's first QE programmes – although this could reflect the fact that the Fed also gave explicit guidance about the future path for policy rates.

The finding that signalling explains only a portion of the impact of QE is consistent with a substantial role for portfolio balance in helping to lower yields by compressing term premia. One of the preconditions for this channel to operate is that some investors view assets as imperfectly substitutable for non-pecuniary reasons. Insurance companies and pension funds (ICPFs), for example, are often thought to have 'preferred habitats' because they tend to hold long-term assets to match their liabilities. In recent research, Giese and colleagues (2024) show that preferred habitat behaviour in the gilt market exists across the term structure and that foreign central banks (at shorter maturities) and ICPFs (at longer maturities) make up some of these preferred habitat investor groups. These investors' gilt holdings are less sensitive to changes in the price of gilts, consistent with the idea that they value these assets for non-pecuniary reasons. In an earlier study, Joyce, Liu and Tonks (2017) found that ICPFs played a significant role in selling gilts to the Bank as part of the QE1 and QE2 programmes. Worlidge (2022) finds a similar result for QE5, in that ICPFs reduced their net acquisition of gilts and increased their net investment in corporate bonds.

Evidence suggests that local supply effects (part of the portfolio balance channel) were important in the first QE programmes. One way to shed light on the role of portfolio balance is to study how the impact of QE announcements varies across individual gilts. If QE lowers gilt yields by shrinking their supply, those gilts more likely to be purchased by the central bank should see larger drops in yields after announcements. McLaren, Banerjee and Latto (2014) find that this was the case for the first two QE programmes. They calculate that this 'local supply' effect explains around half of the total impact of the QE1 and QE2 announcements on medium and long-term gilt yields.[22] Comparable estimates suggest that local supply explains around two-thirds of the response of

[22] Joyce and Tong (2012) find that both the local supply and duration risk channels dominated during QE1, albeit with some variability across different announcements.

US Treasury yields to the Fed's first QE programme.[23] McLaren, Banerjee and Latto (2014) also find that longer-term bonds react more strongly to QE announcements, in line with a duration effect. More recently, Froemel, Joyce and Kaminska (2022), examining the importance of the local supply channel across all Bank programmes to date, find that the yield reductions associated with this channel seem to have become smaller in later purchase rounds and account for a smaller fraction of the overall yield response to announcements.[24]

Quantitative easing has also been found to reduce uncertainty. Kaminska and Mumtaz (2022) find that term premia associated with uncertainty about the future path for Bank Rate fell after QE was introduced in 2009. Feeding this decomposition into a macroeconometric model, they estimate that lower uncertainty translated into lower corporate bond spreads and improved economic outcomes. Using a vector autoregression approach, Weale and Wieladek (2016) also find that proxies for financial market and household uncertainty fell in response to MPC announcements during the first three QE programmes.

There is limited evidence that QE purchases lowered yields by reducing liquidity premia in the gilt market. While asset purchases can improve the liquidity of purchased gilts around auction times, these benefits should be short-lived and limited to periods of poor gilt market liquidity.[25] For example, for the UK, Joyce and Tong (2012) find that during the early stages of the QE1 auctions yields fell most for less liquid gilts, but these effects were small and temporary. But beyond a certain point, by reducing the free float of bonds, central bank purchases may also potentially reduce bond liquidity. The international evidence suggests that asset purchases

23 D'Amico and King (2013). Some studies point to important local supply effects in the euro area as well, although the results are sometimes weaker – possibly because of the relatively calmer market conditions during which the first European Central Bank (ECB) QE programmes were conducted (Arrata and Nguyen (2017), De Santis and Holm-Hadulla (2020) and Altavilla, Carboni and Motto (2021)).

24 These results are robust to controlling for the amount of QE news in each announcement.

25 The presence of a large 'backstop' buyer should reduce the liquidity risk of holding a bond. And if QE leads to portfolio rebalancing, this can also stimulate trading – both for purchased assets and for potential substitutes. These effects should be localised on purchased bonds or their substitutes and concentrated during auction time. A related but distinct channel is for asset purchases to support dealers' balance sheets during periods of market stress, which can improve liquidity more generally.

have a range of impacts on bond liquidity. In Sweden, for example, Grimaldi, Crosta and Zhang (2021) found that the Riksbank's purchases of government bonds improved liquidity as long as the Riksbank held less than 40% of these bonds, but impaired liquidity past that level. These findings are unlikely to be representative of the impact of asset purchases when there is a stress in government bonds and pressure on dealers' ability to intermediate, as was the case in March 2020. In this case, it seems clear that the market functioning channel was of crucial importance. While yields immediately fell in reaction to the MPC announcement of its QE5 programme, market conditions eased only once the auctions had begun, allowing dealers to unclog their balance sheets.

One critique of the body of research on QE announcement effects on yields is that this might be a short-term effect that would reverse before it can have any impact on real outcomes. Bond yields will fluctuate with a range of domestic and global factors, and this can offset any impact from a QE announcement – particularly in an open economy like the UK. But insofar as these factors would exist absent QE, any reversal in yields does not necessarily mean that the effect of QE is transient.[26] In addition, while the full effects would be expected to manifest in gilt yields over a few days, there is evidence that the spillovers to other assets may take place over several weeks.[27] However if QE succeeds in strengthening the economy, there will ultimately be upward pressure on yields. Some studies point to announcement impacts that persist as long as several months or even a few years.[28]

1.5 The Impact of QE on Other Asset Prices and the Real Economy

Lower interest rates across the yield curve should in turn affect other asset prices, thereby easing financial conditions and increasing wealth, which can support demand in the economy by stimulating investment and consumption.

[26] As Bernanke (2020) argues, any impact of QE via a liquidity channel could be transitory in theory, but there is no obvious reason why this should be true for signalling or portfolio balance effects, for which there is more empirical support.

[27] See, for example, Mamaysky (2018) and Greenwood, Hanson and Liao (2018).

[28] See, for example Wright (2012), Wieladek and Pascual (2016), Gambetti and Musso (2020), Swanson (2021), Neely (2022), Rebucci, Hartley and Jimenez (2022) and Eser et al. (2023) for estimates of QE persistence in the US and euro area.

For a fall in interest rates across the yield curve to stimulate demand, it should lower borrowing costs for households and corporates in a sufficiently persistent way. These costs reflect default-free rates plus a credit risk premium. A fall in the yield curve from QE will lower the first component (by lowering expected risk-free rates via the signalling channel and by increasing the demand for corporate bonds via portfolio balance effects – although this effect might materialise more gradually). Quantitative easing can also help to lower the second component by improving the outlook for the economy and therefore decreasing default risk for borrowers.

The evidence is supportive of spillover effects from the impact of QE on the yield curve into other financial market prices. In line with this, event studies for the UK suggest that corporate bond yields fell significantly in response to the announcements of the QE programmes (Joyce et al. (2011); Joyce, Tong and Woods (2011); McLaren, Banerjee and Latto (2014); D'Amico and Kaminska (2019)). High-yield corporate bonds seem to react particularly strongly, suggesting that QE lowered downside tail risks in the corporate sector.[29] In addition, D'Amico and Kaminska (2019) find that after QE announcements, there was a larger drop in the yield on investment-grade corporate bonds with maturities similar to the purchased gilts. This impact peaks after a few months, consistent with portfolio rebalancing into riskier assets occurring gradually and having a persistent impact on financial conditions.

Furthermore, lower interest rates could also put some downward pressure on the exchange rate. The empirical evidence suggests that, consistent with this mechanism, the pound has tended to depreciate in response to QE announcements by the MPC.[30]

While there is strong evidence of QE operating through capital markets, there is no evidence of a material bank lending channel in the UK. By lowering gilt rates, QE will tend to lower rates on bank loans to households and corporates as well as on banks' wholesale funding. All else equal, this should translate into more bank lending.

[29] Joyce et al. (2011); Joyce, Tong and Woods (2011); Haldane et al. (2016).

[30] Joyce et al. (2011), Glick and Leduk (2012), Kenourgios, Papadamou and Dimitriou (2015) and Haldane et al. (2016) focus on the exchange rate impact of QE announcements in the UK. Swanson (2011), Bernanke (2015) and Powell (2018) study the international effects of the Fed's asset purchases. Bluwstein and Canova (2016) and Dedola et al. (2021) study the effect of unconventional monetary policies on the exchange rate in the euro area.

However, there is little to suggest a direct impact on lending through the impact QE has on banks' holdings of reserves and deposits; indeed, the existing evidence suggests that UK banks experiencing a larger influx of reserves during QE1 and QE2 did not increase lending relative to other banks.[31]

While estimating the impact on real activity and inflation is more challenging, the literature suggests that QE programmes provided positive stimulus. Averaging across sixteen studies by academic and central bank researchers, the Bank's QE1 was estimated to have increased UK inflation and annual GDP growth by up to 1.8pp and 1.6pp at its peak, respectively.[32] To put this into context, UK GDP dropped by 4.2% between the start and the trough of the GFC. Controlling for the size of each QE programme relative to GDP, the Fed's first large-scale asset purchase (LSAP1) programme was estimated to have had a larger impact on the economy, especially in terms of GDP (Figure 1.5).

To estimate the macroeconomic impact of QE announcements, researchers typically use models calibrated from historical relationships between bond yields and GDP and inflation. However, these models often embody a limited range of potential transmission channels and their estimates depend on the chosen identification scheme.[33] As Figure 1.5 shows, impact estimates across different studies and programmes vary considerably.[34] More broadly, there is substantial

31 Butt et al. (2014); Miller and Wanengkirtyo (2020); Giansante, Fatouh and Onega (2020). In contrast, there is evidence for a significant bank-lending channel of QE for the US. However, the Fed's purchase programme included mortgage-backed securities (MBS), which represent a large share of the assets of some US banks. Since MBS tend to be relatively less liquid, QE had more scope to 'unclog' banks' balance sheets and stimulate lending. The one Fed programme that only included Treasury purchases does not appear to have stimulated bank lending (Darmouni and Rodnyanksy (2017)). In contrast to QE, there is evidence that the Bank's lending schemes, which explicitly intended to support credit supply by reducing banks' funding costs, significantly stimulated bank lending in the UK (Benetton, Gavazza and Surico (2025)).

32 As the numbers in Figure 1.5 are rescaled to reflect a purchase programme worth 1% of GDP, they must be multiplied by the relevant size of QE1 (13% of GDP) to arrive at the programme's peak impact.

33 Typically, dynamic stochastic general equilibrium (DSGE) models only allow for QE to impact term premia. Vector autoregression (VAR) models can potentially encompass a broader range of channels, depending on the identification scheme they use.

34 Fabo et al. (2021) report estimates for the impact of QE on inflation and GDP across fifty-four studies published by academics and central bankers. The

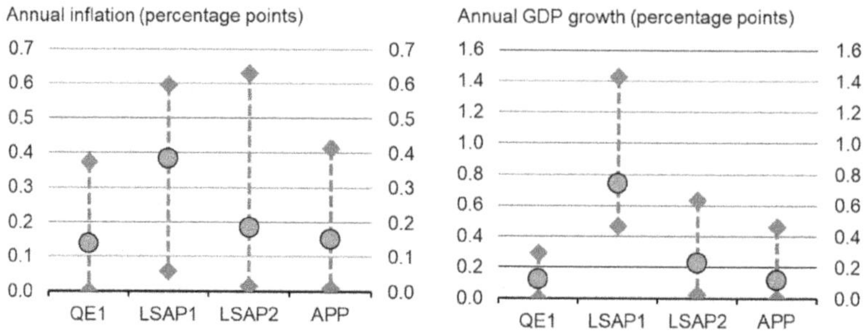

Figure 1.5 Empirical estimates of the peak macroeconomic impacts of different QE programmes.

Notes: Dots show average across empirical estimate. Diamonds and dotted lines show minimum/maximum and range. Estimates are re-scaled to reflect a purchase programme worth 1% of domestic GDP. APP: ECB's Asset Purchase Programme. LSAP: Federal Reserve's Large Scale Asset Purchase programme.

Sources: Fabo et al. (2021) and Bank of England calculations.

uncertainty around each individual estimate (Williams (2014)), leading Borio and Zabai (2016) to argue that, even though the positive effect of QE is clearly present, its size and stability are quite uncertain. Therefore, and unsurprisingly given the identification challenges, there remains room for disagreement about the economic significance of individual QE episodes. This is also consistent with these programmes having operated through a different mix of channels with different impacts on the real economy.

Understanding the strength of different channels is important to quantify the macroeconomic impact of QE. While a majority of existing studies focus on the first QE programmes, Kaminska and Mumtaz (2022) study all of the MPC's programmes before 2020 together and allow for a range of transmission channels (signalling, QE-specific supply, uncertainty). Their results suggest that the impact of QE on economic activity varies in strength with the mix of channels. In particular, the signalling channel can have a persistent impact on interest rates at the short end of the yield curve and so affect the pricing of a broad range of loans and financial assets. Thus a given reduction in long gilt yields is associated with relatively larger changes in the exchange rate, corporate

authors find that studies published by central banks tend to find larger effects on output and inflation.

bond yields, and inflation and activity, when it is driven by signalling rather than channels operating via term premia.

1.6 Conclusions

In the UK, QE has been a key instrument of monetary policy across five different episodes since 2009. While the evidence base for QE remains smaller than that available for assessing conventional interest rate policy, we can nevertheless draw some lessons.

From experience in the UK and elsewhere, we have learnt that QE mainly works through lowering interest rates at various maturities, thereby lowering borrowing costs. It is by lowering yields at longer maturities that QE can ease monetary conditions further once Bank Rate has reached its effective lower bound.

In lowering interest rates, QE operates via a number of channels, which we have described in this chapter. The available evidence suggests that both the absolute and the relative importance of each of these channels has varied through time, as economic circumstances and market conditions have evolved. The impact of QE on interest rates and yields is therefore state contingent. Given all this, it is not surprising that the broader transmission of QE to the real economy and inflation is also uncertain and likely to vary with economic and financial conditions.

While the magnitude of its effect and the strength of the evidence is greatest for the first QE programme, announced in 2009 during the most intense phase of the GFC, later QE announcements also helped to lower longer-term interest rates, albeit to a lesser extent, even when market stress and dysfunction were not as pronounced.

Although there is still much to learn, the evidence suggests that the Bank's QE programmes stimulated activity and supported inflation to varying degrees. But whether and how QE is used in the future remains an open question and will require a fuller cost-benefit analysis, including an assessment relative to other policy tools.

References

Alexander, P., Fakhoury, R., Horn, T., Panjwani, W. and Roberts-Sklar, M. (2023). 'Financial Stability Buy/Sell Tools: A Gilt Market Case Study', *Bank of England Quarterly Bulletin.*

Altavilla, C., Carboni, G. and Motto, R. (2021). 'Asset Purchase Programs and Financial Markets: Lessons from the Euro Area', *International Journal of Central Banking*, 17(4), pp.1–47.

Andrés, J., López-Salido, J. D. and Nelson, E. (2004). 'Tobin's Imperfect Asset Substitution in Optimizing General Equilibrium', *Journal of Money, Credit and Banking*, 36(4), pp.665–90.

Arrata, W. and Nguyen, B. (2017). 'Price Impact of Bond Supply Shocks: Evidence from the Eurosystem's Asset Purchase Program', Working Paper No. 623, Banque de France.

Bailey, A., Bridges, J., Harrison, R., Jones, J. and Mankodi, A. (2020). 'The Central Bank Balance Sheet as a Policy Tool: Past, Present and Future', Bank of England Staff Working Paper No. 899.

Bank of England (2009). Minutes of the Monetary Policy Committee Meeting 4 and 5 March 2009, para 27.

Bank of England (2023). Box A: 'Reviewing the Process of Quantitative Tightening', Monetary Policy Report, August 2023, pp.27–32.

Bank for International Settlements (2019). 'Unconventional Monetary Policy Tools: A Cross-Country Analysis', Report Prepared by a Working Group Chaired by Potter S. M. (Federal Reserve Bank of New York) and Smets F. (European Central Bank).

Bauer, M. D. and Rudebusch, G. D. (2014). 'The Signaling Channel for Federal Reserve Bond Purchases', *International Journal of Central Banking*, 10(3), pp.233–89.

Benetton, M., Gavazza, A. and Surico, P. (2025). 'Mortgage Pricing and Monetary Policy', *American Economic Review* [Preprint]. www.aeaweb.org/articles?id=10.1257/aer.20211229&&from=f (accessed: 3 February 2025).

Bernanke, B. (2015). 'Federal Reserve Policy in an International Context', Paper presented at the 16th Jacques Polak Annual Research Conference.

Bernanke, B. (2020). 'The New Tools of Monetary Policy', *American Economic Review*, 110(4), pp.943–83.

Bhattarai, S. and Neely, C. J. (2022). 'A Survey of the Empirical Literature on US Unconventional Monetary Policy', *Journal of Economic Literature*, 60(2), pp.527–97.

Bluwstein, K. and Canova, F. (2016). 'Beggar-Thy-Neighbor? The International Effects of ECB Unconventional Monetary Policy Measures', *International Journal of Central Banking*, 12(3), pp.69–120.

Borio, C. and Zabai, A. (2016). 'Unconventional Monetary Policies: A Re-appraisal', BIS working papers No. 570.

Busetto, F., Chavaz. M., Froemel, M., Joyce, M., Kaminska, I. and Worlidge, J. (2022). 'QE at the Bank of England: A Perspective on Its Functioning and Effectiveness', *Bank of England Quarterly Bulletin*.

Butt, N., Churm, R., McMahon, M., Morotz, A. and Schanz, J. (2014). 'QE and the Bank Lending Channel in the United Kingdom', Bank of England Working Paper 511.

Chen, H., Ferrero, A. and Curdia, V. (2012). 'The Macroeconomic Effects of Large-Scale Asset Purchase Programmes', *The Economic Journal*, 122(564), pp.F289–F315.

Christensen, J. and Rudebusch, G. (2012). 'The Response of Interest Rates to US and UK Quantitative Easing', *The Economic Journal*, 122(564), pp. F385–F414.

D'Amico, S. and Kaminska, I. (2019). 'Credit Easing Versus Quantitative Easing: Evidence from Corporate and Government Bond Purchase Programs', Bank of England Staff Working Paper No. 825.

D'Amico, S. and King, T. B. (2013). 'Flow and Stock Effects of Large-Scale Treasury Purchases: Evidence on the Importance of Local Supply', *Journal of Financial Economics*, 108(2), pp.425–48.

Darmouni, O. M. and Rodnyanksy, A. (2017). 'The Effects of Quantitative Easing on Bank Lending Behavior', *The Review of Financial Studies*, 30(11), pp.3858–87.

Dedola, L., Georgiadis, G., Gräb, J. and Mehl, A. (2021). 'Does a Big Bazooka Matter? Quantitative Easing Policies and Exchange Rates', *Journal of Monetary Economics*, 117(C), pp.489–506.

De Santis, R. A. and Holm-Hadulla, F. (2020). 'Flow Effects of Central Bank Asset Purchases on Sovereign Bond Prices: Evidence from a Natural Experiment', *Journal of Money, Credit and Banking*, 52(6), pp.1467–91.

Eser, F., Lemke, W., Nyholm, K., Radde, S. and Vladu, A. L. (2023). 'Tracing the Impact of the ECB's Asset Purchase Programme on the Yield Curve', *International Journal of Central Banking*, 19(3), pp.359–422.

Fabo, B., Jančoková, M., Kempf, E. and Pástor, L. (2021). 'Fifty Shades of QE: Comparing Findings of Central Bankers and Academics', *Journal of Monetary Economics*, 120, pp.1–20.

Froemel, M., Joyce, M. and Kaminska, I. (2022). 'The Local Supply Channel of QE: Evidence from the Bank of England's Gilt Purchases', Bank of England Staff Working Paper No. 980.

Gagnon, J. E. 2016. 'Quantitative Easing: An Underappreciated Success', Peterson Institute for International Economics, Policy Brief Number PB16–4.

Gambetti, L. and Musso, A. (2020). 'The Effects of the ECB's Expanded Asset Purchase Programme', *European Economic Review*, 130, pp.1–16.

Giese, J., Joyce, M., Meaning, J. and Worlidge, J. (2024). 'Do Preferred Habitat Investors Exist? Evidence from the UK Government Bond Market', *Economics Letters*, 234 (January), pp.1–4.

Giansante, S., Fatouh, M. and Ongena, S. (2020). 'Does Quantitative Easing Boost Bank Lending to the Real Economy or Cause Other Bank Asset Reallocation? The Case of the UK', Bank of England Staff Working Paper No. 883.

Glick, R. and Leduk, S. (2012). 'Central Bank Announcements of Asset Purchases and the Impact on Global Financial and Commodity Markets', *Journal of International Money and Finance*, 31(8), pp.2078–101.

Greenwood, R., Hanson, S. G. and Liao, Y. (2018). 'Asset Price Dynamics in Partially Segmented Markets', *The Review of Financial Studies*, 31(9), pp.3307–43.

Greenwood, R. and Vayanos, D. (2010). 'Price Pressure in the Government Bond Market', *American Economic Review: Papers and Proceedings*, 100, pp.585–90.

Grimaldi, M., Crosta, A. and Zhang, D. (2021). 'The Liquidity of the Government Bond Market: What Impact Does Quantitative Easing Have? Evidence from Sweden', Sveriges Riksbank Working Paper Series, No. 402.

Haldane, A. G., Roberts-Sklar, M., Wieladek, T. and Young, C. (2016). 'QE: The Story So Far', Bank of England Staff Working Paper No. 624.

Harrison, R. (2012). 'Asset Purchase Policies and Portfolio Balance Effects: A DSGE Analysis', in Chadha, J. and Holly, S. (eds.) *Interest Rates, Prices and Liquidity: Lessons from the Financial Crisis*, Cambridge University Press, pp.117–43.

Harrison, R. (2017). 'Optimal Quantitative Easing', Bank of England Staff Working Paper No. 678.

Hauser, A. (2022). 'Thirteen Days in October: How Central Bank Balance Sheets Can Support Monetary and Financial Stability', Speech given at the ECB's 2022 Conference on Money Markets.

Joyce, M., Lasaosa, A., Tong, M. and Stevens, I. (2011). 'The Financial Market Impact of Quantitative Easing in the United Kingdom', *International Journal of Central Banking*, 7(3), pp.113–61.

Joyce, M., Tong. M. and Woods, R. (2011). 'The United Kingdom's Quantitative Easing Policy: Design, Operation and Impact', *Bank of England Quarterly Bulletin*, Q3, pp.200–12.

Joyce, M. A. S., Liu, Z. and Tonks, I. (2017). 'Institutional Investors and the QE Portfolio Balance Channel', *Journal of Money, Credit & Banking*, 49(6), pp.1225–46.

Joyce, M. A. S. and Tong, M. (2012). 'QE and the Gilt Market: A Disaggregated Analysis', *The Economic Journal*, 122(564), pp. F348–84.

Kaminska, I. and Mumtaz, H. (2022). 'Monetary Policy Transmission during QE Times: Role of Expectations and Term Premia Channels', Bank of England Staff Working Paper No. 978.

Kaminska, I. and Zinna, G. (2020). 'Official Demand for US Debt: Implications for US Real Rates', *Journal of Money, Credit and Banking*, 52, pp.323–64.

Kenourgios, D., Papadamou, S. and Dimitriou, D. (2015). 'On Quantitative Easing and High Frequency Exchange Rate Dynamics', *Research in International Business and Finance*, 34, pp.110–25.

Krishnamurthy, A. and Vissing-Jorgensen, A. (2011). 'The Effects of Quantitative Easing on Interest Rates: Channels and Implications for Policy', *Brookings Papers on Economic Activity*, Fall, pp.215–87.

Lloyd, S. (2020). 'Estimating Nominal Interest Rate Expectations: Overnight Indexed Swaps and the Term Structure', *Journal of Banking and Finance*, 119, pp.1–19.

McLaren, N., Banerjee, R. N. and Latto, D. (2014). 'Using Changes in Auction Maturity Sectors to Help Identify the Impact of QE on Gilt Yields', *The Economic Journal*, 124(576), pp.453–79.

McLeay, M., Radia, A. and Thomas, R. (2014). 'Money Creation in the Modern Economy', *Bank of England Quarterly Bulletin*, Q1, pp.14–27.

Mamaysky. H. (2018). 'The Time Horizon of Price Responses to Quantitative Easing', *Journal of Banking and Finance*, 90, pp.32–49.

Miller, S. and Wanengkirtyo, B. (2020). 'Liquidity and Monetary Transmission: A Quasi-experimental Approach', Bank of England Staff Working Paper No. 891.

Neely, C.J. (2022). 'How Persistent Are Unconventional Monetary Policy Effects?', *Journal of International Money and Finance*, 126, pp.1–16.

Powell, J.H. (2018). 'Monetary Policy Influences on Global Financial Conditions and International Capital Flows.' At 'Challenges for Monetary Policy and the GFSN in an Evolving Global Economy' Eighth High-Level Conference on the International Monetary System sponsored by the International Monetary Fund and Swiss National Bank, Zurich, Switzerland.

Rebucci, A., Hartley, J. S. and Jiménez, D. (2022). 'An Event Study of Covid-19 Central Bank Quantitative Easing in Advanced and Emerging Economies', NBER Working Paper 27339.

Swanson, E. T. (2011). 'Let's Twist Again: A High-Frequency Event-Study Analysis of Operation Twist and Its Implications for QE', *Brookings Papers on Economic Activity*, Spring, pp.151–207.

Swanson, E. T. (2021). 'Measuring the Effects of Federal Reserve Forward Guidance and Asset Purchases on Financial Market', *Journal of Monetary Economics*, 118, pp.32–53.

Vayanos, D. and Vila, J.-L. (2021). 'A Preferred-Habitat Model of the Term Structure of Interest Rates', *Econometrica*, 89(1), pp.77–112.

Vlieghe, G. (2021). 'Running Out of Room: Revisiting the 3D Perspective on Low Interest Rates', Speech given at the London School of Economics on 26 July 2021.

Weale, M. and Wieladek, T. (2016). 'What Are the Macroeconomic Effects of Asset Purchases?', *Journal of Monetary Economics*, 79, pp.81–93.

Wieladek, T. and Pascual, A. G. (2016). 'The European Central Bank's QE: A New Hope', CESifo Working Paper Series No. 5946.

Williams, J. (2014). 'Monetary Policy at the Zero Lower Bound: Putting Theory into Practice', Hutchins Center on Fiscal and Monetary Policy at Brookings.

Worlidge, J. (2022). 'Rolling Substitutions in Financial Markets: Did Quantitative Easing in 2020 Lead to Portfolio Rebalancing?' Bank Underground Post, Bank of England.

Wright, J. H. (2012). 'What Does Monetary Policy Do to Long-Term Interest Rates at the Zero Lower Bound?', *The Economic Journal*, 122(564), pp. F447–66.

2 *US Experience of QE and QT*

NINA BOYARCHENKO AND OR SHACHAR

2.1 Introduction

The Federal Reserve first announced purchases of agency mortgage-backed securities and debt of government-sponsored enterprises (GSE) on 25 November 2008.* More than fifteen years later, the Federal Reserve System's balance sheet remains above $7 trillion as of September 2024. This balance sheet size reflects the ebbs and flows of balance sheet policy implemented in the years since the depth of the 2008–2009 financial crisis, as the US central bank – as well as central banks in other major economies – have faced the challenges of stimulating the economy at the (effective) zero lower bound, controlling both the highs and lows of inflation, and keeping inflation expectations anchored.

In this chapter, we review the recent history of quantitative easing and tightening in the US, focusing on the impact on financial markets. We view the response of financial markets to such balance sheet policies a necessary but not sufficient condition for quantitative monetary policy to have an effect on the real economy. A large literature argues for the relationship between the tightness of financial conditions and future real outcomes, both on average and in the tails. From the perspective of understanding whether balance sheet policy affects real activity, the question then becomes whether the "normal" effect of a loosening in financial conditions occurs independently of the response of the conduct of monetary policy to financial conditions or because of it. In the former case, the pass-through of balance sheet policy through financial conditions to real activity should be at least as strong as the effect of changes in financial conditions due to any other

* The views expressed here are the authors' and are not necessarily representative of the views of the Federal Reserve Bank of New York or the Federal Reserve System.

forces. In the latter case, the pass-through to real activity is likely to be much more subdued.

This chapter considers the different phases of quantitative easing (QE) in the US as well as the potential asymmetry in how effective QE and quantitative tightening (QT) are. Much of the discussion in the literature of the effectiveness of QE and the channels through which QE operates resembles the debates in the pre-crisis monetary policy literature on how the conventional monetary policy target of a level of the federal funds rate is implemented. The debate on whether QE works through primarily the initial announcement effect resembles the early 2000s literature on whether (conventional) monetary policy is implemented via "open market" or "open mouth" operations. The conventional open market operations hypothesis postulated that, under the scarce reserves regime, the Federal Reserve puts downward pressure on interest rates – most directly, the federal funds rate – by increasing the supply of reserves through an open market purchase. This is analogous to the QE intuition of asset purchases removing supply of risky securities from the market, raising asset prices.

Proponents of the "open mouth" hypothesis (Guthrie and Wright, 2000; Taylor, 2001; Thornton, 2004) instead argued that, since open market operations were rarely needed to achieve the federal funds target rate since the Federal Open Market Committee (FOMC) began communicating a target interest rate in 1994, private agents endogenously adjust market interest rates to the monetary policy target. That is, the open mouth hypothesis is similar in its nature to the announcement effect of QE purchases: the expectation of future interventions is sufficient to move interest rates or asset prices today. The literature on the open mouth hypothesis also notes that market participants' expectations for a market intervention have to be fulfilled at some point, loosening the tight temporal link between open market interventions and changes in interest rates or prices but not removing it altogether. As we will discuss in Section 2.3, this is also consistent with the announcement of QE having a larger effect than actual purchases but purchases nonetheless being required to maintain the gains made at announcement.

Clear communication and the consistent fulfillment of market participants' expectations provide important context in comparing the lessons from modern implementation of QE with those from the previous foray of the Federal Reserve System into asset purchases – the so-called Operation Twist 1961. Although the intent behind Operation Twist 1961 – increase capital inflows and strengthen the dollar – was substantively different from the motivation behind QE operations over the last fifteen years, a close examination of the effect of Operation Twist announcements on Treasury yields suggests that the initial impact was on par with the impact of modern QE announcements but was reversed about a month later due to policy reversals and mixed signals from the public sector (Swanson, 2011). This highlights that "open mouth" operations in asset markets are effective only to the extent that there are subsequent open market operations.

The rest of the chapter is organized as follows. In Section 2.2, we lay out the economic forces through which balance sheet policy may affect financial conditions, and the mechanisms that may make the effects of QT asymmetric from the effects of QE. We review the literature on QE in the context of US asset markets in Section 2.3. Section 2.4 discusses the evidence on QT, and Section 2.5 concludes.

2.2 Organizing Framework

To help organize our discussions of the various aspects of QE and QT, we begin by laying out a simple framework that captures the main channels through which purchases of securities by the central bank may affect asset prices in an economy. We follow the preferred habitat framework of Vayanos and Vila (2021) but allow for a leverage constraint on the part of the arbitrageurs in the economy. As in Vayanos and Vila (2021), we consider a continuous time model, with time indexed by t ranging from 0 to infinity. At each point in time, there is a continuum of zero-coupon government bonds (Treasuries), with the remaining time to maturity of each bond lying in the interval $(0, +\infty)$. We denote by $P_t(\tau)$ the time t price of a bond with remaining time to maturity τ, by $y_t(\tau)$ the corresponding yield, and by r_t the short rate (yield with maturity 0) in the economy.

There are two types of private agents in the economy: arbitrageurs and preferred habitat investors. The preferred habitat investors are standard and have preferences for specific maturities, so that investors with habitat τ at time t hold a position

$$Z_t(\tau) = -\beta_0\ (\tau)\ \log\ P_t\ (\tau) - \beta_t(\tau)$$

in the bond with maturity τ. The slope coefficient $\beta_0\ (\tau)$ captures the price sensitivity of the preferred habitat investors with habitats in $[\tau,\ \tau + d\tau]$ while $\beta_t\ (\tau)$ captures the time-varying demand shocks. The demand shocks $\beta_t\ (\tau)$ have a factor structure over the remaining time to maturity τ so that we can represent

$$\beta_t(\tau) = \theta_0(\tau) + \sum_{k=1}^{k} \theta_k(\tau)\beta_{k,t},$$

where $\{\beta_{k,t}\}$ are independent of maturity and $\theta_k\ (\tau)$ are constant maturity-specific loadings.

We denote by $\vec{v}_t = (r_t,\ \beta_{1,t}, \ldots,\ \beta_{K,t})'$ the vector of exogenous random processes in the economy. $\vec{v}_t$ evolves according to an Ornstein-Uhlenbeck process

$$d\vec{v}_t = -\gamma\ (\vec{v}_t - \overline{v})dt + \Sigma dB_t,$$

where B_t is a standard $(K + 1) \times 1$ vector Brownian motion. If we conjecture that bond prices are exponentially affine in the $\vec{v}_t$

$$P_t(\tau) = \exp\Big(- A\ (\tau)' \vec{v}_t - C\ (\tau)\Big),$$

then prices evolve as

$$\frac{dP_t(\tau)}{P_t(\tau)} = \mu_t\ (\tau)\ dt\ -\ A\ (\tau)'\ \Sigma dB_t$$

where the instantaneous expected return $\mu_t\ (\tau)$ is given by

$$\mu_t\ (\tau)\ =\ A\ (\tau)'\ \vec{v}_t\ +\ C(\tau)'\ +\ A\ (\tau)'\ \gamma\ (\vec{v}_t - \overline{v}) + \frac{1}{2}A(\tau)'\ \Sigma\Sigma' A(\tau)$$

The arbitrageurs in the economy instead optimally choose their holdings of the risky assets in the economy and of the short rate. Focusing for now on the case where Treasuries are the only securities available, arbitrageurs choose their holdings $X_t\ (\tau)\ d\tau$ of bonds with maturities in $[\tau, \tau + d\tau]$ to maximize an instantaneous mean-variance objective of wealth

$$\max_{\{Xt(\tau)\}} E_t(dW_t) - \frac{\gamma}{2} V_t(dW_t)$$

where γ is the coefficient of risk aversion. The maximization is subject to a value-at-risk (VaR) constraint $\mathbb{E}\,\mathbb{V}$

$$\alpha\sqrt{\frac{1}{dt}\left\langle\int_0^{+\infty} X_t\ (\tau)\ \frac{dP_t\ (\tau)}{P_t(\tau)}\ d\tau^2\right\rangle} \leq W_t,$$

so that the arbitrageurs are required to have enough wealth to cover a certain fraction of asset losses. While in reality arbitrageurs and intermediaries may be subject to a much wider set of leverage constraints, the VaR constraint provides a convenient illustration of changes in the tightness of leverage constraints affecting equilibrium asset prices and the impact that asset purchases can have through changing the tightness of the constraint.

With these assumptions, the dynamic budget constraint of the intermediaries is given by

$$\begin{aligned} dW_t &= W_t r_t dt + \int_0^{+\infty} X_t\ (\tau)\ \left(\frac{dP_t\ (\tau)}{P_t(\tau)}\ \ r_t dt\right)\ d\tau \\ &= W_t r_t dt + \int_0^{+\infty} X_t\ (\tau)\ \left(\mu_t(\tau) - r_t\right)\ d\tau dt - \int_0^{+\infty} X_t(\tau)'\ \Sigma d\tau dB_t\,. \end{aligned}$$

Using the conjectured dynamics of bond returns from above, we can thus rewrite the arbitrageurs' problem as

$$\max_{\{Xt(\tau)\}}\ \int_0^{+\infty} X_t(\tau)\ \left(\mu_t(\tau) - r_t\right)\ d\tau - \frac{\gamma}{2}\left(\int_0^{+\infty} X_t(\tau)\ A\ (\tau)'\ d\tau\right)'$$

$$\Sigma'\Sigma\ \left(\int_0^{+\infty} X_t(\tau)\,A\,(\tau)'d\tau\right)$$

$$W_t \geq \alpha\sqrt{\left(\int_0^{+\infty} X_t\ (\tau)\ A\ (\tau)'\ d\tau\right)'\Sigma'\Sigma\left(\int_0^{+\infty} X_t\ (\tau)\ A\ (\tau)'\ d\tau\right)}\quad .$$

Denote by $\lambda_t/2$ the Lagrange multiplier on the date t VaR constraint. Then the first order condition for the arbitrageurs' allocation is given by

$$\mu_t(\tau) - r_t = (\gamma + \lambda_t)A(\tau)'\Sigma\Sigma'\left(\int_0^{+\infty} X_t\ (\tau)\ A\ (\tau)'\ d\tau\right).$$

When the arbitrageurs are unconstrained – that is, when their wealth is high relative to the riskiness of bond returns – the Lagrange multiplier $\lambda_t/2$ is zero and the first order condition for the arbitrageurs' problem collapses to the one in Vayanos and Vila (2021). When arbitrageur wealth is low, instead, their portfolio allocation is constrained, raising the equilibrium expected excess returns on government bonds, and lowering the government bond price. In general, the arbitrageurs' first order condition relates the expected excess on a bond with maturity τ to the riskiness of the bond $-A(\tau)' \Sigma$ and the vector of risk prices in the economy

$$\eta_t = -(\gamma + \lambda_t)\, \Sigma' \left(\int_0^{+\infty} X_t(\tau)\, A(\tau)' d\tau \right).$$

Risk prices are high when the arbitrageurs' effective risk aversion $\gamma + \lambda_t$ is high, when uncertainty (Σ) is high, or when arbitrageurs hold large positions in bonds (so that $\{X_t(\tau)\}_{\tau \geq 0}$ are large).

The arbitrageurs' first order conditions together with market clearing

$$Z_t(\tau) + X_t(\tau) = 0$$

provide the intuition for the mechanisms through which the central bank's balance sheet policy can affect equilibrium asset prices. First, the most straightforward, is the "pure" purchase effect: *ceteris paribus*, central bank purchases reduce the net supply of bonds that arbitrageurs have to absorb. To the extent that new supply enters the marketplace, either through changes in the preferred habitat investors' preferences (leading to sales by such investors) or through new issuance by the fiscal authority, the pure purchase effect would also explain a flow effect of QE.

Second, by pre-specifying a pace and duration of purchases, the central bank can reduce the uncertainty associated with the demand shocks $\vec{v}_t$ of the preferred habitat investors. Reducing uncertainty Σ has two effects. Lower uncertainty directly reduces the risk prices η_t in the economy and the bond risk exposure $A(\tau)'\Sigma$. Lower uncertainty further relaxes the arbitrageurs' VaR constraint, again by reducing the bond risk exposure that enters into the calculation of the VaR constraint. By relaxing the arbitrageurs' VaR constraint, central bank purchases reduce arbitrageurs' effective risk aversion, further reducing the prices of the risk factors in the economy. The impact of central bank purchases on uncertainty in the economy can generate both an announcement effect – with private agents in the economy anticipating that future central bank purchases will reduce demand shock volatility in the future – and a purchase effect – by actually delivering on the anticipated reduction in demand shock volatility. Furthermore, the uncertainty channel can explain an asymmetric effect of QE and QT. A predictable QT program does not necessarily increase the uncertainty associated with the demand shocks of preferred habitat investors and, assuming that arbitrageurs are sufficiently capitalized, does not necessarily make arbitrageurs' leverage constraints bind. Finally, a QE effect through uncertainty rationalizes why the first announcement of QE has the largest impact: It is fully unanticipated by market participants, whereas subsequent QE announcements may be anticipated by market participants as part of the "new normal" toolkit of monetary policy.

Related to the reduction of uncertainty channel, central bank purchases can also act as a signal that the central bank plans to maintain a low level of interest rates going forward. Through the lens of the simple framework we laid out at the beginning of this section, this translates into a lower level of the unconditional level of interest rates, lowering the expected excess returns to holding bonds. This again has the effect of lowering the risk prices in the economy, enabling arbitrageurs to take on more leverage and to intermediate more end investors' demand.

The third channel through which central banks' balance sheet policy may have an effect on risky asset prices in the economy is through a rebalancing effect. By relaxing arbitrageurs' leverage constraints, central bank purchases enable arbitrageurs to take on larger positions in other risky assets. To the extent that other risky assets have risks correlated with those of government bonds – for example, other fixed income securities – decreases in risk prices η_t further decrease the risk premia on these risky assets with risk exposures correlated to those of the government bonds. By decreasing the supply of government bonds of a particular maturity, central bank purchases may also induce investors with preferences for those maturities to reallocate to holding other fixed income securities – for example, corporate bonds – of the same maturity. This again lowers the equilibrium risk premia on those securities, further relaxing arbitrageurs' leverage constraints. The rebalancing effect of central bank purchases, especially if it acts through the portfolios of preferred habitat investors, is also likely to be asymmetric between QE and QT. While removing supply of a particular maturity can induce preferred habitat investors to seek alternative securities, adding supply does not necessary induce those investors to sell out of their existing corporate bond positions, particularly when those investors are buy-and-hold. This is the case with US insurance companies and pension funds, leading to little reallocation away from existing corporate bond positions when new Treasury supply is introduced.

Finally, it is worth noting that central bank purchases increase the size of central bank balance sheets and thereby increase the overall level of reserves in the economy. Thus, for central bank purchases to relax arbitrageurs' constraints, arbitrageurs cannot be indifferent between holding reserves and holding Treasuries. Under the VaR constraint we examined here, reserves, which have zero remaining time to maturity, expose arbitrageurs to less duration risk than government bonds, thereby relaxing the VaR constraint. More generally, any differences in either the regulatory treatment of reserves and Treasuries, differences in how positions can be used in market transactions (for example, due to uses as collateral) or differences in the distribution of reserves and Treasury holdings will translate into non-neutrality of central bank purchases for arbitrageurs' constraints.

2.3 Quantitative Easing

Quantitative easing in the US has been a significant part of monetary policy since the 2008–2009 global financial crisis. We start by reviewing the timeline of QE programs in the US and then turn to discussing the approaches that the literature has taken to evaluate their impact on asset prices.

2.3.1 QE Timeline

2.3.1.1 QE1

The modern history of QE by the Federal Reserve began on 25 November 2008, with the Federal Reserve announcing purchases of agency debt and agency mortgage-backed securities (MBS) "to reduce the cost and increase the availability of credit for the purchase of houses, which in turn should support housing markets and foster improved conditions in financial markets more generally." The initial press release announced purchases of \$100 billion in agency debt and \$500 billion in agency MBS. QE1 was further expanded on 18 March 2009, with an announcement of additional purchases of \$100 billion of agency debt, \$750 billion of agency

MBS and $300 billion of long-term Treasury securities, bringing the overall size of QE1 purchases to $1.75 trillion.

2.3.1.2 QE2

By November 2010, the FOMC judged that "the pace of recovery in output and employment continue[d] to be slow," and announced on the 3 November 2010 FOMC statement an expansion of its securities holdings. In particular, the 3 November 2010 statement announced the purchase of a further $600 billion of longer-term Treasury securities by the end of the second quarter of 2011, at a pace of about $75 billion per month. The same FOMC statement also introduced a notion of data-dependence into both the size and the pace of purchases, noting that, "The Committee will regularly review the pace of its securities purchases and the overall size of the asset-purchase program in light of incoming information and will adjust the program as needed to best foster maximum employment and price stability." The November FOMC statement was largely anticipated due to Chairman Bernanke's communication in late August 2010, reminding the markets that the FOMC could purchase more assets if conditions warranted, and the September 2010 FOMC statement reiterating concerns about low inflation. The November 2010 FOMC statement also reconfirmed the committee's policy of reinvesting principal payments from securities holdings into Treasuries.

2.3.1.3 Maturity Extension Program (MEP)

Shortly after the completion of QE2 purchases in June 2011, the FOMC announced the Maturity Extension Program and Reinvestment Policy. Instead of expanding QE, the MEP, also known as "operation twist," involved selling short-term Treasury securities and using the proceeds to buy longer-term Treasury securities. The program aimed to flatten the yield curve and lower longer-term interest rates. Under the program, the Federal Reserve sold $400 billion of short-term securities and purchased $400 billion of long-term securities, prompting commentary that the "Fed twists again." Together with the 21 September 2011 MEP announcement, the FOMC also announced that it would begin reinvesting agency MBS and agency debt principal into agency MBS holdings, rather than Treasuries. The MEP was extended further in June 2012, with the FOMC announcing on 20 June 2012 that the program would purchase an additional $267 billion of long-term securities with offsetting sales of short-term securities.

2.3.1.4 QE3

In September 2012 the FOMC judged that the continued weakness in inflation and slow pace of economic recovery required further interventions, announcing on 13 September 2012 additional purchases of agency MBS at a pace of $40 billion per month through the end of 2012. QE3 was further expanded on 12 December 2012, with the continuation of the $40 billion a month agency MBS purchases and the announcement that the $45 billion a month purchases of long-term Treasuries conducted as part of MEP would no longer be offset by sales of short-term securities. While QE1 and QE2 involved purchases at a given pace up to a predetermined overall size of each program, the December 2012 FOMC statement left the total amount of securities purchases and their duration open-ended, specifying instead that "the Committee will continue its purchases of Treasury and agency mortgage-backed securities . . . until [outlook for the labor market improves substantially] in a context of price stability." QE3 purchases continued at the monthly pace of $40 billion agency MBS and $45 billion long-term Treasuries until 18 December 2013, when the FOMC announced a tapering of the pace of purchases, reducing the pace by $10 billion (split evenly between agency MBS and Treasuries) at every subsequent meeting. QE3 purchases concluded in October 2014, with $790 billion of Treasury securities and $823 billion of agency MBS purchased overall throughout the duration of the program.

Prior to the "official" announcement of the tapering of QE3, on 22 May 2013, then Fed Chair Ben Bernanke indicated for the first time that the Fed was considering slowing down its asset purchases as the economy showed signs of recovery. This potential reduction in QE sparked concerns among investors about the future of liquidity and economic growth, leading to a sharp rise in interest rates and a sell-off in bond markets during which ten-year US Treasuries rose from around 2 percent in May 2013 to around 3 percent in December 2013. This episode highlighted the crucial role of clear and effective communication in the context of unwinding QE, shaping the deliberate and precise communication of the Fed's eventual ending of QE and the start of QT.

2.3.1.5 QE4

The on-set of the COVID-19 pandemic brought substantial dislocations in global asset markets, including the US Treasury and US agency-backed MBS markets. As part of the response to these broad market dislocations, the FOMC announced on 15 March 2020 that it would increase its holdings of Treasuries by at least $500 billion and its holdings of agency MBS by at least $200 billion to support market functioning. As such, the policy rationale was similar to the one for QE1: These asset purchases were conducted to stabilize markets, thereby restoring the flow of credit to households, rather than implementing a further loosening of the stance of monetary policy in the context of the effective zero lower bound on the policy rate. QE4 was further expanded on 23 March 2020, with the FOMC announcing that it would continue to purchase securities "in the amounts needed" to support market functioning and effective transmission of monetary policy. These announcements made QE4 unprecedented in the speed and scale of the intervention. During the height of the dislocations in Spring 2020, purchases reached $100 billion per day and totaled more than $2 trillion by 30 April 2020. QE4 purchases also included agency commercial mortgage-backed securities (CMBS), extending the market stabilization objective to that important market as well.

Market conditions improved rapidly after the introduction of the various market interventions in March 2020, and the pace of purchases declined to $18 billion daily in late April and $9.5 billion daily in late May 2020. By the June 2020 FOMC meeting, purchases were proceeding at a monthly pace of $80 billion Treasuries and $40 billion agency MBS, a pace that was maintained until the start of tapering in November 2021. QE4 purchases were completed by March 2022, totaling around $4.6 trillion purchased securities.

2.3.2 *Measuring the Impact of QE*

Empirical macroeconomics has long studied the question of how to measure the impact of monetary policy on financial markets and real activity. With the FOMC announcing policy rate decisions publicly at every meeting starting in 1994, the literature studying the connection between conventional monetary policy changes and financial conditions has largely converged to an empirical strategy that measures the monetary policy surprise associated with every policy meeting and the corresponding change in broader financial conditions in a relatively narrow window – ranging from a few minutes to a couple of days – around the policy announcement. Such empirical strategies are broadly speaking inaccessible to researchers evaluating the impact of a central bank's balance sheet policy on financial markets.

The empirical literature on evaluating the effects of large-scale asset purchases on financial markets has instead primarily focused on an event study strategy. The event study strategy is particularly suited to evaluating the effect of *surprise announcements* of monetary policy actions as the forward-looking nature of financial markets means that changes in the expected future supply of securities and the future path of interest rates are reflected in today's asset prices. As such, the QE1 announcements in November 2008 and March 2009 have proven to provide the most fruitful information on the effectiveness of central bank purchases as the novelty of QE1 plausibly sets it apart from subsequent QE announcements.

While different event studies use different sizes of event windows, from 30 minutes to three days bracketing the announcements, the estimates of the impact on government bond yields from event studies focusing on the QE1 announcement are largely not sensitive to the size of the event window.[1] Various studies (Gagnon et al., 2011; Krishnamurthy and Vissing-Jorgensen, 2011; D'Amico et al., 2012; D'Amico and King, 2013; Bauer and Neely, 2014; Neely, 2015) estimate that, for purchases equivalent to 10 percent of GDP, ten-year yields decline by forty to ninety basis points. Such purchases imply a similar reaction of yields on lower-rated corporate bonds (Gilchrist and Zakrajˇsek, 2013) and a somewhat smaller reaction of foreign sovereign debt yields (Neely, 2015). A surprise announcement of purchases of long-term bonds also lowers MBS yield, by around sixty-six basis points per $1 trillion of purchases announced, as well as mortgage rates (Krishnamurthy and Vissing-Jorgensen, 2011; Hancock and Passmore, 2014); lower the value of the USD and raise both domestic and international stock prices (Kiley, 2014; Bowman et al., 2015; Neely, 2015); and reduce option-implied tail risk (Hattori et al., 2016) and the liquidity risk premium in agency MBS (Boyarchenko et al., 2019).

Other studies have attempted to measure the long-term effects of QE announcements and whether the effect is persistent. Wright (2012) takes a structural vector autoregression approach to identify days on which the variance of monetary policy shocks was especially high. He

[1] See also the literature surveys in Bhattarai and Neely (2022) and Gagnon (2016).

measures the total effects of FOMC news, although QE is clearly the dominant tool used during the paper's sample period, from November 2008 to December 2010. Over that period, it is estimated that monetary policy shocks have a significant effect on ten-year yields that wear off over the next few months. Similarly, Greenlaw and colleagues (2018) find a smaller policy impact compared with the event studies due to reversal of the initial reaction on subsequent days to the announcement. They point out the caveat that QE1 is not a good natural experiment for how QE works in normal times as it was a period of severe market dislocation and illiquidity, as well as the difficulty to control for investors' expectations ahead of QE. These empirical findings are supported to some extent by theory. For example, using a standard New Keynesian model, Curdia and Woodford (2011) argue that QE is generally ineffective, but that targeted asset purchases by a central bank can instead be effective when financial markets are sufficiently disrupted.

Besides measuring the overall effect of QE announcements, the academic literature has tried to disentangle the channels through which those announcements operate, focusing on portfolio rebalancing and signaling channels. Bauer and Rudebusch (2011), Christensen and Rudebusch (2012), Swanson (2021) and Christensen and Rudebusch (2016) separate the announcement effect into signaling and portfolio channels, and find that the portfolio channel accounts for around fifteen to forty-five basis points of the overall effect of the QE announcement. Haddad and colleagues (2024) instead attribute the overall announcement effect to a reduction in uncertainty about future purchases; that is, to a priced-in insurance effect of future central bank interventions.

It is important to note that an event study approach by definition focuses only on the announcement effect of QE and cannot measure, for example, the impact of the flow of purchases or the impact of the overall size and composition of the Federal Reserve's balance sheet. An alternative approach is to use time series data, leveraging cross-sectional security heterogeneity to estimate the differential impact of central bank asset purchases. D'Amico and King (2013) study the flow effects of QE1 using security-level transactions and find small microstructure effects on the liquidity of the securities being purchased. Kandrac and Schlusche (2013), however, argue that these effects were confined to the early large-scale asset purchases (LSAPs) but not necessarily economically significant and not present during QE2 or MEP. While Kandrac and Schlusche interpret their findings as suggesting that LSAPs in general do not have systematic liquidity flow effects, an alternative interpretation is that LSAP purchases have liquidity effects only when Treasury (and MBS) market functioning is impaired. Indeed, the literature that has studied the effect of market functioning purchases during the early stages of QE4 (Fleming et al., 2022; He et al., 2022) found that such purchases substantially improved market functioning in March and April 2020. While the debate on the overall impact of QE4 and other COVID-19-era interventions is very far from settled (see e.g. Levin et al., 2022, for a more critical view of QE4), the market functioning purchases during QE1 and QE4 had important stabilization effects not just for the Treasury and agency MBS markets but also for other securities markets where Treasuries are used as collateral and for financial conditions globally.

Finally, recent studies have pursued a "shock identification" strategy to try to quantify the portfolio rebalancing channel or, in other words, the preferred habitat channel. Ray and colleagues (2024) use high frequency identification from Treasury auctions to construct demand shocks for Treasuries in the primary market that mimic QE and are plausible transmitted through the preferred habitat channel only. Using such demand shocks, Ray and colleagues (2024) argue that the preferred habitat channel accounts for the majority of the response of financial markets to QE, especially during periods of market stress. Selgrad (2023) likewise constructs QE shocks – based on differences between predicted and actual purchased amounts of individual securities – and finds a large role for the portfolio rebalancing channel, with investors rebalancing toward corporate bonds within their preferred maturity segment in response to Treasury purchases. Such rebalancing leads to a substantial reduction in corporate bond yields, with \$100 billion of Treasury purchases corresponding to a 7.8 basis points decline in average bond yields.

2.4 Quantitative Tightening

While an expansion of the central banks' balance sheet may be necessary to stabilize financial markets during periods of stress and to transmit monetary policy easing when the policy rate is at the effective zero lower bound, tightening of monetary policy also requires management of the balance sheet size. The US has so-far experienced two episodes of QT – declines in the size of the Federal Reserve's balance sheet. In both cases, that reduction was achieved through a slow-down of reinvestment of the maturing principal on the existing portfolio of securities rather through outright sales. In other words, the evolution of the Federal Reserve's balance sheet has three phases. During the expansion phase, or the QE phase, the Federal Reserve actively buys additional securities, increasing the size of the balance sheet. When purchases concluded, the Federal Reserve can choose to keep the size of the balance sheet constant. During this holding phase, Treasury securities and agency debt held may mature and agency MBS may either mature or be prepaid early, resulting in all cases in a repayment of the principal. To keep the face value of securities held constant, the Federal Reserve replaces matured or prepaid securities with purchases of other securities. When the Federal Reserve reduces the size of the balance sheet, it does so by slowing the replacement rate of matured or prepaid securities, so that principal payments are not used one-for-one for purchases of new securities. The two QT programs in the US were conducted as follows.

2.4.1 *QT1*

Starting in October 2017, the FOMC began to reduce the size of its securities holdings by decreasing the reinvestment of principal payments. To ensure a gradual decline in the size of the Federal Reserve balance sheet, the FOMC capped the monthly amount of securities that were allowed to mature and not be replaced. As described in the 14 June 2017 addendum to the policy normalization principles, the initial cap was $6 billion per month for Treasury redemptions and $4 billion per month for agency MBS and agency debt redemptions. These caps increased gradually every quarter by $6 billion and $4 billion for Treasuries and agency MBS, respectively, until they reached $30 billion and $15 billion monthly. In March 2019, the FOMC reduced the cap on Treasuries redemptions to $15 billion monthly, effective in May 2019, and balance sheet run-off ended altogether in August 2019. Between October 2017 and August 2019, the Federal Reserve's balance sheet declined by $0.7 trillion.

2.4.2 *QT2*

The FOMC outlined balance sheet reduction principles in January 2022, and a specific pace of balance sheet reduction in May 2022. The May 2022 announcement outlined that the amount of securities held by the Federal Reserves would be allowed to decrease up to certain monthly limits ("caps"), with the pace of the run-off increasing after an initial three-month period. The initial cap on the run-off in Treasury securities was set at $30 billion per month, increasing to $60 billion monthly after three months. The initial cap on the run-off in agency MBS was set at $17.5 billion per month, likewise doubling to $35 billion monthly after a three-month period. The run-off in Treasury securities was targeted first at Treasury coupon securities (that is, longer-term securities), with a run-off in Treasury bills allowed only to the extent that coupon maturities are less than the monthly cap. In May 2024, the FOMC announced a slowing of the run-off, lowering the cap on Treasury redemptions to $25 billion effective June 2024 but maintaining the $35 billion monthly redemption cap on agency MBS and agency debt. Overall, between the start of QT2 in June 2022 and July 2024, the Federal Reserve's securities holdings declined by $1.75 trillion, with a $1.36 trillion reduction in Treasury securities holdings and $0.39 trillion in agency MBS holdings.

There are a number reasons why one would expect the effects of QT to not simply be an unwinding of the QE effects. First, QT is conducted against the background of well-functioning financial markets while QE1 and QE4 were conducted during periods of market stress. Indeed, the taper tantrum episode illustrates the potential adverse effects on markets if QT were conducted before market conditions fully stabilized as even a misconstrued announcement without actual removal of accommodation led to large movements in fixed income prices. More generally, the economic conditions during which monetary policy is tightened are substantively different from the economic environment that necessitates policy easing. Thus, the removal of liquidity through a gradual QT approach is less likely to, for example, substantially increase levered investors' effective risk aversion. Second, announcement effects are likely to be much more muted under QT than QE as QT announcements are largely anticipated and the pace of QT has been much slower than the pace of QE. Third, buy-and-hold preferred habitat investors who adjusted their portfolios toward other securities to fulfill their preferred maturity habitat holdings are unlikely to sell out of those securities in response to QT. Similarly, the regulatory environment has changed substantially since the start of QE in 2008, potentially changing the impact that an increased supply of Treasury and MBS securities may have. Finally, while the bulk of post-crisis QE programs were conducted simultaneously across a large number of advanced economies, QT1 was done by the US in isolation.

Smith and Valcarcel (2023) study the effects of QT1 on financial conditions. They argue that the primary transmission channel of QT is through the market for bank reserves. They document that the relationship between the federal funds – interest on excess reserves spread and the overall amount of reserves is much steeper during the QT1 period. This reduction in the liquidity available to the banking sector translates into an overall tightening of financial conditions, even though QT announcement effects on financial conditions were largely absent.

2.5 Conclusion

As the Federal Reserve navigates the transition from an abundant to an ample reserves regime, the question of how the central bank's balance sheet affects financial conditions and through which channels is ever more salient. Before the global financial crisis, the Federal Reserve's balance sheet was substantially smaller than current levels, and monetary policy was implemented through open market operations that kept the federal funds rate at the FOMC's target. The global financial crisis and the post-crisis sluggish recovery of the economy precipitated the need for new approaches to setting and implementing monetary policy. In the "new normal" of monetary policy, the Federal Reserve's balance sheet is an integral tool for stabilizing financial conditions during periods of stress and adjusting the stance of monetary policy beyond that which can be achieved through the federal funds target range alone.

In this new normal, both the asset side and the liabilities side of the Federal Reserve's balance sheet have a role. Increasing the overall size of the balance sheet can help ease financial conditions by providing liquidity in stressed markets and easing the stance of monetary policy at the effective zero lower bound. Changing the composition of the balance sheet – in terms of the types of securities and the duration of the portfolio held – can shift which market and, thus, which market participants are affected the most directly. In other words, shifts in the composition of the Federal Reserve's balance sheet may translate into a differential transmission of monetary policy, even when the overall size of the balance sheet remains the same.

The Federal Reserve's liabilities serve as safe assets for the rest of the global financial system. Reserves and non-reserve deposits at the

Federal Reserve support liquidity risk management and fulfill regulatory liquidity requirements for member-banks of the Federal Reserve System, as well as designated financial market utilities and foreign central banks. In the current implementation of monetary policy, the Federal Reserve also lends the securities from its balance sheet to money market mutual funds through the overnight reverse repo facility, with the interest rate in the facility helping to support interest rate control. The size and the composition of the central bank's balance sheet thus also affects the transmission of monetary policy through the composition of the central bank's liabilities.

The benefits of the central bank's balance sheet policies have to, however, be balanced against the possible risks. Any official sector intervention into financial markets raises moral hazard concerns, with market participants anticipating future interventions, leading to a slippery slope of underestimation of risks and expectations of interventions in response to ever less exigent circumstances. In the case of purchases of Treasuries and agency debt and agency MBS, an additional risk is the perception of a switch to a fiscally dominated monetary policy regime and the specter of a monetization of government debt. More research is necessary to understand the longer-run costs and benefits of monetary policy implementation through the size and composition of the balance sheet.

References

Bauer, M. D. and C. J. Neely (2014): "International channels of the Fed's unconventional monetary policy," *Journal of International Money and Finance*, 44, 24–46.

Bauer, M. and G. Rudebusch (2011): "Signals from unconventional monetary policy," *FRBSF Economic Letter*, 36.

Bhattarai, S. and C. J. Neely (2022): "An analysis of the literature on international unconventional monetary policy," *Journal of Economic Literature*, 60, 527–597.

Bowman, D., J. M. Londono and H. Sapriza (2015): "US unconventional monetary policy and transmission to emerging market economies," *Journal of International Money and Finance*, 55, 27–59.

Boyarchenko, N., A. Fuster and D. O. Lucca (2019): "Understanding mortgage spreads," *The Review of Financial Studies*, 32, 3799–3850.

Christensen, J. H. and G. D. Rudebusch (2012): "The response of interest rates to US and UK quantitative easing," *The Economic Journal*, 122, F385–F414.

(2016): "Modeling yields at the zero lower bound: Are shadow rates the solution?" in *Dynamic Factor Models*, Emerald Group Publishing Limited, vol. 35, 75–125.

Curdia, V. and M. Woodford (2011): "The central-bank balance sheet as an instrument of monetary policy," *Journal of Monetary Economics*, 58, 54–79.

D'Amico, S., W. English, D. Lo´pez-Salido and E. Nelson (2012): "The Federal Reserve's large-scale asset purchase programmes: rationale and effects," *The Economic Journal*, 122, F415–F446.

D'Amico, S. and T. B. King (2013): "Flow and stock effects of large-scale treasury purchases: Evidence on the importance of local supply," *Journal of Financial Economics*, 108, 425–448.

Fleming, M. J., H. Liu, R. Podjasek and J. Schurmeier (2022): "The Federal Reserve's market functioning purchases," *Economic Policy Review*, 28, 210–241.

Gagnon, J. E. (2016): "Quantitative easing: An underappreciated success," *PIIE Policy Brief*, 16, 1–7.

Gagnon, J., M. Raskin, J. Remache and B. Sack (2011): "The financial market effects of the Federal Reserve's large-scale asset purchases," *International Journal of Central Banking*, 7, 45–52.

Gilchrist, S. and E. Zakrajˇsek (2013): "The impact of the Federal Reserve's large-scale asset purchase programs on corporate credit risk," *Journal of Money, Credit and Banking*, 45, 29–57.

Greenlaw, D., J. D. Hamilton, E. Harris and K. D. West (2018): "A skeptical view of the impact of the Fed's balance sheet," Tech. rep., National Bureau of Economic Research.

Guthrie, G. and J. Wright (2000): "Open mouth operations," *Journal of Monetary Economics*, 46, 489–516.

Haddad, V., M. Moreira and T. Muir (2024): "Asset purchase rules: How QE transformed the bond market," Tech. rep., National Bureau of Economic Research.

Hancock, D. and S. W. Passmore (2014): "How the Federal Reserve's large-scale asset purchases (LSAPs) influence mortgage-backed securities (MBS) yields and US mortgage rates," Feds working paper no. 2014-12, Federal Reserve Board of Governors.

Hattori, M., A. Schrimpf and V. Sushko (2016): "The response of tail risk perceptions to unconventional monetary policy," *American Economic Journal: Macroeconomics*, 8, 111–136.

He, Z., S. Nagel and Z. Song (2022): "Treasury inconvenience yields during the COVID-19 crisis," *Journal of Financial Economics*, 143, 57–79.

Kandrac, J. and B. Schlusche (2013): "Flow effects of large-scale asset purchases," *Economics Letters*, 121, 330–335.

Kiley, M. T. (2014): "The response of equity prices to movements in long-term interest rates associated with monetary policy statements: Before and after the zero lower bound," *Journal of Money, Credit and Banking*, 46, 1057–1071.

Krishnamurthy, A. and A. Vissing-Jorgensen (2011): "The effects of quantitative easing on interest rates: Channels and implications for policy," *Brookings Papers on Economic Activity*, 43, 215–287.

Levin, A. T., B. L. Lu and W. R. Nelson (2022): "Quantifying the costs and benefits of quantitative easing," Working Paper N. 30749, National Bureau of Economic Research.

Neely, C. J. (2015): "Unconventional monetary policy had large international effects," *Journal of Banking and Finance*, 52, 101–111.

Ray, W., M. Droste and Y. Gorodnichenko (2024): "Unbundling quantitative easing: Taking a cue from treasury auctions," *Journal of Political Economy*, 132(9): 3115–3172.

Selgrad, J. (2023): "Testing the portfolio rebalancing channel of quantitative easing," Working paper, New York University.

Smith, A. L. and V. J. Valcarcel (2023): "The financial market effects of unwinding the federal reserve's balance sheet," *Journal of Economic Dynamics and Control*, 146, 104582.

Swanson, E. T. (2011): "Let's twist again: a high-frequency event-study analysis of operation twist and its implications for QE2," *Brookings Papers on Economic Activity*, 151–188.

(2021): "Measuring the effects of Federal Reserve forward guidance and asset purchases on financial markets," *Journal of Monetary Economics*, 118, 32–53.

Taylor, J. B. (2001): "Expectations, open market operations, and changes in the federal funds rate," *Federal Reserve Bank of Saint Louis Review*, 83, 33–48.

Thornton, D. L. (2004): "The Fed and short-term rates: Is it open market operations, open mouth operations or interest rate smoothing?" *Journal of Banking and Finance*, 28, 475–498.

Vayanos, D. and J.-L. Vila (2021): "A preferred-habitat model of the term structure of interest rates," *Econometrica*, 89, 77–112.

Wright, J. H. (2012): "What does monetary policy do to long-term interest rates at the zero lower bound?" *The Economic Journal*, 122, F447–F466.

3 *Measuring and Modelling the Effects of QE and QT in VAR models*

TOMASZ WIELADEK

3.1 Introduction

Vector autoregressions (VARs) have become the standard empirical tool for examining the effects of monetary policy on the economy in the past four decades. In his seminal work, Sims (1980) proposed this approach to study the effects of money supply shocks on the US economy as an alternative to the large-scale empirical models of the day. Since his initial work, many studies have used this approach subsequently. The approach has been refined in many different ways. Techniques to improve estimation such as using Bayesian methods, (Litterman, 1986) including a much larger amount of information (Bernanke, Boivin and Eliasz, 2005) and allowing for more theory consistent identification of macroeconomic shocks (Canova and De Nicolo, 2002) have been developed over time. However, at the core, the approach has remained the same for the past four decades. For conventional monetary policy, there is a broad consensus of how to model the transmission of monetary policy and which policy instrument to focus on. But for quantitative easing (QE) there is no consensus on how to model this policy in a VAR. The question does arise whether different approaches provide different answers. This is one of the questions this chapter proposes to tackle, by examining the empirical effects of eight different VAR models, based on the major approaches proposed in the literature.

Previous papers have provided surveys of the different approaches to the econometric modelling of QE. Borio and Zabai (2018) provide a comprehensive survey of the different approaches used to study QE in VAR and dynamic stochastic general equilibrium (DSGE) models. They argue that results from these studies need to be taken with a pinch of salt. Vector autoregression studies are heavily data-dependent and often need to extrapolate from pre-QE data, which may affect the reliability of these results and make it less clear what they are actually capturing. Their critique of DSGE models is that while these models may illustrate the transmission channels better, they are unlikely to be able to model all of them, meaning that their quantitative results may not fully reflect the policy. More recently, Fabo, Janckova, Pastor and Kempf (2021) collect estimates of the inflation and output impact of QE across a wide range of QE studies. Among other evidence, they use these data to show that central bank authors systematically report higher QE multipliers with OLS regressions. Of course, these datasets can also be applied to investigate whether different measures of QE produce different answers in VAR models. In Figures 3.1 and 3.2, I present VAR estimates for peak gross domestic product (GDP) and CPI effects in response to the same size QE shock from that paper. This shows that there is significant heterogeneity across country and studies. Vector autoregression QE effects range from very large to very small.

This analysis in this chapter aims to understand whether this large heterogeneity in estimates is due to specific QE measures or the VAR modelling approach adopted in each of these studies. I estimate eight different VAR models, based on the eight most popular measures of unconventional monetary policy in the academic literature. I estimate these models for the Euro Area, UK and US, but only on data when

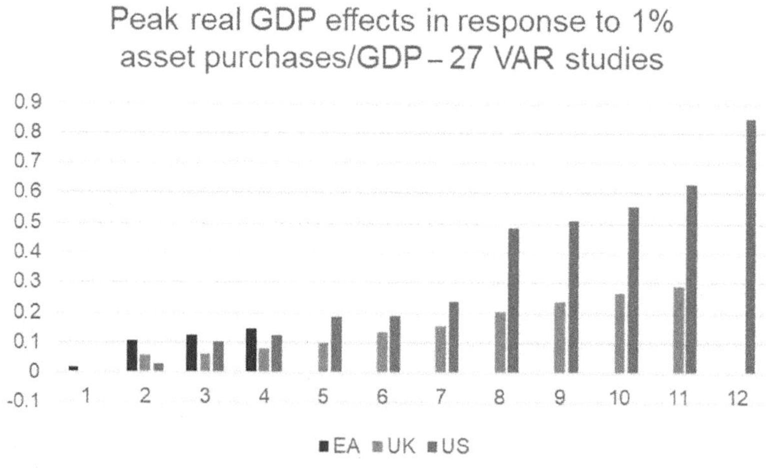

Figure 3.1 Peak GDP effects in response to QE across VAR studies and countries.

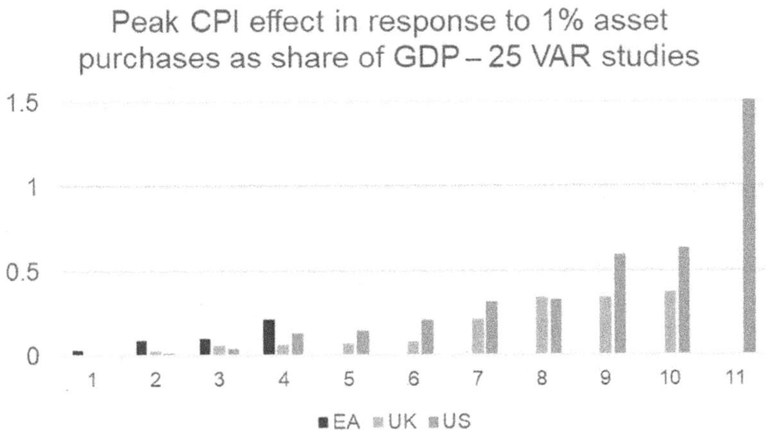

Figure 3.2 Peak CPI effects in response to QE across VAR studies and countries.

these economies were at the Zero Lower Bound and their central banks actively engaged in QE. This addresses the criticism of Borio and Zabai (2018) that time-series studies of QE conflate the effects of QE with policy before the zero lower bound. Importantly, different studies usually use different VAR specifications. This makes the comparison of effects across studies difficult because it is impossible to know if different effects are due to a different measure of QE or due to a different VAR modelling approach. In contrast, I use the same VAR specification throughout my analysis. This allows for a much cleaner comparison of whether different measures of QE produce different results or not.

Given the current state of macroeconomic policy and debate, interest in QE is fading and interest in quantitative tightening (QT) is rising. Given the very limited time series available to date, it is not possible to apply VAR methods to study the effects of central banks' most recent QT. Even the Federal Reserve's QT episode in 2018 is hard to examine, since that datapoint is so close to the Covid-19 pandemic. However, it is possible to reverse-engineer QT multipliers from QE multipliers.

Economic theory suggests several transmission channels for QE. The portfolio rebalancing channel relies on the idea that active central bank purchases can lower long-term yields, as there are so-called preferred habitat investors who need to purchase government debt at certain maturities. Central bank purchases raise the scarcity of debt available at these maturities, thereby pushing up prices and lowering yields. An alternative transmission channel, proposed by Bauer and Rudebush (2014) is the idea that QE signals that the policy rate will stay lower for longer. Quantitative easing is also likely to depreciate the exchange rate. Weale and Wieladek (2016) highlight the economic uncertainty channel: in times of great economic uncertainty, QE is a signal to the general public that the central bank will do whatever it can to bring inflation back to target. This means that consumers need to save less for precautionary reasons and firms don't need to hold off on investment. A channel frequently mentioned by policymakers is the market stabilisation channel: QE supports normal financial market activity during a market dislocation such as 2008 or 2020. Finally, QE is financed by the issuance of central bank reserves. A loosening in reserve requirements should boost lending via the bank lending channel. The portfolio balance, bank lending and exchange rate channels should also operate with QT. If it were possible to therefore remove the signalling, market stabilising and economic uncertainty channel effects from multipliers of QE, the residual effects should roughly be reflective of QT. The second significant contribution of this chapter is to illustrate how to do that.

The results of my analysis show that the effects of QE are similar across measures. Where there are meaningful differences in the peak effects on output and inflation, the difference often isn't statistically significant. When I repeat this approach with the meta-data collected by Fabo, Janckova, Pastor and Kempf (2021), I get similar results.

My calculations suggest that QT is roughly 25% as powerful as QE, once the uncertainty, market stabilising and signalling channels are removed from QE estimates. When all of the Bank of England's QT announcements are taken into account, Bank of England QT raised the ten-year gilt yields by 60 bps. This seems much larger than the 10–15 bps estimated by the Bank of England in the August 2024 Monetary Policy report. I show that this can be reconciled through the large rise in foreign official investors ownership of Gilts since QT started. My back-of-the-envelope calculation is just that. It isn't estimated on the data. The Bank of England's figures are estimates. However, foreign official buyers bought roughly two-thirds of Gilts that became available as are result of QT. The private sector therefore only had to absorb one-third of the announced QT. This is how the Bank of England's estimates and my own can be reconciled.

These results have important macroeconomic policy implications. At the moment, central banks are in the process of cutting interest rates but maintaining QT at the same time. Put simply, central banks are easing with one hand but tightening with the other. Clearly, no central bank wants to unintentionally engineer significant deviations from its inflation target, given the experience of the last couple of years. However, to avoid policy mistakes, central banks need to get a better understanding of the tightening effect of QT. The best way to get these answers in a manner that encourages intellectual diversity is to crowd source them from outside. Central banks should therefore be leading the debate on how large or small the tightening effect of QT is.

3.2.1 Literature Review

This section reviews the ways that previous papers have modelled QE in VAR models. Vector autoregression models are one of many ways of modelling QE.[1] However, the advantage of VAR models is that they are the standard workhorse empirical model of monetary policy and provide estimates of monetary policy effects with the minimal structural and identification assumptions. Those are the reasons why this literature review will focus on the main ways in which QE has been modelled in previous VAR studies.

The first generation of QE VAR models relies on the idea that when the short-term rate reached the zero lower bound, central banks tried to reduce the long-term interest rate to stimulate their economies. Baumeister and Benati (2013) and Kapetanios, Mumtaz, Theodoris and Stevens (2012) model QE as shock that lowers the spread between the long-term and short-term interest rate and raises real GDP the CPI as a result. However, because these were the first papers written on this topic, their models are heavily reliant on macroeconomic data from before when QE was introduced. This is significant caveat, because spread shocks were not an instrument of monetary policy before that date. To address this issue both studies use models that allow coefficients to change over time. Baumeister

1 See Gertler and Karadi (2011, 2013) and Sims and Wu (2020) for DSGE approaches to modelling QE.

and Benati (2013) use a Bayesian VAR (BVAR) model with time-varying coefficients, while Kapetanios, Mumtaz, Theodoris and Stevens rely on a Markov-Switching BVAR model. While in theory these approaches should address the fact that these models are mostly estimated on data prior to the QE period, it is unclear if that is the case in practice.

An alternative approach, proposed by Krippner (2015) and Wu and Xia (2016) is to infer what the monetary policy rate would have been, given the slope of the yield curve, had the zero lower bound constraint not been present. The resulting 'shadow' policy rates can take negative values. Analytically, this is a very intuitive concept: the shadow rate is the policy rate that takes into account all of the additional balance sheet easing. Because it is expressed on the same scale as the conventional policy rate, it is much easier to interpret. Despite these advantages, shadow rates have one significant caveat: they are all dependent on the model of the yield curve that they are estimated from. Christensen, Oomen and Podolskij (2014) shows that the estimated shadow rates can differ significantly based on seemingly innocuous model choices. Aruoba, Mlikota, Schorfheide and Villalvazo (2022) rely on a three-variable structural VAR (SVAR) model with an occasionally binding constraint and find that inflation shows a stronger reaction to unconventional monetary policy relative to conventional policy, but upon impact only. Mavroides (2021) uses a similar approach to identify unconventional monetary shocks for the US but concludes that unconventional monetary policy is less effective than conventional monetary policy. The literature hasn't, as of yet, come with a way to provide shadow rate estimates which are robust to model choice.

The third generation of QE models relies on the central bank's balance sheet. The advantage of this approach is that all of the relevant studies rely only on data when the policy was actually implemented. Gambacorta, Hofman and Peersman (2014) estimate a panel VAR model on the balance sheets of several countries to show that balance sheet shocks have a statistically significant effect on output and prices in those countries. Weale and Wieladek (2016) go one step further and introduce a series of asset purchase announcements by central banks as the main measure of QE in their VAR models. They also show that small scale VAR models can be estimated just on data when the policy was implemented and find that asset purchase announcements raise real GDP and CPI in the UK and the US.[2] An important conceptual advantage of using asset purchase announcements, the actual policy decision, as the measure of QE in a VAR model is that this is more likely to pick up all of the relevant transmission channels. After all, monetary policy isn't just transmitted to the real economy through financial markets but also by affecting the expectations and behaviour of agents in the real economy.

The latest generation of measuring unconventional monetary policy relies on high-frequency shocks around the monetary policy announcement. Gertler and Karadi (2011, 2013) collect the change in future rates priced in financial markets around the monetary policy announcement for the US. They use the resulting time series of identified shocks as an instrument in a proxy-SVAR model to identify the monetary policy shock. An important advantage of this 'high-frequency' approach to examining monetary policy is that the shock series is the same for both conventional and unconventional monetary policy. This makes the comparison of the effects of conventional and unconventional monetary policy easier. However, Jarocinski and Karadi (2020) show that high-frequency shocks contain both the policy and an information shock. The information shock is the central bank's view on the future of economy and therefore future policy rates. Bu, Rogers and Wu (2021) introduce a new measure of high-frequency shocks, based on the Fama-Macbeth (1973) approach applied to bond markets. They show that their measure of monetary policy is free from information shocks and hence only contains the effects of monetary policy. As before, their measure can be used to compare the effects of conventional and unconventional monetary policy. Nevertheless, one issue with measures which are only derived from financial markets around the policy announcement is that they only capture the transmission through financial markets. But macroeconomic theory puts consumers' and firms' expectations of the future at the heart of the output and inflation reaction to monetary policy. It is unclear whether these measures derived from financial markets reactions to central bank announcements capture the expectations' reaction of firms and households well.

[2] Wieladek and Garcia-Pascual (2016) extend this approach to study the ECB's QE and find similar results. Haldane, Roberts-Sklar, Wieladek and Young (2016) extend this approach to study the effects of QE across countries.

None of these measures is likely to be flawless individually, but they are likely to be useful in assessing the effects of QE on the macroeconomy collectively.

3.2.2 VAR Methodology

The idea in this chapter is to compare different measures of QE within the same VAR model. Clearly, a suitable VAR model needs to include at least the minimum amount of relevant financial and monetary variables. But given the short period of the effective lower bound, short time series limit the number of variables that can be included. I use the model of Weale and Wieladek (2016). They argue that including the long-term interest rate and real share prices alongside the policy variable is important to capture the relevant monetary policy transmission mechanism. This VAR model only requires five variables and Weale and Wieladek (2016), Wieladek and Garcia-Pascual (2016) and Hesse, Hofmann and Weber (2018) have shown that this model can be successfully applied to study monetary policy transmission in small samples.

I estimate the following VAR model on monthly data:

$$Y_t = \alpha + \sum_{k=1}^{L} A_k Y_{t-k} + e_t \qquad e_t \sim N(0, \Sigma) \tag{1}$$

where Y_t is a vector of the following endogenous variables: the monetary policy indicator; the log of CPI; the log of real GDP; the yield on the ten-year government bond and the log of real equity prices at time t. A_k is the array of coefficients associated with the corresponding lagged vector of variables for lag k. e_t is a vector of residuals at time t. This is assumed to be normally distributed with variance-covariance matrix Σ. A non-informative normal inverse-Wishart prior is used, with the VAR estimated in levels following the approach in Uhlig (2005).[3] The lag length, L, is determined by the Bayesian Information Criterion (BIC) and *ex post* tests of VAR residuals.[4]

[3] Sims, Stock and Watson (1990) argue that 'Bayesian inference need take no special account of non-stationarity'. They point to the superconsistency of non-stationary VARs, meaning that estimated coefficients converge twice as fast to population moments, an advantage in the small samples in this chapter. Uhlig (1994) argues that including a time trend could lead to interdependencies between this prior and the VAR roots. I follow Uhlig (2005) and omit the time trend.

[4] I first estimate the VAR with the lag length implied by the BIC. As VAR residuals are meant to be uncorrelated shocks, we test them for serial correlation. I then

A second important consideration in VAR models is the identification of the shock of interest. The literature on identifying monetary policy shocks in VAR model is large. Multiple approaches exist and they have different advantages and disadvantages. On the one hand, researchers can impose precise restrictions on the impact matrix of the VAR model to identify monetary policy shocks. For example, the popular triangular identification Choleski decomposition scheme imposes zeros on the impact matrix in a lower triangular fashion. But for this identification scheme to be valid, the researcher needs to be certain that these are indeed the right identification restrictions. This is frequently a subject of controversy in the academic literature. Many applications of these precise identification restrictions in VARs have given rise to a number of puzzles, including the prize puzzle, which results in a rise in prices in response to a monetary policy contraction. This is clearly a counterintuitive result. The literature has suggested that this is a function of omitted variables in the model.

On the other side of the spectrum is the sign restriction approach to identification, pioneered by Canova and De Nicolo (2002) and Uhlig (2005). Rather than relying on one particular specification, this approach searches over all possible identification schemes of the impact VAR matrix. Those identification schemes which satisfy economically consistent restrictions are kept. For example, all impulse responses which lead to a decline in output and prices following a rise in the short-term interest rate are kept and interpreted as a monetary policy shock. In many ways, this is a more comprehensive approach to identification, since it enables the researcher to search over and show all possible impulse responses which are consistent with a monetary policy shock. But a valid critique is that showing the median of many different identification schemes may not reflect the median identification scheme but rather an amalgamation of models, which doesn't reflect any particular econometric model. That is seen as the major flaw of this methodology.

In recent years, the proxy SVAR approach has become popular. In this approach, impact coefficients are identified using a monetary policy shock series derived from changes in financial market pricing around the monetary event window as an instrument. The advantage

add lags until we cannot reject the H0 of no serial correlation. Generally, ECB/UK/US QE models are estimated with 3/2/2 lags, while the conventional policy VAR models are estimated with 4/3/3 lags, respectively.

Table 3.1 *Identification scheme.*

	Log CPI	Log Real GDP	MP Policy Indicator	Long-term Interest Rate	Log Real Equity Price
Aggregate Supply Shock	0 ≤	≥ 0			
Aggregate Demand Shock	≥ 0	≥ 0	≥ 0		
Monetary Policy Shock	≥ 0	≥ 0	0 ≤	0 ≤	≥ 0
Central Bank Information Shock*				≥ 0	≥ 0

Note: This table shows the restrictions imposed to identify QE and conventional monetary policy shocks. The sign for the MP policy variable is dependent on the policy indicator in the model. It is positive for the balance sheet and an asset purchases announcement variables and negative for all other monetary policy indicators.
*To identify the information shock separately from the other shocks, I require that this shock explains the largest fraction of the variance decomposition of real share prices upon impact.

of this approach is that the shock can interpreted as a monetary policy shock by definition rather than by inference as with the sign restrictions approach. Which high-frequency financial market price to use for the identification of conventional monetary policy shocks is clear. But this is still debated for QE.

Clearly, all of these methods have strengths and weaknesses. But an important advantage of the sign restrictions identification approach is that it can be applied to many different monetary policy indicators. Since the purpose of this chapter is to compare VAR effects in response to many different QE indicators, I therefore choose the sign restrictions approach for identification in this chapter.

The restrictions I use to identify a monetary policy, aggregate demand, aggregate supply and central bank information shock are summarised in Table 3.1. Quantitative easing economic theories concur that a rise in asset purchases will lead to a fall in the long-term interest rate.[5] This is

[5] See Harrison (2012), Vayanos and Villa (2021), Eggertson and Woodford (2003) and Sims, Wu and Zhang (2022).

also likely to lead to higher equity prices, as investors reallocate their portfolios from bonds to equities. Output and prices rise in response to a QE shock.[6] The other identified shock is an aggregate demand shock, which leads to a rise in prices, output and a tightening of the monetary policy indicator. An aggregate supply shock is identified as a rise in output and fall in prices. A central bank information shock is identified as a shock that raises the long-term interest rate and real share prices, in line with the original definition of this shock in Jarocinski and Karadi (2020). To distinguish this shock from the others, I also require that the information shock explains the maximum share of the variance decomposition of real share prices upon impact. Monetary theory implies that these same restrictions can be applied to identify monetary policy, aggregate demand, aggregate supply and central bank information shocks during the conventional monetary policy period. Importantly, the sign restriction on the monetary policy variable depends on the monetary policy indicator and is always imposed to identify a monetary policy expansion. Therefore, the imposed sign is positive if asset purchases are the monetary policy indicator, but negative if the short-term interest rate is the monetary policy indicator. Similarly, in response to an aggregate demand shock, the monetary policy indicator is restricted to not rise for the balance sheet and asset purchase announcement variables but not fall for the all the other variables. This identification scheme is implemented with the QR approach presented in Rubio-Ramirez, Waggoner and Zha (2010). All sign restrictions are imposed upon impact and one month thereafter with the exception of the monetary policy variable, where I impose the sign restriction upon impact and for five months thereafter, in line with Weale and Wieladek (2016).

For the description of the data used in this chapter, please see Wieladek (2023), who uses the same dataset to investigate if QE generates more inflation that conventional monetary policy.

[6] Relative to Weale and Wieladek (2016), I also impose restrictions on output and prices in the QE shock identification scheme. This is because Baumeister and Hamilton (2015, 2018) and Watson (2019) argue that the Rubio-Ramirez, Waggoner and Zha (2010) algorithm can assign higher probability to certain impulse responses randomly. The implication therefore is that all variables of interest should be sign restricted to have the right theoretical sign as part of the identification scheme.

3.2.3 Main Results

This chapter aims to compare the effects of QE on output and inflation across different QE measures within the same VAR framework. This will allow us to better understand whether the difference in effects observed in previous studies were due to different measures of QE. In this chapter, I aim to compare the effects of conventional monetary policy on output and inflation to the effects of QE on these variables.

An important challenge in this exercise is how to compare different QE measures to each other across models. After all, the scale of the asset purchase announcement and the shadow rate series are very different and hence not comparable. This is not a straightforward problem, but the solution is easier than it appears at first sight. I use a one-standard deviation shock to compare the effects across measures. Clearly each measure will have different statistical properties. The means and standard deviations will differ across measures. But a one-standard deviation shock always measures the reaction of CPI and GDP to a one standard deviation shock in that particular measure. Comparing effects in response to a one-standard deviation shock across measures therefore allows for comparing of effects across QE measures, alleviating the need to express all QE measures in the same scale.

There are eight VAR models, each one with a different measure of QE, and each VAR has five variables. The models are estimated on three different monetary areas, the Euro Area, the UK and the US. Altogether, these are 120 impulse responses. Cleary that is too much information to show in a chapter, otherwise it would be hard to see the wood for the trees. For this reason, I choose to summarise the relevant information from the VAR models in a more efficient way: I show the peak effects of output and CPI in response to a one-standard deviation shock for each measure.

Figures 3.3 and 3.4 show the results from this exercise. For the European Central Bank (ECB), a one -standard deviation shock leads to a rise of 0.1% in GDP for the Bu, Rogers and Wu (2021) – BRW measure. The effects to one-standard deviation shocks of the other measure are probably the same. The exception is the use of the balance sheet and high-frequency identification measure. There the effects on GDP are clearly smaller. However, for the remaining candidate measures of QE, the results are roughly the same. Given that in six out of

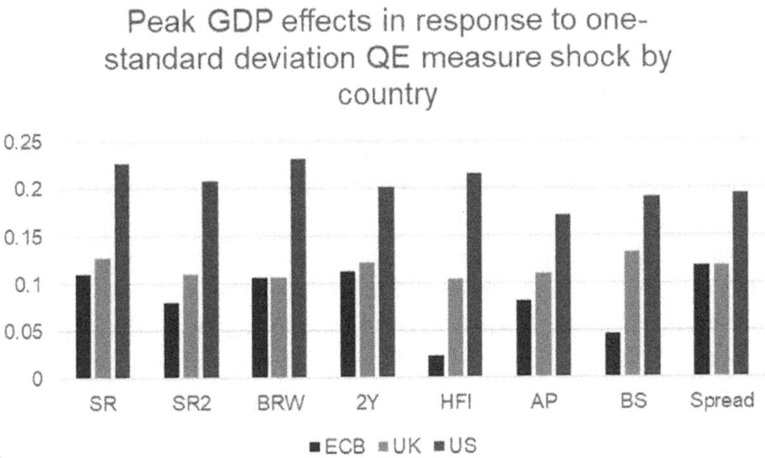

Figure 3.3 Peak GDP effects in response to one-standard deviation QE measure shock by country.

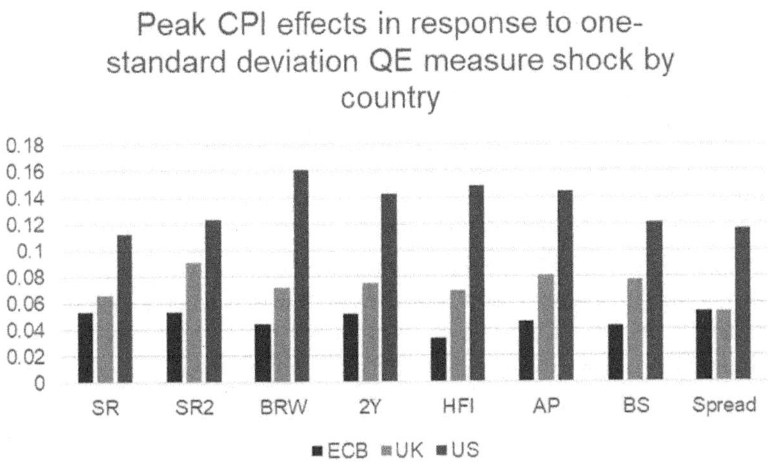

Figure 3.4 Peak CPI effects in response to one-standard deviation QE measure shock by country.

Notes (Figures 3.3 and 3.4): SR is Wu and Xia shadow rate; SR2 is Krippner shadow rate; BRW is Bu, Rogers & Wu indicator; 2Y is two-year yield; HFI is Gertler and Karadi indicator; AP is Asset purchases announcement/GDP; Gambcorta, BS is log of balance sheet. Spread is a specification that replicates the term spread approach of Baumeister and Benati (2013), where we apply a shock to the Long rate.

eight cases the results are roughly we similar, I conclude that ECB QE GDP effects are roughly similar across measures. The effects of ECB QE on CPI differ between 0.04% and 0.05%, implying similar results regardless of QE measure. For the UK, the effects of a one-standard deviation QE shock on real GDP range from 0.1% to 0.15%. For CPI the effects vary from 0.05% to 0.09%. For the US, the effects are larger across the board. The effects of a one-standard deviation shock on GDP is about 0.2% on GDP across QE measures. Quantitative easing CPI effects for the US vary between 0.11% and 0.16%.

Overall, these are much smaller variation in effects than seen in Figures 3.1 and 3.2. Figure 3.1 shows that for GDP QE effects the largest effect is 100 times, 10 times and 5 times the size of the smallest effect for the US, the UK and Euro Area, respectively. Figure 3.2 shows that for CPI QE effects the largest effect is 75 times, 29 times and 8 times the size of the smallest effect for the UK, the US and Euro Area, respectively.

The results presented here therefore show that the estimated effects in response to eight different QE measures across three different monetary areas are roughly the same. It doesn't matter which measure is used: they all give roughly the same answers. The only difference to previous studies is that the VAR model stays the same throughout. This suggest that the heterogeneity in estimates in the literature is mainly due to different VAR modelling approaches, not due to differences in QE indicators.

We can also use this dataset to compare the effects of QE shocks across countries. Figures 3.3 and 3.4 hint that effects in the US are larger than in other countries. However, the estimates presented in Figures 3.3 and 3.4 cannot be used for this exercise, because they show responses to one-standard deviation shocks within each country. But what a one-standard deviation shock for each measure is in each country can of course differ. To compare the results across countries, it is necessary to calibrate all measures to size of the standard deviation in one specific country. I scale all of the effects such that they respond to the one-standard deviation size shocks of the ECB. I then average the responses across countries. These results are reported in Figure 3.5. Once the peak effects are scaled in response to ECB-sized shocks, the US and UK CPI peak effects in response to QE are five and two times the ECB effects. The difference in effects is even starker for real GDP: The UK and US effects

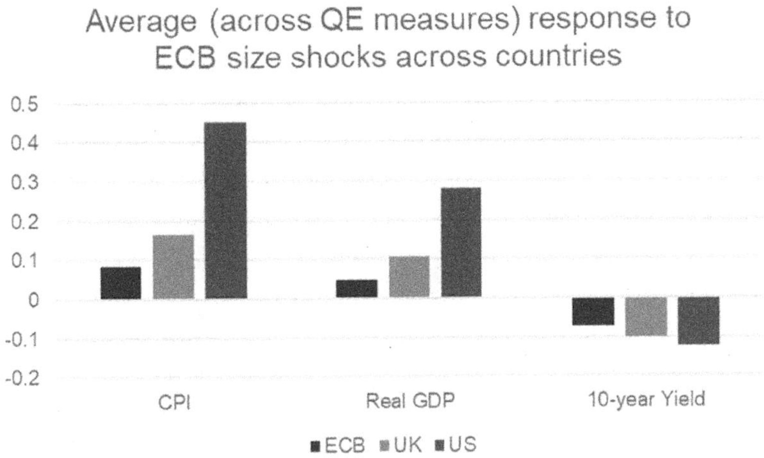

Figure 3.5 Peak QE effects in response to ECB-sized shocks by country.

are two-and-a-quarter and six times larger than peak ECB QE effects. However, the effect on the long-term interest rate is broadly similar.

The finding that ECB QE effects are smaller than those in the UK and the US are not just confined to this chapter. Figure 3.6 shows the peak effect of CPI, real GDP and the ten-year yield in response to a 1% QE as share of GDP shock for the ECB, UK and US averaged across twenty-seven previous VAR studies. As in this chapter, the peak QE CPI and real GDP effects in the UK and the US are meaningfully larger than for the ECB. But the impact on the ten-year yield is the same.

3.2.4 *What Can We Learn from QE Studies for QT?*

Why are the ECB QE effects so much smaller than in the UK and the US? Economic theory sheds some light on why this may be the case.

Ben Bernanke famously said that QE doesn't work in theory but in practice. Nevertheless, a number of theoretical channels have been proposed and discussed in the academic literature. The main channel initially proposed is the portfolio rebalancing channel. The idea is that central bank purchases of governments bonds push investors into different assets classes. This idea has been around since the 1960s (Modigliani and Sutch, 1966), but goes against the friction free expectations theory of the term structure that was predominant when QE was

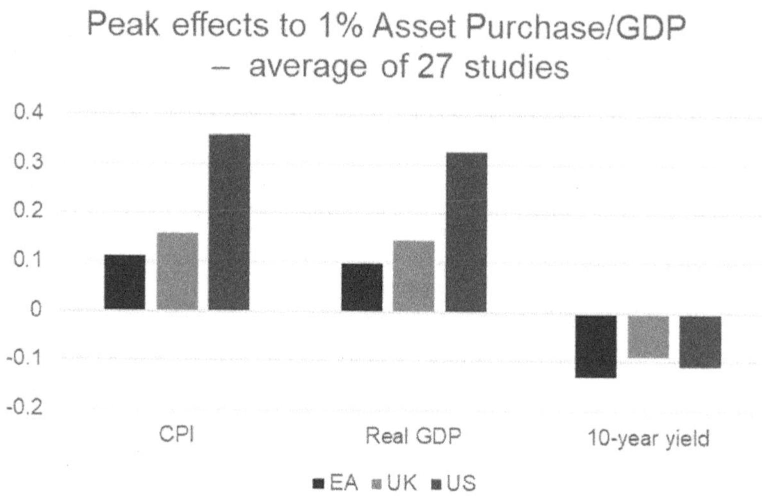

Figure 3.6 Peak QE effects by country as an average across up to twenty-seven studies.

first introduced. For this channel to emerge in theory, a friction is necessary. Vayanos and Vila (2021) introduce preferred habitat investors, agents who have a strong preference for one particular segment of the yield curve, to allow QE to have an impact on the yield curve.[7] The intuition is simple: if certain investors prefer the long-end of the yield curve, they will require a premium to sell their bonds. As a result, QE can move yields and induce allocations to other asset classes. An alternative transmission channel is the signalling channel. This channel is consistent with the expectations theory of the yield curve. The idea is that QE announcements signal that the short-term interest rate will stay at the zero lower bound for longer. Bauer and Rudebusch (2014) find that this channel accounted for 50% of move down in yields after the Federal Reserve's first QE announcements. The last major channel is the market stabilising channel. Quantitative easing is believed to be particularly powerful in times of bond market crisis. By providing liquidity to bond markets as a buyer of last resort, QE calms bond markets and leads to a large move lower in yields. This last channel has been a popular explanation of the Covid-19 pandemic-era QE among

[7] This idea was first introduced by Modigliani and Sutch (1966).

policymakers, but likely also played an important role during the global financial crisis. A related channel is the idea that by announcing QE, the central bank sends a signal to households and firms that it will do whatever it takes to save the economy thereby changing their behaviour, first discussed in Weale and Wieladek (2016).

Figure 3.7 shows QE announcements in by the ECB, Bank of England and Federal Reserve plotted against the VIX, a measure of financial market stress. In high VIX times, financial markets are typically stressed. Figure 3.7 shows that before the Pandemic, the Federal Reserve and the Bank of England typically implemented QE when the VIX was elevated. This suggests that the transmission of QE in those countries benefitted from a powerful market stabilising channel. The experience in the Euro Area was different. The ECB only implemented QE much later than the Bank of England and the Federal Reserve. When the ECB implemented QE, the VIX index was at lower levels, implying the absence of major market stress. As a result, it is unlikely that ECB QE was transmitted through the market stabilising channel in any major way. However, the other channels, like the signalling and portfolio rebalancing channel, were likely still effective. Returning to the question at the beginning of this section, the best explanation for

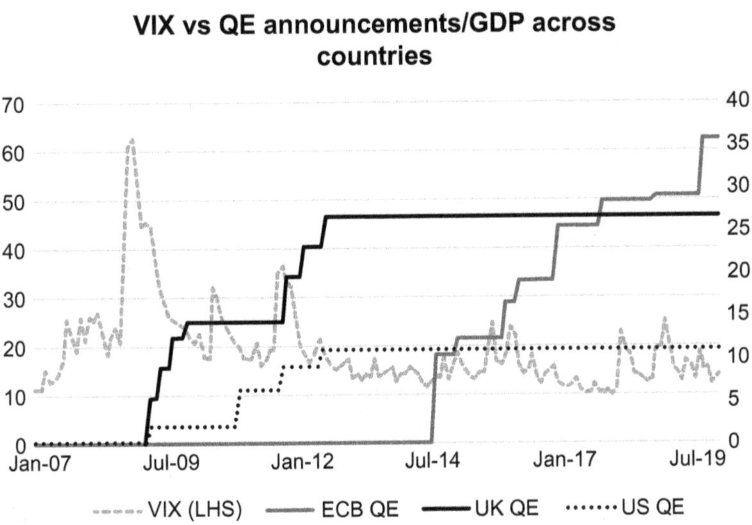

Figure 3.7 VIX vs QE announcements/GDP across countries.

the smaller size of ECB QE multipliers, relative to those in the UK and US, is the absence of the market stabilising channel.

This difference in central bank transmission channels of QE policy can be used to infer the potential effects of QT. Quantitative tightening has three key differences to QE: it is anticipated, is not a policy tool and is implemented in stable market conditions. These operational differences to QE mean that the signalling and a market stabilising channel are likely absent. However, the portfolio balance channel should continue to remain effective. If there was a way to remove the effects of the market stabilising and signalling channels from QE estimates, whatever is left as a residual is reflective of the portfolio rebalance channel and therefore QT. It turns out there is way to do this.

To infer a QT multiplier we need to remove the market stabilising and policy signalling channels from QE effects. Removing the first is fairly easy. I argued that pre-pandemic ECB QE effects do not contain market stabilising effects. This means we can treat ECB QE multipliers as QE multipliers without the market stabilising effect. But to derive a QT effect, the signalling channel still needs to be removed. Bauer and Rudebusch (2014), some of the most vocal proponents of the signalling channel, estimate that 50% of the Federal Reserve QE initial effects on yields was due to the signalling rather than portfolio balance channel. These are some of the highest estimates of the signalling channel in the academic literature. To remove the signalling channel, I therefore reduce the ECB QE estimates by 50% to obtain a back-of-the-envelope estimate of QT.

In sum, I propose a simple approach to infer QT multipliers from previous QE studies. This consists of the recognition that pre-pandemic ECB estimates likely to do not contain the market stabilising effect. To remove the signalling channel, I reduce ECB QE estimates by another 50%. This suggests that a 1% rise in QT as a share of GDP reduces GDP by 6 bps and CPI by 6 bps. This is roughly 75% smaller than the effect of QE in the UK.

3.2.5 Foreign Official Investors as an Important QT Mitigating Factor

Figure 3.8 shows the total effect of QT in the Euro Area, UK and US, based on the multipliers derived in Section 2.4. The effects in the UK stand out as particularly large. This is because the Bank of England has

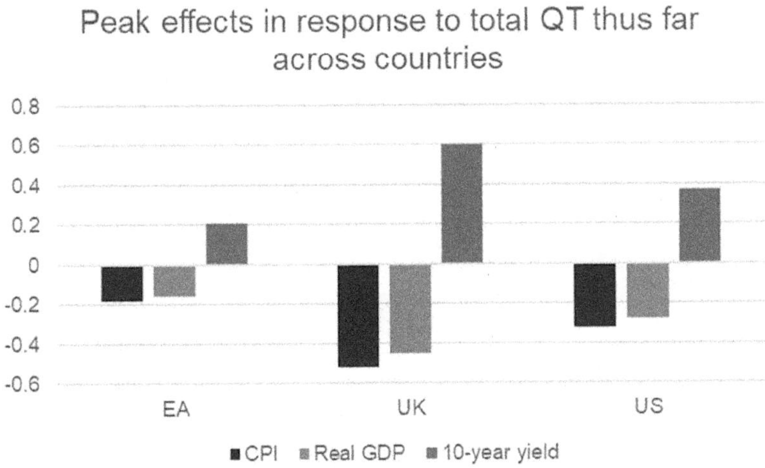

Figure 3.8 Peak effects in response to total QT thus far across countries.

announced and implemented a more aggressive QT programme than other central banks. The effects of UK QT are roughly double those of policy announcements by the ECB. But the effect on the ten-year yield is triple. Indeed, the 60 bps effect is as large as that reported by the recent of event study in Du, Forbes and Luzzetti (2024).

However, the UK results are much larger than those reported by the Bank of England. In the August 2024 monetary policy report, the Bank of England argued that the QT effects on yields were at most 10–20 bps, depending on approach and model. Similarly, Du, Forbes and Luzzetti (2024) use a two-day window for their event study, in line with the first studies of the yield effect of QE. But if that event window is reduced to half an hour, ten minutes before and twenty minutes after the event, the standard in more recent event studies, then the total yield effect of QT is only about 16 bps.

How can our model predictions for the UK be reconciled with reality? It is important to realise that the UK estimate is based on a back-of-the-envelope calculation of what should happen, all else equal. However, in the case of the UK, all else was not equal. What matters for the transmission of QE and QT to the bond market via the sovereign debt channel is the change in the free float, the share of government debt held by the private sector. Normally, one pound in

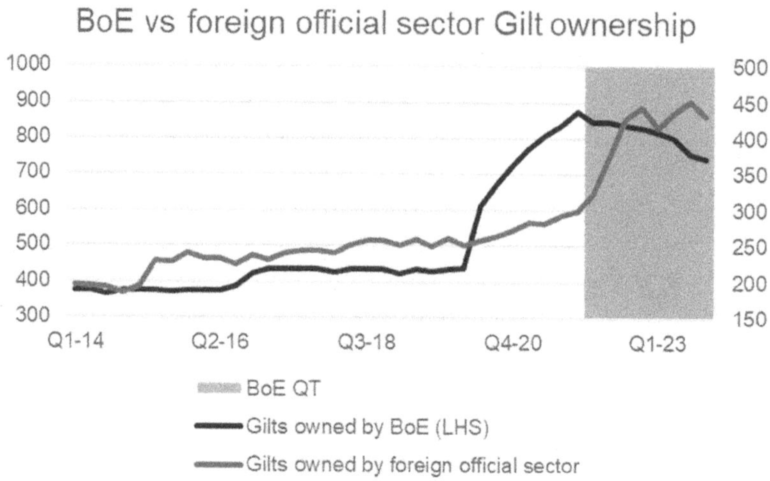

Figure 3.9 BoE vs foreign official sector gilt ownership.

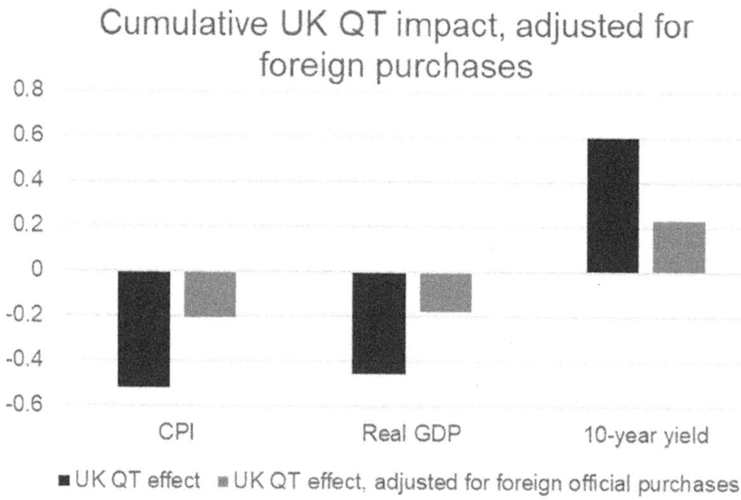

Figure 3.10 Cumulative UK QT impact, adjusted for foreign purchases.

QT should translate to a one-pound rise in the free float. But in the UK, there was an important mitigating factor. Figure 3.9 shows that when the Bank of England began QT, the amount of Gilts held by foreign official investors surged by £132 billion. Normally, the effects of the

Bank of England's QT would be to raise the free float, the amount of Gilts private sector investors need to absorb, by £217 billion. But purchases by foreign official investors partially offset these effects: The private sector only needed to absorb 85 billion worth of Gilts, or only roughly 40% of the total QT amount.

Figure 3.10 shows UK total QT effects adjusted for rise the foreign official sector purchases. After this adjustment, the total effect on ten-year Gilt yields is 24 bps, much closer to the estimates proposed by the Bank of England.

3.3 Conclusion

It has been fifteen years since QE was introduced to ease monetary policy at the zero lower bound. Despite all of this time and many econometric studies of this policy, a consensus remains to be reached on how to model and estimate the effects of this policy. Indeed, there are at least eight different measures of unconventional monetary policy in the academic literature. Similarly, there is a wide range of estimates of what QE does to the macroeconomy in previous studies in the literature varying up to a factor of 100 for GDP and 75 of CPI. This is a much larger range of effects than reported for conventional monetary policy. However, it is unknown if this large range in effects is a result of different measures of QE or different approaches to VAR modelling. I explore this question in this chapter.

I estimate the same monthly VAR model for eight different measures of QE used in previous academic studies for the Euro Area, the UK and the US. These estimates of the CPI and GDP effects are broadly similar across measures within each country. This suggests that the heterogeneity in estimates reported in the literature are a function of the VAR model, rather than the QE measures themselves. Future research should therefore focus on what the right VAR model is to capture all of the relevant channels for QE, rather than what the right QE measure is.

A result that is robust in both this study and the literature is that ECB QE effects are roughly 50% smaller than those reported for the UK and the US. The most probably explanation for this difference is that the ECB only implemented QE when financial markets were stable, which the Bank of England and the Federal Reserve implemented QE in response to financial market distress. The effects of this market stabilising channel are therefore not present in the ECB's estimates. I use this finding to derive QT estimates from previous studies of QE estimates.

Unlike QE, QT was anticipated, implemented in stable market times and central banks were clear from the start that QT as a policy doesn't provide a signal about the future path of the policy rate. *Ex post*, this has been verified since QT has continued regardless of whether central banks were hiking or cutting the policy rate. If there was a way to remove the market stabilising and policy signalling channel from QE estimates, then the remainder would be the effect of QT. It turns out that there is. I take ECB QE estimates as QE estimates which exclude the market stabilising channel. To further take out the signalling channel, I reduce ECB QE estimates by 50%, the share of transmission to yields that Bauer and Rudebusch (2014) have shown the signalling channel to be responsible for. This back of the envelope calculation suggests that QT effects are 75% smaller than QE effects in the UK and the US.

This simple calculation suggests that the ten-year Gilt yield rose by 60 bps in response to the Bank of England's QT up until September 2024. The Bank of England's analysis suggested that the effect is between 10 and 15 bps. However, the QT calculation is just a prediction of what would have happened all else equal. But in the UK, foreign official investors significantly reduced the impact of QT, such that only the private sector had to absorb only 40% of the Bank of England's QT. This means that the predicted effect on Gilt yields is 24 bps, not 60 bps. This is more in line with the estimates that the Bank of England reported. However, it is unlikely that the foreign official investors come to the rescue again, meaning that future rounds of QT will likely have a larger impact on Gilt markets.

This chapter has answered some questions about QE and QT, but raised many others along the way. Understanding which variables to include in QE VAR models, how to estimate the effects of QT and what role foreign official investors play in the transmission of QT are all important research areas going forward.

References

Altavilla, C., L. Brugnolini, R.S. Guerkaynak, R. Motto and G. Ragusa (2019). 'Measuring euro area monetary policy'. *Journal of Monetary Economics*. 108. 162–179.

Aruoba, S.B., M. Mlikota, F. Schorfheide and S. Villavazo (2022). 'SVARs with occasionally-binding constraints'. *Journal of Econometrics*. 231. 477–499.

Bauer, M. D. and G. Rudebusch (2014). 'The signaling channel for Federal Reserve bond purchases'. *International Journal of Central Banking*. 10(3). 233–289.

Bauer, M. D. and E. T. Swanson (2023). 'A reassessment of monetary policy surprises and high-frequency identification'. *NBER Macroeconomics Annual*. 37. 87–155.

Baumeister, C. and L. Benati (2013). 'Unconventional monetary policy and the great recession: Estimating the macroeconomic effects of a spread compression at the zero lower bound'. *International Journal of Central Banking*. 9. 165–212.

Baumeister, C. and J. D. Hamilton (2015). 'Sign restrictions, structural vector autoregressions, and useful prior information'. *Econometrica*. 83(5). 1963–1999.

Baumeister, C. and J. D. Hamilton (2018). 'Inference in structural vector autoregressions when the identifying assumptions are not fully Believed: Re-evaluating the role of monetary policy in economic fluctuations'. *Journal of Monetary Economics*. 100. 48–65.

Baumeister, C. and J. D. Hamilton (2020). 'Drawing conclusions from structural vector autoregressions identified on the basis of sign restrictions'. *Journal of International Money and Finance*. 109. 48–65.

Bernanke, B., J. Boivin and P. Eliasz (2005). 'Measuring the effects of monetary policy: A factor-augmented vector autoregressive (FAVAR) approach'. *The Quarterly Journal of Economics*. 120(1), February. 387–422.

Borio, C. and A. Zabai (2018). 'Unconventional monetary policies: A re-appraisal'. In *Research Handbook on Central Banking*. Ed. P. Conti-Brown and R. M. Lastra. 398–444.

Bu, C., J. Rogers and W. Wu (2021). 'A unified measure of Fed monetary policy shocks'. *Journal of Monetary Economics*. 118. 331–349.

Canova, F. and G. Nicolo (2002). 'Monetary disturbances matter for business fluctuations in the G-7'. *Journal of Monetary Economics*. 49(6). 1131–1159.

Carney, M. (2020). A framework for all seasons? Speech. 9 January 2020.

Cesa-Bianchi, A., G. Thwaites and A. Vicondoa (2020). 'Monetary policy transmission in the United Kingdom: A high-frequency identification approach'. *European Economic Review*. 123. 1–19.

Christensen, K., R. Oomen and M. Podolskij (2014). 'Fact or friction: Jumps at ultra high frequency'. *Journal of Financial Economics*. 114(3). 576–599.

Debortoli, D., J. Gali and L. Gambetti (2020). 'On the empirical (ir)relevance of the zero lower bound constraint'. *NBER Macroeconomics Annual 2019*. 34(1). 141–170.

Du, W., K. Forbes and M. Luzzetti (2024). 'Quantitative tightening around the globe: What have we learned?' NBER Working Paper 32321.

Eggertson, G. B. and M. Woodford (2003). 'The zero bound on interest rates and optimal monetary policy'. *Brookings Papers on Economic Activity*. 34. 139–235.

Fabo, B., M. Jancokova, E. Kempf and L. Pastor (2021). 'Fifty shades of QE: Comparing findings of central bankers and academics'. *Journal of Monetary Economics*. 120(C). 1–20.

Fama, E. F. and J. D. MacBeth (1973). 'Risk, return and equilibrium: Empirical test'. *Journal of Political Economy*. 81(3). 607–636.

Gambacorta, L., B. Hofmann and G. Peersman (2014). 'The effectiveness of unconventional monetary policy at the zero lower bound: a cross-country analysis'. *Journal of Money, Credit and Banking*. 46. 615–642.

Garin, J., R. Lester and E. Sims (2019). 'Are supply shocks contractionary at the ZLB? Evidence from utilization-adjusted TFP data'. *The Review of Economics and Statistics*. 101(1). 160–175.

Gertler, M. and P. Karadi (2011). 'A model of unconventional monetary policy'. *Journal of Monetary Economics*. 58. 17–34.

Gertler, M. and P. Karadi (2013). 'QE 1 vs. 2. Vs. 3 . . . : a framework for analyzing large-scale asset purchases as a monetary policy tool'. *International Journal of Central Banking*. 9. 5–53.

Gertler, M. and P. Karadi (2015). 'Monetary policy surprises, credit costs and economic activity'. *American Economic Journal: Macroeconomics*. 7. 44–76.

Haldane A., M. Roberts-Sklar, T. Wieladek and C. Young (2016). QE: The story so far. Bank of England Working Paper 624.

Harrison, R. (2012). Asset purchase policy at the effective lower bound for interest rates. Bank of England Working Paper 444.

Hesse, H., B. Hofmann and J. M. Weber (2018). 'The macroeconomic effects of asset purchases revisited'. *Journal of Macroeconomics*. 58. 115–138.

Inoue, A. and L. Killian (2022). 'Joint Bayesian inference about impulse responses in VAR models'. *Journal of Econometrics*. 231(2). 457–476.

Jorda, O. and F. Nechio (2023). 'Inflation and wage growth since the pandemic'. *European Economic Review*. 156. Article 104474.

Jarocinski, M. and P. Karadi (2020). 'Deconstructing monetary policy surprises: The role of information shocks'. *American Economic Journal: Macroeconomics*. 12(2). 1–43.

Kapetanios, G., H. Mumtaz, I. Stevens and K. Theodoridis (2012). 'Assessing the economy-wide effects of quantitative easing'. *Economic Journal*. 122. F316–F347.

Krippner, L. (2015). 'A comment on Wu and Xia (2015), and the case for two-factor Shadow Short Rates'. CAMA Working Papers 2015–48.

Litterman, R. B. (1986). 'Forecasting with Bayesian vector autoregressions: Five years of experience'. *Journal of Business & Economic Statistics*, 4(1). 25–38.

Mavroeides, S. (2021). 'Identification at the Zero Lower Bound'. *Econometrica*. 89. 2855–2885.

Modigliani, F. and R. Sutch (1966). 'Innovations in interest-rate policy'. *American Economic Review*. 56. 178–197.

Romer, C. D. and D. H. Romer (2004). 'A new measure of monetary shocks: Derivation and implications'. *American Economic Review*. 94(4). 1055–1084.

Rubio-Ramírez, J., D. Waggoner and T. Zha (2010). 'Structural vector autoregressions: Theory of identification and algorithms for inference'. *Review of Economic Studies*. 77. 665–696.

Rusnak, M., Havranek, T. and R. Horvath (2013). 'How to solve the price puzzle? A Meta-Analysis'. *Journal of Money, Credit and Banking*. 45. 37–70.

Sims, C. A. (1980). 'Macroeconomics and reality'. *Econometrica*, 48(1), 1–48.

Sims, E. and J. C. Wu (2020). 'Are QE and conventional monetary policy substitutable?' *International Journal of Central Banking*. 16(1). 195–230.

Sims, E., J. C. Wu and J. Zhang (2022). 'The four-equation new Keynesian model'. *Review of Economics and Statistics*. 105(4). 931–947.

Sims, C. A., J. H. Stock and M. W. Watson (1990). 'Inference in linear time series models with some unit roots'. *Econometrica*. 58. 113–144.

Swanson, E. (2023). 'The macroeconomic effects of the Federal Reserve's conventional and unconventional monetary policies'. NBER Working paper 31603.

Swanson, E. and J. Williams (2014). 'Measuring the effect of the zero lower bond on medium-and longer-term interest rates'. *American Economic Review*. 104(10). 3154–3185.

Uhlig, H. (1994). 'What macroeconomists should know about unit roots: A Bayesian perspective'. *Econometric Theory*. 10(3–4). 645–671.

Uhlig, H. (2005). 'What are the effects of monetary policy on output? Results from an agnostic identification procedure'. *Journal of Monetary Economics*. 52. 381–419.

Vayanos, D. and J.-L. Vila (2021). 'A preferred-habitat model of the term structure of interest rates'. *Econometrica*. 89. 77–112.

Watson, M (2019). 'Comment on "On the empirical (ir)relevance of the zero lower bound" by D. Debortoli, J. Gali and L. Gambettií'. *NBER Macroeconomics Annual*. 34. 182–193.

Weale, M. and T. Wieladek (2016). 'What are the macroeconomic effects of asset purchases?' *Journal of Monetary Economics*. 79. 81–93.

Weale, M. and T. Wieladek (2022). 'Financial effects of QE and conventional monetary policy compared'. *Journal of International Money and Finance*. 127(C). 102673.

Wieladek, T. (2023). 'Does QE generate more inflation than conventional monetary policy?' CEPR Discussion Paper No. 18463.

Wieladek, T. and A. Garcia-Pascual (2016). 'The European central bank's QE: A new hope'. CEPR Discussion Paper No. 11309.

Wu, J. C. and F. D. Xia (2016). 'Measuring the macroeconomic impact of monetary policy at the zero lower bound'. *Journal of Money, Credit and Banking*. 48. 253–291.

4 *The Old Lady's QE Story*

The Evolving View of the Transmission Mechanism of QE at the BoE

RICHARD BARWELL

Like almost every question in macroeconomics, there is uncertainty around the transmission mechanism of quantitative easing (QE). A reasonable person should therefore expect that the views of a committee of economists on how QE works would evolve through time as both the facts and the people who sat on that committee change. This chapter documents how the views of the Monetary Policy Committee (MPC) and the staff of the Bank of England (BoE) on this subject have changed since QE was used as a policy tool. There has been a shift in the importance attached to the different transmission channels: faith in the power of the portfolio balance channel outside moments of market stress has declined somewhat, and the importance attached to the signalling channel has correspondingly increased. There is no Groupthink about the transmission channels of QE within the MPC – there have been significant differences of opinion, particularly in recent years – but there is a tendency to vote the same way on QE programmes. The big unanswered question is how exactly MPC members think the signalling channel of QE works: the precise mechanism through which asset purchases lend added credence to any private information that the MPC discloses, or what exactly that information is.

4.1 Introduction

This chapter reviews the BoE's experience with QE. The stock of asset purchases financed by the issuance of central bank reserves had reached £895 billion by the end of 2021, with a £20 billion stock of sterling non-financial investment-grade corporate bonds and a £875 billion stock of government bonds. These assets were acquired in a series of purchase programmes, with the first launched in the immediate aftermath of the financial crisis in March 2009 and the last launched during the acute phase of the pandemic (see Bailey et al. (2020) for more details on the QE timeline).

The objective of the chapter is not to discuss whether or how QE works – in theory or in practice – or with the benefit of hindsight to second-guess specific decisions, either about design choices or the flow of purchases. This chapter has a more modest ambition: to establish what the institution thought about QE during the period that the Bank was buying bonds, and to document any fundamental change in view over that period. The final section of this chapter offers some personal reflections on the Bank's evolving QE narrative, but these are incidental to the core objective of the chapter: to establish what Bank staff and Bank policymakers thought at different points in time.

It is to be expected that the Bank's official position on QE would have evolved over this period. At the outset, there were relatively few observations on the effectiveness of QE although plenty of relevant theory, so a rational policymaker would naturally have updated his or her priors on the transmission mechanism as new facts arrived. Moreover, the composition of the MPC changed across this period – including changes in all the key positions (the Governor and the Deputy Governor for Monetary Policy, and the Executive Directors for Markets and Monetary Analysis) – and it is reasonable to assume that different people, with different backgrounds and expertise, would have different positions on this topic. The purpose of this chapter is simply to document when key views changed, and as far as possible, to attribute those changes to individual policymakers. Three key themes stand out.

First, policymakers attach less importance now to portfolio balance effects, where increases in the stock of bond purchases can have a lasting impact on bond yields and the broader constellation of asset prices. Over time, policymakers increasingly made the argument that this transmission channel was less effective when financial markets were orderly. For some, the portfolio balance effect was perceived as modest and transitory in those circumstances.

Second, policymakers attach more importance now to the signalling channel, where the power of asset purchases to move prices is derived from the private information (about the state of the economy or the future conduct of policy) that is revealed to the market alongside the decision to buy bonds. The increased importance attached to the signalling channel raises supplementary questions about the nature of the information that policymakers believed was revealed to the market and the precise mechanism through which a decision to purchase assets alongside lent additional credibility or relevance to that signal. This chapter does not provide a satisfactory answer to that question.

Third, there is no consensus (or Groupthink) on the transmission mechanism of QE within the Bank. There appears to be a diverse range of views on the relative importance of these channels across the Committee, particularly regarding the portfolio balance channel. Several external MPC members have made it clear that they have little faith in this channel outside moments of market stress. However, the content of staff publications on QE (including one co-authored by the Governor) suggests that other members of the Committee still believe in this channel. Another related and unresolved question in the Bank's QE story is how members of the Committee with fundamentally different views on the transmission mechanism managed to vote the same way on asset purchases.

The rest of this chapter is organised as follows. Section 4.2 describes the information set that was used to write this chapter, and the limitations with this approach. Sections 4.3 and 4.4 are devoted to what the Bank thought before and at the outset of QE respectively. Sections 4.5 and 4.6 cover the first reflections of the staff and the Committee. Section 4.7 reviews the QE programmes that took place between the Global Financial Crisis (GFC) and the pandemic, and Section 4.8 covers the Haldane 'story so far' paper. Sections 4.9 and 4.10 focus on a sequence of important contributions by Jan Vlieghe and the intervention by Governor Bailey. Section 4.11 discusses the response to the Independent Evaluation Office (IEO) review of QE and Section 4.12 draws on relevant comments by the Deputy Governor for Monetary Policy for the latter half of this period (Ben Broadbent). Section 4.13 reviews an important speech by external member Silvana Tenreyro which is arguably the most pessimistic take on the QE transmission mechanism published by an MPC member (although Vlieghe may run that close). Section 4.14 discusses the rise of financial stability QE or what the Bank used to refer to as a market maker of last resort (MMLR), and Section 4.15 reviews where the Bank stands on the stock versus flow QE debate. Section 4.16 offers some personal reflections and Section 4.17 concludes.

4.2 Source Material

This is a chapter about what BoE officials thought about the transmission mechanism of QE. The text is dominated by extensive quotes from policymakers and members of staff on this subject to establish a narrative about their views on this subject. Whether that narrative is compelling or not will hinge on the choices that are made over the source material.

The chapter is primarily structured around the 'considered' on-the-record comments of MPC members, official minutes of MPC meetings and significant articles published by the staff that are devoted to the topic of QE. Speeches should provide a polished description of the settled view of individuals policymakers. Articles published by the Bank should likewise present the prevailing view within the institution. On occasion, the chapter will draw on the spoken comments of policymakers, either to Parliament or in the Q&A session that follows a press conference or speech.

There is a limit to what can be learned from speeches and articles. For a start, some policymakers have spoken in much more detail about QE than others. We cannot be sure that the views of those MPC members who have spoken in detail about QE reflect the views of the MPC members who have not done so. At a stretch, we might assume that those who remained silent were broadly comfortable with the 'house view'.

Nor can we be certain that those policymakers who do speak are giving their personal assessment when they speak about the transmission mechanism of QE. They may instead be defending the 'house view'. Indeed, that is likely to be the case where the articles published by Bank staff and the speeches of the internal MPC members are concerned. It is more likely to be the external members, like Vlieghe and Tenreyro, who will give a personal assessment. Even here, it is possible that external members might self-censor their remarks concerning disagreements over the effectiveness of a policy instrument, and perhaps to a greater extent than would be the case with a disagreement over the conjuncture.

In the final section of this chapter, we discuss the merits of creating an alternative, far richer and more compelling source of information on this subject: an oral history of the MPC. That would require a series of in-depth interviews with former members of the MPC, where policymakers are asked about the nature of the decision-making process on the Committee during their tenure: which issues were discussed; how the debate was framed; how decisions were reached; how individuals thought about dissenting views and votes, and so on. In this case, it would be interesting to learn how MPC members thought QE worked, how their thinking evolved through time and the extent to which their views were influenced by the views of the staff, other members of the MPC or external voices, why they voted the way they did, and how comfortable they were expressing dissent. The eighteen interviews that Dylan Cassar conducted with senior figures at the Bank, including the Governor, Deputy Governors, the Chief Economist, and external members of the MPC, illustrate what could potentially be achieved here. Indeed, Cassar (2023) argues that, on the basis of his interviews, there were profound differences of opinion within Threadneedle Street about the transmission mechanism of QE, so this should be interest in exploring these questions in more detail.

4.3 What the BoE Thought about QE before It Began Doing QE

The BoE did not start thinking about QE as Bank Rate was being cut towards the lower bound in the acute phase of the financial crisis. Years earlier, senior Bank officials had already turned their thoughts to what should happen at the lower bound, in part motivated by events in Japan at that time. Indeed, almost a decade before the launch of QE, the then Deputy Governor Mervyn King reflected on monetary policy choices at the lower bound and the merits of asset purchases (King (1999)):

> What is the mechanism by which increases in base money affect demand and output when short-term interest rates are zero? It is hard to believe that an increase in real money balances induces a sizeable wealth effect – they are too small relative to other forms of wealth. Their impact must come, at least in part, from a change in the yields on other assets. In turn that is likely to reflect changes in risk premia. With short rates stuck at zero, the pure expectations theory of the term structure of interest rates and the uncovered interest parity arbitrage theory of exchange rates provide no way for monetary policy to affect other yields. Those theories ignore risk premia. A full explanation of the transmission mechanism of monetary policy at zero interest rates will require a general equilibrium theory of risk premia and how those risk premia are affected by monetary policy ... Since short-term government instruments have now become almost perfect substitutes for cash, open

market operations should, so it is argued, concentrate on purchases of long-term government bonds, private sector financial assets and foreign currency. Such purchases would change relative asset yields, including the exchange rate, and produce a rise in private sector demand.

King would return to the same theme when as Governor he gave the Ely lecture to the American Economic Association (AEA) (King (2004)):

> I shall assume that, when interest rates are zero, monetary policy takes the form of open market purchases or sales of government securities using central bank money. A well-known policy prescription, which has become known as unconventional monetary policy, is that the central bank should buy long-term Government bonds rather than the more conventional short-term bills. The Bank of Japan did indeed follow this prescription.

King went on to explain how he thought this policy works, with an argument rooted in squeezing liquidity premia:

> Long-term bonds are likely to contain a significant premium to compensate investors for their lack of liquidity – the fact that, in practice, investors face significant costs when switching between bonds and goods. When the central bank offers to buy illiquid long-term bonds, it increases the average liquidity of the private sector's portfolio, replacing less liquid with more liquid securities. The private sector will therefore be more willing to hold other illiquid instruments, such as private sector bonds and equities. As a result, liquidity premia fall across a broad category of securities, raising their market value. That will stimulate spending by firms and consumers.

The same year, Paul Tucker discussed QE in the speech where he set out the Bank's new framework for monetary operations (Tucker (2004)):

> Faced with a liquidity trap, the Bank could in principle make purchases of securities to inject base money, which would be within our vires and technically would be 'excess reserves'. We would need to do so in a way that preserved the integrity of our balance sheet.

Interestingly, in terms of the topic of this chapter (the Bank's evolving view on the transmission mechanism), Tucker highlighted that the modalities of any future asset purchase programme should reflect views on the nature of the problem and how asset purchases work:

> the recipe would of course depend on the diagnosis of the problem; and on views about the transmission mechanism and, in particular, the role of money within it. We would, for example, need to form a view – or individual

views – on whether the injection of base money was expected to work through affecting the risk-free rate, or risk and liquidity premia on other financial assets, or both. But that lies beyond my scope today.

Given the shifts in beliefs about the transmission mechanism that this chapter will document, one interesting feature of the discussion of asset purchases for monetary policy purposes in both speeches was the stress placed on the need for coordination between monetary policy and debt management policy, or at least the importance of the latter not consciously undoing the work of the former (King (2004), Tucker (2004)):

> The purchase of a long-term bond by the central bank is equivalent to a combination of two other operations: a purchase of a short-term bill, followed by an operation that swaps the short-term bill for the long term bond. . . . The first of these two operations, the purchase of a short-term bill, is neutral in its effect as it replaces one private sector asset, a short-term bill, with another, cash, that is a perfect substitute for it. The second is debt management, which is normally seen as the responsibility of the finance ministry. So when interest rates are zero unconventional quantitative operations and debt management are indistinguishable. . . . when rates are at their zero bound then the central bank no longer has instrument independence. Indeed, because its actions can be offset by appropriate sales or purchases in the government debt market, it loses goal independence too. It becomes crucial that fiscal and monetary authorities cooperate.
>
> there would potentially be a need to co-ordinate with government debt management, since that by definition also involves the exchange of securities for cash. In a world where OMOs [open market operations] were conceived as an instrument to control the path of reserves, the question of such co-ordination was familiar – as is apparent from Milton Friedman's writings. Most of the time these days, it is not a practical issue. But it is an issue that we have identified, and there is nothing in our planned new framework that would inhibit such questions being explored if they ever needed to be.

Around the same time, the full range of monetary policy options at the lower bound was discussed in an influential staff paper by a senior member of Bank staff, Tony Yates. In the section dealing with assets purchases, Yates (2003) makes the case for purchasing illiquid private sector assets:

> the central bank could stimulate the economy by buying assets less similar to cash than normal: illiquid assets like infrequently traded bonds, or even claims on the private sector like shares or corporate bonds. An exchange

like this would involve the private sector giving up an illiquid asset and taking a more liquid one, cash, in return ... Having something that is more readily (more cheaply) turned into a good that can be consumed is valuable. Following an exchange of cash for illiquid bonds or shares the private sector would have more 'liquidity' and would therefore be better off. This would stimulate spending. By announcing that the central bank is prepared to engage in operations in formerly illiquid assets, these assets would themselves become more liquid. That would cause their prices to rise, make private sector holders of those assets better off, and increase demand.

In passing, discussion of central bank purchases of long-dated government bonds was relegated to a footnote in that article, and 'signalled as a possibility' in remarks by Ben Bernanke. Cassar (2023) describes how a range of options for how to stimulate the economy at the lower bound were still being considered as the moment of decision approached – including forward guidance and purchases of private sector assets – and it was only late in the day that the Bank settled on purchases of government bonds as the preferred option.

4.4 In the Beginning, There Was Portfolio Balance

The decision to create central bank reserves to finance the purchase of assets for explicitly monetary policy purposes was not taken until the start of March 2009, but the Governor had already signalled the direction of travel in a speech on 20 January (King (2009)):

[the MPC] may need to move beyond the conventional instrument of Bank Rate and consider a range of unconventional measures. They would take the form of purchases by the Bank of England of a range of financial assets in order to expand the amount of reserves held by commercial banks and to increase the availability of credit to companies. That should encourage the banking system to expand the supply of broad money by lending to the private sector and also help companies to raise finance from capital markets.

The conventional approach to such unconventional measures is to buy assets, such as government securities or gilts, which are traded in liquid markets to boost the supply of money. Provided the additional reserves are not simply hoarded by banks, as happened to some extent in Japan earlier in this decade, such asset purchases can increase the supply of broad money and credit and the liquidity of private sector portfolios, raising spending.

King draws a clear distinction in that speech between purchases of gilts ('conventional unconventional') and what he labels the 'unconventional unconventional' approach, defined as follows:

> The objective of such purchases would be not only to boost the supply of broad money but also to increase liquidity and trading activity in the markets for those assets. A reduction in the illiquidity premium for a particular credit instrument might help to stimulate issuance by corporate borrowers and the resumption of capital market flows, thus reducing reliance on bank lending. It could also raise the values of assets that are currently under-priced because of high illiquidity premia, helping to strengthen the balance sheets of banks and other financial institutions.

The March 2009 minutes set out the official narrative on how purchases of government bonds would stimulate the economy, which is clearly rooted in what would become known as the 'portfolio rebalancing' narrative (BoE (2009b)):

> By increasing the supply of money in the economy, these operations should, over time, cause nominal spending to rise. Sellers of assets to the Bank would find that their portfolios were now more heavily weighted towards highly liquid, low-yielding assets. To rebalance their portfolios, they would be likely to spend some or all of the proceeds buying other types of asset. This would tend to increase the relative prices of those assets, and hence wealth, and would, by stimulating the demand for corporate credit instruments, improve the supply of funds to the corporate sector. The purchases would also mean that the banking system would be holding a higher level of reserves in aggregate, which might cause it to increase its lending to companies and households. There could also be positive impacts on expectations and confidence from these operations to increase the money supply, as businesses and individuals became more confident about an eventual recovery.

The primacy of the portfolio balance channels was consistent with the broad consensus within the central banking community at that time. At the very least, Ben Bernanke reached a similar conclusion in his speech at the 2010 Jackson Hole speech (Bernanke (2010)):

> I see the evidence as most favorable to the view that such purchases work primarily through the so-called portfolio balance channel, which holds that once short-term interest rates have reached zero, the Federal Reserve's purchases of longer-term securities affect financial conditions by changing the quantity and mix of financial assets held by the public. Specifically, the Fed's strategy relies on the presumption that different financial assets are not

perfect substitutes in investors' portfolios, so that changes in the net supply of an asset available to investors affect its yield and those of broadly similar assets.

The March 2009 minutes also made the following interesting observation about the uncertainty *within* the Committee about the effectiveness of QE (BoE (2009b)):

> there was a range of views about the desirable size of the initial programme of asset purchases. But Committee members agreed that the differences between their preferred scale of purchases were small relative to the degree of uncertainty surrounding these estimates.

The institutional arrangements for QE also acknowledged the concerns raised before the fact by Tucker and King about coordination of monetary policy and debt management policy. The Chancellor's letter of 3 March makes clear that there would be no attempt to adjust issuance to take advantage of the impact of the Bank's purchases (Darling (2009)):

> I recognise the importance of ensuring that debt management policy is consistent with the aims of monetary policy. I am today confirming that the Government's debt management objective remains to minimise, over the long term, the costs of meeting the Government's financing needs … the Government will not alter its issuance strategy as a result of the asset transactions undertaken by the Bank of England for monetary policy purposes.

This may seem like much ado about nothing for those who believe that QE largely works via a signalling mechanism, and the quantity of purchases is neither here nor there. But for those who believe – as the MPC clearly did at the outset – that the quantity of purchases and portfolio rebalance is central to the transmission mechanism of asset purchases, this agreement was 'crucial' (BoE (2009a)).

A *Quarterly Bulletin* article devoted to QE that was published in June 2009 discussed the transmission mechanism in more detail (Benford et al. (2009)). The section on 'economic channels' begins with a very clear statement about the core transmission mechanism:

> Injecting money into the economy, in return for other assets, increases the liquidity of private sector balance sheets. This is the fundamental mechanism through which such a monetary expansion influences spending and hence inflation.

The Benford and colleagues article goes on to highlight four key channels of transmission:

- asset prices and the portfolio balance effect: if those financial companies selling assets to the Bank do not 'regard this extra money to be a perfect substitute for the assets it has sold, this would imply that it is now holding excess money balances', leading to a series of transactions that 'should bid up asset prices' until 'the value of the overall asset portfolio has risen sufficiently to bring the share of money relative to all assets to its desired level' – a process 'sometimes known as the portfolio balance effect'.
- bank lending effects: injections of reserves into the system 'could encourage them to extend more new loans than they would otherwise have done' or 'may contribute to a decline in the interest rate that banks pay to borrow from each other'.
- quantity effects: the deposit holdings of households and companies will increase and that could lead to higher spending 'if their money balances are pushed above the desired level' in 'an analogous way to the portfolio effect'.
- expectations effects: by signalling that the Bank 'will do whatever it takes to meet the inflation target' QE could help to anchor inflation expectations' keeping real interest rates low. Moreover, higher inflation expectations could 'influence price-setting behaviour by firms' and a 'perceived improvement in the economic outlook is likely to boost confidence and make people more willing to spend'.

The bank lending channel might have featured in this official list of transmission channels, but it would play a peripheral role in the Bank's evolving narrative on QE. In fact, the MPC had been sceptical from the start about this channel, noting at the March 2009 meeting (BoE (2009b)):

> The current strains in the financial system, and in particular the pressures on banks to reduce the size of their balance sheets, meant banks were less likely to increase their lending substantially following an increase in their reserves. That would reduce the extent to which a given increase in banks' reserves would generate a correspondingly larger rise in the stock of broad money and credit.

Bank staff would go on to publish a couple of papers on this topic in 2014: the former establishing the presence of a weak channel, and the latter arguing that it was unlikely to have been operative during this period (Joyce and Spaltro (2014), Butt et al. (2014)):

> We found that the deposit ratio has a small but statistically significant effect on bank lending growth, which suggests that QE may have led to an increase in bank lending through this channel. These effects, however, are likely to have been limited, both because the estimated marginal effects through deposits are small and also because we assumed there was a full pass-through from QE to deposits, which seems likely to overstate the impact.
>
> We find no statistically significant evidence ... that those banks who received increased deposits from QE lent more, all else equal ... Our results do not preclude a bank lending channel, but if the effect were very powerful it seems unlikely there would be no evidence of it in our tests ... This is consistent with the idea that there was no bank lending channel from QE precisely because portfolio rebalancing was occurring and is therefore consistent with other studies which show that QE boosted aggregate demand and inflation. UK policymakers did not rely on QE to boost bank lending and our evidence lends support to the use of other policies, rather than QE, to attempt to improve the supply of credit.

We end this section with remarks given by the Chief Economist, Spencer Dale, who reflected on the 'theoretical foundations' in his 'one year on' speech in March 2010. Dale name-checks James Tobin, reasserts the portfolio balance narrative and highlights the key channels of transmission from the Bank's perspective (Dale (2010)):

> in the real world it seems plausible that demand curves for assets, in addition to money, are downward sloping to some degree, in which case changes in their relative supplies can affect their relative prices. It is this which gives quantitative easing its traction.
>
> we placed weight on three key channels of monetary transmission: the impact of imperfect substitutability and the portfolio rebalancing channel on relative prices, the role of financial market liquidity, and the importance of expectations.

His comments on the final channel – expectations – are worth emphasising. Dale argues that asset purchases must have 'an economic impact' if they are to influence expectations:

> The importance of expectations also played a central role in the design of our asset purchase programme. It was vitally important that the Monetary Policy Committee was able to introduce a new policy instrument at the point at which Bank Rate reached its effective lower bound. This

instrument had to be credible, both in terms of its economic impact and the willingness of the Committee to use the instrument in force. My own view is that the speed with which the asset purchase programme was introduced and the scale of the programme played an important role in reaffirming the MPC's commitment to achieving the inflation target and reinforcing the belief in our ability to do so.

4.5 The Staff Reflects on QE: The Signalling Channel Is Referenced but Not Yet Embraced

The natural place to look for timely commentary by Bank staff about the critical first leg of the transmission mechanism of QE – the impact of asset purchases on financial markets – is the regular 'Markets and operations' chapter of the *Quarterly Bulletin* that was prepared by staff in the Markets directorate. This is the place where Bank staff would routinely discuss market developments in the context of shifts in the conduct of central bank policy, the broad state of capital markets and the macroeconomic backdrop, both at home and abroad. For example, in the 2009 Q3 *Bulletin* we find this discussion of long-term bond yields and the transmission mechanism of QE (BoE (2009c)):

> Official purchase schemes could be thought to affect government bond yields by inducing investors to rebalance their asset portfolios. Specifically, central bank purchases may, in the absence of substitute assets, encourage investors to pay more for particular bonds, which, other things being equal, would reduce their yields.
>
> Since this factor should not affect OIS [overnight index swap] rates, its impact may be evident from moves in the spread between bond yields and equivalent-maturity OIS rates (to the extent that the latter proxy default-free rates). Indeed . . . since the MPC's asset purchase programme was announced, gilt-OIS spreads have narrowed. The fact that these spreads fell further than equivalent spreads in other currencies may reflect the relatively large size of the Bank's gilt purchase programme. The MPC's £175 billion purchase programme represents around 30% of the outstanding stock of gilts, while the US Federal Reserve's intended purchase of $300 billion of US Treasuries represents less than 5% of the outstanding stock.
>
> Moves in government bond yields may also reflect changes in investors' perceptions of macroeconomic prospects (which themselves could be affected by policy announcements about the scale of asset purchases). However, contacts suggested that, in general, perceptions of the macroeconomic outlook

improved over the period, which, all other things being equal, would have tended to increase bond yields.

To get a sense of the evolving staff view on the broader transmission into the real economy we have to look to the article published by Bank staff in the *Quarterly Bulletin* in 2011, which focused on the design, operation and impact of BoE QE. The article references the signalling channel – indeed, it is the first channel to be mentioned in the section on transmission channels working through asset prices (Joyce, Tong, and Woods (2011)):

This channel includes anything economic agents learn about the likely path of future monetary policy from asset purchases. For example, asset purchases may have led market participants to expect policy rates to remain low for longer than otherwise by signalling the MPC's determination to meet the inflation target .... More generally, policy announcements on asset purchases might contain 'news' about the underlying state of the economy, for example if agents relied on central bank analysis to inform their views on the economy.

Indeed, the article mentions (in a footnote) how signalling is all that matters in certain intellectual frameworks:

In conventional New Keynesian models, asset purchases can only work to the extent that they change agents' expectations of the future path of policy rates (see, for example, Eggertsson and Woodford (2003)). Asset purchases on their own do not change behaviour because the assumptions made imply the distinction between public and private asset holdings is unimportant.

However, the article goes on to stress the limited sense in which the MPC had used QE as a direct signal about the future rath path, and instead to argue that the signal works by convincing people that monetary policy is not impotent at the lower bound for the policy rate by demonstrating that the central can still loosen the stance through asset purchases.

The MPC has not used the asset purchase programme explicitly to signal future intentions about the likely path of policy rates. It emphasised its ongoing commitment to meet the inflation target using its normal communication channels, for example, the minutes of MPC meetings and the Inflation Report. That said, asset purchases gave a clear signal that the Bank would continue to be able to loosen monetary policy and stimulate demand even when Bank Rate is effectively at its lower bound, which could have had strong expectations effects. This signal could have substantially changed the distribution of future macroeconomic outcomes, reducing the chance of further large falls in asset prices and hence reducing risk premia more generally, as well as having the sort of broader confidence effects discussed above.

Bank staff produced a lot of research into the impact of QE over this period. A paper published in the *International Journal of Central Banking* investigates the impact of QE on a wide range of asset prices, but it is the core result for the reaction of long-term bond yields in the immediate aftermath of QE announcements that is probably the most widely cited of all Bank research in this area (Joyce et al. (2011)):

> Based on market reactions to news about QE purchases, we found that medium to long-term gilt yields were about 100 basis points lower than they would otherwise have been as a result of QE which our estimates suggest mainly came through a portfolio balance effect.

Over time, it would becoming increasingly difficult to identify the impact of changes in the target stock from the immediate market reaction to an announcement, because the market was increasingly able to predict future changes in the target stock. A separate strand of Bank research (McLaren et al. (2014)) exploited operational changes in the conduct of QE to circumvent this problem. At several points, the Bank released market notices that contained news about which bonds the Bank would buy (i.e. at which maturities), allowing Bank staff to test for the presence of portfolio balance channel via the impact of news on 'local' supply on relative gilt yields, and whether the potency of that channel had diminished over time (by comparing the impact of notices in 2009 and 2012). The results were positive and moreover suggest no diminution of this channel over the first few years of the QE era.

> The local supply effects we identify appear to be important: they may account for around half of the total impact on gilt yields in these events, and are passed through to yields of related assets.

4.6 The Committee Reflects Too, and Changes . . .

The MPC narrative on what was originally considered to be the primary transmission channel of QE – portfolio rebalancing – gradually evolved through time. Policymakers would sound increasingly sceptical about the capacity of bond purchases to move bond prices through this channel in normal market conditions, and more supportive of the signalling channel.

Monetary Policy Committee members had long been open about the fact that the effectiveness of QE could vary according to the state of the market. Charlie Bean discussed both the time- and state-contingent nature of the transmission mechanism in his Jackson Hole speech (Bean et al. (2010)):

This imperfect asset substitutability may be both time-varying – in particular, the scope for asset substitution may be rather greater in the long run than in the short run – and state-contingent, as traders may be less able to arbitrage between assets in times of economic and financial distress. But as long as there is some period of imperfect asset substitutability to exploit, purchases by the central bank can push up asset values, which in turn boosts aggregate demand and encourages increased issuance of the assets whose prices have risen ... The theoretical case for an effect from asset purchases rests on there being frictions that prevent the Eggertsson-Woodford neutrality result holding. During a financial crisis, when credit is hard to come by, arbitrageurs may find it difficult to find the wherewithal to correct any excessive compression of the spread between government bond yields and expected policy rates. During normal times, such credit will be easier to come by and the activities of arbitrageurs may therefore lead to the attenuation of the effectiveness of asset purchases as a monetary policy tool.

Likewise, external member Adam Posen highlighted this point in his testimony to Parliament in 2010 (Posen (2010)):

part of the benefits of QE that the Bank rightly undertook in 2009, before I joined the committee, is to deal with panic in markets and to deal with lock-up in markets. Thankfully we don't have that now but, therefore, you don't have the benefit of that. Secondly, because of the panic going away, thanks in part to the Bank of England policy, the amount of desire people have for gilts versus other securities goes down, or rather they're more willing to substitute other things for gilts. And the power of QE, as explained in speeches by Spencer Dale and by my colleague David Miles, is in part when you think that there's an imperfect substitutability, that your buying people really want to hold gilts, and so when you buy gilts from them it causes a lot of changes to their portfolio. Now that we're in more normal times there's more substitutability. So, to me, the mechanism is less potent than it was, say, a year and a half ago.

The following year Posen would make an interesting intervention on the broader topic of the optimal design of central bank asset purchase programmes, in a speech titled 'How to Do More'. Posen made the case for credit easing as the appropriate response to the specific problems facing the UK economy at that time. However, Posen's argument was not predicated on the belief that QE was ineffective. On the contrary, Posen challenges some of the common criticisms of QE in that speech, concluding that the problem with QE was that not enough had been done. Consistent with his remarks to Parliament, he does acknowledge that the effectiveness of QE might have declined but concludes the appropriate response is to do more (Posen (2011)):

> It is as though the fact that the British economy (or the American, for that matter) is not fully recovered after our previous rounds of QE is evidence that QE failed to work. Even on the face of it, that is a strange type of logic. We know that infusions of QE to the economy have been closely associated with large falls in interest rates out the yield curve of comparable size in the UK and the US. We know that the relative price of riskier assets has gone up, indicating greater demand for them, when QE has been undertaken. And we know that banks have received increased deposits and investors and households have expressed increased confidence in the wake of each round of additional QE . . .
>
> Bottom line, the MPC and our counterparts in the G7 central banks can do more QE without any delay, and should. It will help by affecting risk appetite, relative asset prices, liquidity, confidence, and available fund to banks significantly, even if the bank lending channel is still impeded. If anything, that is an argument to do more QE than we did before. If it will take somewhat more purchases to have the same effect as when the economy was in overt crisis, but we know that effect is significantly greater than zero, we should simply up the dosage. There is no sign that negative side effects of this medicine increase with dosage, or are really evident at all.

Fast forward to 2014 and external MPC member David Miles would make the case for reduced efficacy of the portfolio balance channel a little more forcefully, in both a speech (Miles (2014)) and a working paper co-written with a member of Bank staff (Miles and Schanz (2014)), labelling the channel 'weak':

> If financial markets work well, households choose between money and bonds on the basis of their payoff properties. These payoff properties do not seem sufficiently different to allow central bank asset purchases to cause bond yields to fall significantly.

Our overall finding is that the portfolio balance effect of central bank asset purchases is weak in a wide range of environments. That is not to say that the big expansion of central bank balance sheets in recent years has been ineffective. Our finding is rather that the portfolio balance channel evaluated in an environment of normally functioning (though nonetheless incomplete) asset markets is weak . . . So our results are not inconsistent with the evidence that large-scale asset purchases by central banks since 2008 have had significant effects, because those purchases were made when financial markets were – to varying extents – dysfunctional.

External MPC member Martin Weale published a research paper in the same year, also co-written with a member of Bank staff (Weale and Wieladek (2014)), which examined the macroeconomic impact of QE. They find statistically significant results – that purchases equivalent to 1% of GDP raise UK GDP by 0.18%, and CPI by 0.3% – but more importantly for our purposes, they find evidence consistent with the signalling channel. Weale and Wieladek (2014) find a statistically significant, negative impact of QE on interest rate futures, and also document a reduction in implied volatility.

In the UK an important transmission channel seems to be through signalling that interest rates will stay lower for longer and a reduction in financial market uncertainty.

Finally, it is worth flagging that this period was one of significant change in the leadership of the Bank and that could have had implications for Bank thinking on QE, absent any new information arriving on the transmission mechanism. Of course, the membership of the MPC is forever changing. But the departure of Mervyn King and Paul Tucker within a matter of months in 2013, and then Charles Bean the following year, was likely more consequential for the Bank view on monetary policy strategy than the regular turnover of external members. Meanwhile, the new Governor certainly appeared to shift the Bank view on the merits of forward guidance and perhaps other questions too; Cassar (2023) quotes a member of staff saying 'Carney's arrival was a big, big change. He didn't buy the money stuff' (a reference to the underlying debate on Monetarism versus other schools of thought). As we shall go on to discuss, the Bank view on the merits of corporate bond purchases certainly appears to shift around this time. In any case, only two of the nine MPC members who voted to launch QE4 in August 2016 were present on the Committee in October 2011 when it voted to launch QE2, and those two joined in 2010 and 2011, long after the launch of QE1 (when presumably the key issues were discussed at length within all central banks). It is not unreasonable to think that the Bank's thinking on the transmission mechanism of QE could have shifted – and perhaps significantly – over this period.

4.7 QE between the GFC and Covid-19

Between 2011 and 2016 there were three distinct QE interventions: QE2, QE3 and QE4 respectively – although the first two can be reasonably thought of as a response to a common cause (the crisis in the Eurozone), while the latter was a response to the Brexit referendum. This section will briefly review the motivations for these programmes and what the MPC and the Bank thought about the likely impacts.

The minutes of the October 2011 meeting explained the rationale for resuming asset purchases (BoE (2011)):

> The pace of global expansion had evidently slackened, especially in the United Kingdom's main export markets. And heightened awareness of the vulnerabilities associated with the indebtedness of several euro-area governments and banks had led to a further deterioration in demand prospects. While the worst risks had not crystallised, the threat of them doing so had resulted in severe strains in bank funding markets and financial markets more generally. These tensions in the world economy appeared to have already affected consumer and business confidence and could result in a further tightening of credit conditions, posing a threat to the recovery in the United Kingdom.

Interestingly, the minutes highlighted that financial conditions were easing in anticipation of a policy response, with a clear delineation between the impact of changed expectations for the path of the policy rate and the role of asset purchases, suggesting an additional transmission from the latter (over and above the expectations channel):

> There had already been some stimulus imparted from the substantial downward movements in interest rates across the term structure over the past two months, although part of that was likely to have been in anticipation of policy rates remaining unchanged for longer than previously expected and further asset purchases by the Committee.

Furthermore, the minutes assert that the impact of QE2 was likely to be similar to QE1:

Evidence on the impact and transmission channels of the first round of asset purchases, reviewed in the Bank's 2011 Q3 *Quarterly Bulletin*, indicated that, while there was considerable uncertainty about the magnitudes, the earlier asset purchases had had economically significant effects. There appeared to be no strong reason to expect the economic effect of further asset purchases to be materially different, but their impact would need to be kept under review. The size of the asset purchase programme could be adjusted if there were evidence that its marginal effects were different than past experience suggested.

The language used to describe the situation in the Eurozone around the launch of QE3 – in the May Inflation Report press conference (King (2012a)) and the July 2012 minutes (BoE (2012)) respectively – was even more stark:

there is another storm coming towards us from the euro area . . .. our biggest trading partner – the euro area – is tearing itself apart without any obvious solution.

notwithstanding the initial positive market reaction to the political developments within the euro area, very substantial risks there remained. These could, if they crystallised, have a considerable impact on economic activity in the United Kingdom and the stability of the global banking system. There were increasing signs that the threat of a disorderly resolution of the financial tensions in the euro area was affecting growth at home.

When challenged on the likely effectiveness of gilt purchases in the August Inflation Report press conference, the Governor was insistent that QE was still effective (King (2012b)):

I don't accept the premise of the question that asset purchases are having a diminishing effect, I don't believe that . . . they create money in the economy and that can have an effect. And in particular it can have an effect in reducing the higher interest rates on risky assets, which are still well above zero, and that's something that we can help to influence.

In August 2016 the MPC voted to increase the stock of asset purchases as part of a package of measures designed to support to the economy in the aftermath of the Brexit referendum result. The innovation in that QE announcement was the decision to include the purchase of up to £10 billion of UK corporate bonds, rather than relying entirely on purchases of government bonds.

To return to the beginning and the terminology Carney's predecessor has used in a speech in January 2009, an 'unconventional unconventional' measure had seemingly transformed into a conventional unconventional measure. In passing, this shift raises an interesting hypothetical question as to whether an earlier cohort of MPC members might have looked to a MMLR solution to manage any perceived issue in credit markets in 2016. Indeed, In his review of the effects of the corporate bond purchase scheme (CBPS), it is interesting to note that the Executive Director for Markets, Chris Salmon, would later frame the scheme as an effective way of insulating the corporate bond market and hence the monetary transmission mechanism from a potential source of destabilising stress, as opposed to, say, delivering additional monetary stimulus through that transmission mechanism (Salmon (2017)):

> Stepping back, the big picture is of a discernible impact on the cost of funding for firms and a strong second half of the year for issuance, despite a big uncertainty challenge. The introduction of the CBPS has helped ensure that downside risks following the referendum did not materialise and that the market remained robust in the face of wider market volatility.

In any case, Governor Carney explained the rationale for the 2016 decision, and the focus on corporate bonds, in his letter to the Chancellor (Carney (2016)):

> The Committee judged it was appropriate to purchase corporate bonds in order to improve credit conditions for companies by lowering their cost of borrowing. The Committee expects that a corporate bond purchase programme will encourage further issuance of private debt securities. On balance, it expects corporate bond purchases to impart more stimulus that the equivalent amount of gilt purchases. However, the size of the existing outstanding stock of sterling corporate bonds means that the pace of purchases in that market will be limited. So the Committee also judged it appropriate to conduct further purchases of gilts, which will stimulate demand in the economy by increasing a broad range of asset prices, reducing borrowing costs, and by affecting expectations and confidence.

The impression given here is that the Committee would have exclusively focused on corporate bonds had it not been constrained by the size of the market. Interestingly, three MPC members did not support the decision to expand asset purchases and one voted against the purchases of corporate bonds, given concerns around injecting excessive stimulus into the system. The minutes of the August decision describe the expected impact of the announcement in language rooted in portfolio balance (BoE (2016a)):

The expansion of the Bank of England's asset purchase programme for UK government bonds will impart monetary stimulus by lowering the yields on securities that are used to determine the cost of borrowing for households and businesses. It is also likely to trigger portfolio rebalancing into riskier assets by current holders of government bonds, further enhancing the supply of credit to the broader economy. Purchases of corporate bonds could provide somewhat more stimulus than the same amount of gilt purchases. In particular, given that corporate bonds are higher-yielding instruments than government bonds, investors selling corporate debt to the Bank could be more likely to invest the money received in other corporate assets than those selling gilts. In addition, by increasing demand in secondary markets, purchases by the Bank could reduce liquidity premia; and such purchases could stimulate issuance in sterling corporate bond markets.

Once again, the natural place to look for an initial staff assessment of the impact of QE4 is the Markets and operations QB article that was published the following month (BoE (2016b)):

Long-term interest rates fell further following the announcement. The gilt forward curve fell by 5–20 basis points across maturities, with the largest falls in the five to fifteen-year sector. Part of the fall in forward rates likely reflected lower Bank Rate expectations as a result of both the MPC's guidance on further Bank Rate cuts and the signalling channel of asset purchases. But the fall may also have reflected a reduction in term premia. Long-term interest rates appeared to have stabilised by the end of the review period ... likely helped in part by some improvement in UK data.

Contacts attributed the relatively greater fall in sterling investment-grade spreads to the package of measures announced by the MPC in August, particularly the decision to purchase up to £10 billion of sterling non-financial investment-grade corporate bonds over the next 18 months. On the day of the announcement, sterling-denominated investment-grade non-financial corporate bond spreads fell by around 10 basis points, whereas the euro and US dollar-denominated equivalents were little changed. Contacts also noted strong inflows into sterling bond investment funds following the MPC announcement.

Subsequent research by a member of Bank staff (co-authored with an economist from the Federal Reserve system) would argue that while there is a significant pass-through from gilt purchases to corporate bond prices, that the stimulus is transmitted via risk-free component of the all-in corporate yield. In contrast, corporate bond purchases can reduce credit spreads, particularly at the riskier end of the spectrum and can rapidly stimulate issuance (D'Amico and Kaminska (2019)).

It would appear that the MPC believed that the QE4 intervention had a significant macroeconomic impact. Looking back on the eve of the Covid-19 crisis, Carney (2020) argued that the combined envelope of corporate bond and government bond purchases in the summer of 2016 replicated the impact of a non-trivial conventional monetary policy response:

> A growing body of research shows that asset purchases led to substantial, long-lasting, reductions in long-term yields, providing support to activity when policy rates were constrained. Bank staff estimate that the MPC's £60 billion of asset purchases in August 2016 were equivalent to a Bank Rate cut of around 50 basis points.

4.8 Haldane's 'Story So Far': *Cherchez La Friction*

In the months that followed the 2016 QE decision, the Chief Economist, Andy Haldane, published a working paper (co-authored with several members of Bank staff) that aimed to both review the international evidence on the impact of QE on both financial markets and the real economy, and add to that literature.

Haldane's paper has a brief section devoted to how QE works, which begins with the observation that QE is ineffective in many standard macroeconomic models, so we need to add in 'market frictions and distortions' to create an environment in which QE might work in theory (Haldane et al. (2016)):

> the transmission mechanism for QE can be thought to comprise two legs: an expansion of the central bank's balance sheet, creating new reserves to purchase short-term bills; and a maturity extension programme, swapping these bills for longer-term bonds. In many standard macroeconomic models, neither leg has an effect on economic activity. . . . In order to understand how QE might work, we need to depart from these standard models by adding in various market frictions and distortions.

This observation – the importance of framing the discussion around the transmission mechanism of QE in terms of specific frictions – speaks to the debate that would follow and the focus of this chapter. The state contingent transmission mechanism narrative is present in the text, even if that phrase is not used:

> As with any policy intervention, the effectiveness of QE depends on the extent of distortions or frictions in the functioning of various markets. Because these frictions may change over time, depending on the state of the economy and financial system, so too will the effectiveness of QE . . . there is evidence (at least for the US) that the effect of QE may vary over time, depending on the state of the economy and financial system, as theory would suggest. Specifically, the impact of QE is greater the weaker the economy and the more disturbed the state of financial markets. This state-dependency in the impact of QE is potentially important to our understanding of how QE has worked in the past and the circumstances in which it is likely to be effective in the future.

The comments regarding the signalling channel are of particular interest. First, the paper elaborates on the 'information frictions' that underpin the mechanism:

> These might arise from private agents having less than perfect information either about the future monetary policy reaction function of the authorities and/or about the future course of the macro-economy.

Second, the paper cites specific academic references to underpin the discussion of the signalling channel. The key issue to explain here is how the act of purchasing assets can lend credence to private information that the central bank has disclosed – and thereby move market prices – particularly if those purchases have little to no direct effect on market prices. Two of the papers cited by Haldane and co-authors are worthy of comment here:

- Clouse and colleagues (2003), in which the credibility of the signal derives from the fact that balance sheet operations, such as purchases of long-term debt, are understood to change the reaction function of the central bank, which is now keen to keep rates low to avoid losses.
- Eggertsson and Woodford (2003), which discusses the 'management of expectations' at the lower bound and the importance of credible commitments to a low for too long strategy, perhaps by adopting a history-dependent price-level targeting rule.

Finally, with benefit of hindsight – and in particular thinking about the Bank's operations in the gilt market at a time when the MPC was trying to tighten the stance (see Section 4.16.1) – the Haldane paper reaches an interesting conclusion on the link between the motive for central bank asset purchase programmes and their macroeconomic impact:

> there is clear evidence that not all central bank balance sheet expansions are created equally, at least in terms of their impact on activity and growth. There is a clear split here between those countries whose central bank balance sheet expansions were for reasons of liquidity provision (in this sample, Canada, the ECB and Sweden) and those where the purpose has been a loosening of monetary policy (Japan, UK and US). Only in the latter cases do central bank balance sheet expansions appear to have had a significant impact on activity and prices. In other words, it is not balance sheet expansions per se, but their purpose and, prospectively, method of execution that matters for determining their impact on nominal spending. Only interventions badged as monetary policy – or QE – appear to have reliably boosted activity and prices. This suggests that the expectational effects of QE – for example, operating through the signalling and uncertainty channels – may be particularly potent.

4.9 Vlieghe: The Primacy of the Signalling Channel and Limits on Effectiveness

During his time on the MPC, external member Jan Vlieghe made several significant contributions to the debate on the transmission mechanism of QE within the Committee, shifting the narrative away from portfolio balance, towards signalling. In his speech about monetary policy and long-term interest rates, Vlieghe explains how he thinks that signal works (Vlieghe (2016)):

> Asset purchases were a powerful signal about central banks' reaction functions: central banks demonstrated they were willing and able to provide further stimulus even when the policy rate had reached its effective lower bound. Moreover, by carrying out further asset purchases even when the policy rate had been at its effective lower bound for several years, the action was also a signal that either the economy was even weaker than previously thought, or that low interest rates were providing less of a stimulus than previously thought (i.e., the natural rate was lower) ... if one thought that asset purchases work primarily through term premia, this might give credence to the idea that central bank bond purchases are 'distorting' long-term interest rates. But, as the data show, most of the fall in long-term interest

rates was not due to risk premia, but due to expectations of the future path of policy rates.

A couple of years later, Vlieghe returned to discuss QE and reasserted his view on the transmission mechanism (Vlieghe (2018)):

> I have argued that QE works mainly by influencing expectations of future monetary policy, underpinned by the strong signal that immediate policy action sends about the central bank's reaction function and its assessment of the economy, as well as by strong liquidity effects during times of financial stress .... QE policy works primarily via expectations of future monetary policy, with important liquidity effects which are temporary ... liquidity effects are far less important when markets function well and its participants are well capitalised.

Three years later, on the eve of the pandemic, Vlieghe argued that the MPC could be approaching the limits of the effectiveness of QE, given the proximity of expectations of the policy rate to the effective lower bound over an extended horizon (Vlieghe (2019)):

> there are also limits to the effective stimulus imparted by such asset purchases. Ten year government bond yields in the UK are around 0.5% right now. There is just not that much room for these yields to fall further. ... In the limit, once the policy rate hits its effective lower bound and is expected to stay there for many years, such that longer term rates are also close to the effective lower bound, buying even more government bonds is unlikely to provide significant further stimulus.

There would soon be a significant expansion in the stock of asset purchases in the pandemic period. As we will go on to discuss, the MPC decided to 'go big and go fast' at the start of the pandemic, increasing the stock of asset purchases 'as soon as is operationally possible' by £200 billion. The MPC would increase the stock of asset purchases by a further £100 billion in June 2020 and another £150 billion in November 2020. Vlieghe reflected on what could realistically have been expected from that latter £¼ trillion of asset purchases in speeches in the spring and summer 2021 (Vlieghe (2021a), Vlieghe (2021b)):

> But when market functioning is restored, and if long term yields already at very low levels with inflation expectations near the target, in my view the ability for QE to impart additional macro-economic stimulus is limited. In other words, the impact of QE is state-contingent. I therefore voted in favour

of the subsequent rounds of QE in June and November last year largely because I thought they served as insurance against a renewed episode of tightening in financial conditions due to market dysfunction, rather than because I was expecting to achieve an outright further easing in the monetary stance.

Once market functioning is restored, however, continued purchases at a fast pace are not necessary anymore, and slow purchases likely have little effect beyond their signalling value that future rate hikes are still some way off. This is why I pointed out in my last speech ... that I did not expect the additional QE beyond last year's period of market disruption to add additional stimulus to the economy. It provided some insurance against a withdrawal of stimulus that might otherwise have taken place, either via unwarranted expectations of near-term rate hikes, or via a renewed period of market disruption.

In other words, Vlieghe argues that the purpose of the final £¼ trillion of QE was to reduce the risk of a resumption of financial stress in the near-future and to act a signal that rates won't rise in the near future. The latter signal works presumably because the market expects the Committee to complete any programme of asset purchases once it has been announced and does not expect the MPC to raise rates while that programme is still ongoing – points to which we will return at the end of this chapter.

4.10 Bailey: Go Big and Go Fast in a Crisis

Interventions by the Governor on any topic are obviously significant for understanding how the Bank acts. Governor Bailey would reflect on the Bank's approach to QE in a speech at the (virtual) Jackson Hole conference of 2020, and in more detail in a working paper (co-authored with several members of Bank staff). Bailey's intervention at this point is particularly important both because the Bank was undertaking a major increase in the target stock of purchases and because we are once again at a point in the Bank's QE story where the leadership of the Bank has changed, and that could, in principle, lead to a change in the Bank view.

Bailey reiterates the prevailing wisdom on the state contingent nature of the transmission mechanism of QE and the case for accumulating a lot of assets in a short space of time in those moments where QE is most effective (Bailey (2020)):

> Standing back from the Covid crisis, and looking at the UK case, there indeed is some evidence that the impact of QE over the past decade has been largest at times of market dysfunction and illiquidity . . . In the decade ahead, I think we need to take on board the message the Covid crisis has reiterated, namely that our tools may be state contingent in their effects. And with that in mind, let's not ignore the need to manage central bank balance sheets to enable such state contingency to take effect. There are times when we need to go big and go fast.

Turning to the 'how', the working paper acknowledges that the precise mechanism through which the central bank delivers a credible signal is not 'well established' (Bailey et al. (2020)):

> The 'signalling channel' was perhaps the most natural explanation for an impact of QE in the early literature, without substantial deviation from the baseline model. While the precise mechanisms for the signalling channel are less well established in the theoretical literature, the explanation tends to centre on QE as a way to mimic a commitment by the policymaker to hold rates lower for longer than they otherwise would.

This comment is supplemented by an interesting footnote, which expands on the theory and clarifies its relevance – or lack thereof – to the UK circumstance:

> In theory, holding large quantities of long-term debt on its balance sheet exposes the central bank to interest rate risk, in principle creating an incentive to keep the short-term policy rate low to avoid balance sheet losses. Bhattarai, Eggertsson and Gafarov (2015) provide the clearest theoretical exposition of this channel. They show how the role of government debt as a state variable may influence the behaviour of future policymakers, building on the earlier insights of Eggertsson (2006) and Berriel and Bhattarai (2009). As noted in footnote 5, asset purchases decided by the MPC are undertaken by the APF [asset purchase facility], which is indemnified by HM Treasury. As such, interest rate risk associated with changes asset values is borne by the Treasury.

Meanwhile, the paper offers a theoretical defence of the portfolio balance channel:

> the portfolio balance channel can be generated in any theoretical framework in which changes in the relative quantities of assets held by the public has an effect on financial conditions. Indeed, a macroeconomic role for QE via such effects has been established in a number of ways. Replacing the assumption of perfectly efficient markets with one of limits to arbitrage, market

segmentation, or preferred habitats can generate downward sloping demand curves for individual assets. In turn, this means that changing relative asset supplies for the private sector through QE purchases will affect relative returns ... Even when investors are rational and markets are efficient, generalising the form of investors' utility functions can lead to a role for portfolio compositions in determining asset prices ... A wide range of mechanisms have therefore been studied, all of which are consistent with a broad characterisation of the portfolio balance mechanism and many of which imply similar macroeconomic effects of QE.

The working paper summarises the Bank's view on the evidence of the effectiveness of QE as follows:

On balance, the literature provides evidence of ongoing QE transmission to the macroeconomy in later rounds of purchases and is supportive that at least some of the associated transmission channels are persistent. However, this need not suggest that all QE channels are equally powerful and persistent in all states of the world ... While the debate continues over the relative importance of each channel, the balance of evidence suggests that each has contributed to the overall effectiveness of QE. It seems likely that the three broad transmission channels have often operated together. As set out above, a number of strands of the literature credibly identify portfolio balance mechanisms in action. Other studies have found that QE impacts the path of expected interest rates, supporting the signalling channel. The role for different channels will surely have varied depending on the precise nature of the QE programme, the jurisdiction and the economic context.

4.11 An Independent Review and a Response

In 2019, the Bank's Court of Directors commissioned an evaluation of the Bank's QE programme by the Bank's IEO. The first set of recommendations of that review were around the Bank advancing and applying its understanding of QE, namely (IEO (2021)).

- Produce a prioritised work plan for future investment in analysis to fill QE knowledge gaps.
- Maintain a summary of the rationale and evidence supporting each practical QE design decision.
- Provide a forum to allow regular MPC discussions on how QE (as part of the wider monetary policy toolkit) would be used in the event of a big shock.

- At an appropriate horizon/frequency, update technical audience on the Bank's latest collective thinking on QE and proactively foster external engagement with that.

In the context of this chapter, a few of the comments in review stand out:

> Establishing and communicating the economic rationale for QE – which is to stimulate the economy by lowering longer-term interest rates – has not been straightforward. The nature of the QE transmission mechanism remains uncertain and the Bank's emphasis has evolved over time.
>
> The Bank has advanced its understanding of QE since 2009 but there remain open debates about how exactly QE works. Most market practitioners thought this was a sensible response to the evolving evidence base on QE. But we also heard that the Bank has not sufficiently drawn out the implications of its evolving view ... There is also a desire for the Bank to do more to signpost and explain changes in its views, as well as to reflect the uncertainties about QE in its public communications.
>
> There is, however, a lack of published material on the Bank's collective view on QE, particularly recently. For example, we heard that there was not much agreed material to draw on when writing about QE in official publications such as the MPC minutes. In part, this may reflect the fact that there is understandably not a settled collective view on exactly how QE works.

The official response to the review came in part in the form of a *Quarterly Bulletin* article that, according to Huw Pill's introduction, was 'authored by Bank staff at the request of the MPC' but 'does not seek to give a single MPC view about how QE works'.

Consistent with the Bailey and colleagues (2020) working paper, the official response to the IEO is more supportive of the portfolio balance channel (and the compression of term premia) than the arguments of several MPC members reviewed elsewhere in this chapter (Busetto et al. (2022)):

> Most of these channels initially affect gilt yields, which can be decomposed into two components: the expected policy rate over the bond's term to maturity, and a term premium that captures compensation for the investor from interest rate and illiquidity risk, and also potentially from the impact from demand/supply imbalances. QE can lower the expectations component by conveying information about the future path for the policy rate (signalling channel). QE can also lower term premia via several channels. By shrinking the supply of longer-term bonds, QE can push some investors to rebalance

their portfolios towards other bonds and thereby lower their yields, as well as increasing the price of other assets (portfolio balance channel). QE can also reduce any liquidity premia on purchased assets (liquidity channel). In stressed circumstances, QE can improve market liquidity more broadly by lowering risks to dealers who are intermediating trades (market functioning channel). In addition, QE can mitigate uncertainty in financial markets and the real economy (uncertainty channel), which may also reduce term premia, as well as having wider effects. And under some conditions QE can stimulate credit supply by increasing banks' holdings of reserves (bank lending channel).

The article goes on to insist that QE can still be effective outside moments when markets are dysfunctional:

The evidence suggests that QE announcements can also lower yields when markets are not stressed ... The impact of QE appears to vary across programmes, even if one allows for what had been expected beforehand. The response to the surprise component of QE – the announced target less what markets had anticipated – was much greater in March 2009 than at other times ... But there was still a measurable impact of QE surprises on other occasions, even when markets were functioning well.

The article also offers a particular rationale for the signalling mechanism:

When the central bank engages in QE, markets may infer that the central bank is credibly committing to a period of protracted low policy rates. One reason for this belief could be related to the expectation by market participants that the central bank will not raise policy rates before the end of the QE programme.

Finally, the article notes the existence of significant differences of opinion within the MPC:

the article does not seek to give a single MPC view about how QE works. Individual MPC members, in line with the wider academic and economic community, naturally have their own views about which transmission channels of QE are likely to prove most important, about how that assessment may vary across different economic circumstances, and about the effectiveness of QE in easing financial conditions and stimulating the economy.

Despite the growing body of evidence, state-contingency and the limited number of observations mean that there remains considerable uncertainty about the strength of different channels and the overall real-economy impact of QE. Therefore, there will likely be differences in view across policymakers in assessing the desirability and calibration of any QE programme.

4.12 Broadbent: On Commitments to Low for Too Long and Private Information

In a speech on the history and future of QE, Deputy Governor Ben Broadbent set out his view on the relative importance of the different transmission channels at different points in time. He argued that the portfolio balance channel was likely less effective once market conditions normalised after the immediate stress during the financial crisis (Broadbent (2018)):

> The first two – the 'bank lending' and 'portfolio balance' channels – rely, in their different ways, on markets being sufficiently imperfect that the neutrality result no longer applies. But markets are more impaired at some times than others ... It was when things started to seize up, and markets became more dysfunctional, that these transactions really mattered. With fewer assets considered liquid, the demand for central bank money went up. With preferred habitats more entrenched, the effect of asset purchases on prices were larger. You might therefore have expected QE, at least through these channels, to have become more important. Conversely, you might also expect their impact to diminish once more normal market conditions are restored.

Broadbent argued that the power of the signal associated with any given QE decision depends on what other information the central bank communicates at the same time:

> it surely makes sense that the strength of the 'signalling effect' – what markets infer from QE decisions about future interest rates, and the central bank's intentions regarding its overall policy stance – depends on what it communicates alongside its decision.

Of course, this observation inevitably prompts a couple of questions. First, what role is played by the asset purchases themselves in terms of easing financial conditions, over and above the release of the information that the central bank implicitly or explicitly discloses alongside? Second, what information have Broadbent and his colleagues chosen to communicate alongside those decisions to purchase assets?

Although he was not discussing QE, Broadbent's speech on communication and commitment at 'The MPC at 25' conference provides a partial answer to the second question. In the speech, Broadbent discusses the mechanism referenced in the Bailey paper 'a way to mimic a commitment by the policymaker to hold rates lower for longer than they otherwise would'. Broadbent argues that very few policymakers have attempted to make such a commitment in practice, and not the MPC (Broadbent (2022a)):

> It's striking that this 'Odyssean' guidance has received much more attention in the economics literature – but, in the real world, and despite often being right up against the lower bound, central banks have used it only rarely ... On these grounds, and even with a fairly liberal interpretation of these requirements, it's difficult to pick out many episodes that clearly count as pre-commitment. Perhaps the US Fed's communications during and in the years after the financial crisis came the closest, though the shift to more Odyssean-like guidance was as much evolutionary as revolutionary ... Anyhow, these episodes aside, most guidance seems to me to be pretty clearly 'Delphic' in nature: it's about the central bank's view of economic outlook (a forecast) and about policy conditional on it (a 'reaction function') ... As for the UK, the few times the MPC has issued formal guidance about policy, it's very clearly of this type. If ever it's said something about future policy, it's always been in the context of, and dependent on, the outlook for the economy and inflation at the time.

In the Q&A that followed his speech, Broadbent turned to a more general discussion of the Bank's capacity to send additional signals on the path of rates beyond publishing a forecast and making comments about policy linked to that forecast. Broadbent was sceptical about the mechanics of the Bank releasing signals about the rate path, given that policy is set by a Committee of nine (rather than one single decision maker), and whether there was any additional private information that the Committee could release (over and above what is currently put in the public domain) that would lend credibility to such a signal (Broadbent (2022b)):

> this comes back to the point of whether you can commit, we are in a Committee of nine people. I am not going to try and pin down or even suggest ... not just my future vote but eight other people. The only way you could ever do it ... even a simulated path of interest rates ... was to make clear it is completely automatic, it is some feedback rule, it is no more than an expression of the forecast, it is nothing else, nothing else at all. There is no information value other than the forecast on which it is based. That's all you could ever do. There is no single policymaker in this set-up. There are lots. I have found that even making the few statements that we do about future policy, that you need something akin to a super majority on the Committee. It is not enough to have five people bullying the other four into saying something. It is not enough. So, they are very difficult to make ... My prediction would be

that if we tried to do this Committee we could spend a week discussing it and still not, it could only be completely automatic with a whole disclaimer saying that's what it is and therefore have zero information content other than the forecast on which it is based . . . that is the reality of it . . . Even a simulation . . . I certainly don't see it as some sort of salvation that would make everything clear or give private information that we have, because we don't have it. The private information we have we publish in the forecast.

In short, when it comes to sending explicit signals about the future path of rates, Broadbent believes that: the Committee has sent only a few statements during his tenure; it would be extremely difficult to say more; and the message would in any case carry no additional information (over and above the published forecast).

4.13 Tenreyro: Small and Temporary Effects

In one of her final speeches as an external MPC member, Silvana Tenreyro discussed how she believed QE can help the MPC achieve its inflation target. Like Vlieghe, Tenreyro is a sceptic on the portfolio balance channel and the idea that QE had a persistent impact on yields (Tenreyro (2023)):

The correct observation is that the market had to absorb a lot of additional long-term debt, and yet term premia fell, which is the opposite of what the portfolio balance view would predict . . . Shocks can push up term premia when arbitrageurs' capacity is temporarily constrained (and QE may have limited those spikes relative to the no-QE counterfactual). But eventually arbitrageurs do their job, so there is no clear persistent effect.

Tenreyro then turns to discuss the signalling channel and dismantles some of the common mechanisms that have been proposed by the literature: a commitment to 'low for too long' or concerns around losses on the bond portfolio changing behaviour:

For the commitment-based signalling channel to work, undertaking QE would need to make it more costly for the central bank to raise rates quickly once inflation rises above target . . . it is not clear that QE really adds an additional hurdle: the same reputational damage could result from breaking forward guidance promises; after all, the announced tightening sequencing itself is a form of forward guidance . . . Some have proposed balance-sheet concerns behind the commitment. If a central bank holds many long-term government bonds because of QE, raising rates would generate financial losses on these exposures ... But in the UK, as in other countries, there are arrangements in place specifically designed to ensure that monetary policy makers focus exclusively on the appropriate monetary policy, and do not worry about the narrow financial implications of QE for the public sector.

Tenreyro then highlights the importance of beliefs about the effectiveness of QE as a tool *over and above any signal it conveys*:

A precondition for this expectations channel is that QE does work through other, non-signalling channels, or at least that the central banker believes this to be the case. [footnote: More precisely, market participants need to believe that the central banker believes this to be the case.] If QE had no material effects on yields, output or inflation, then QE would always be costless for the policymaker and hence could not send a more credible signal than words about the state of the economy or the central bank reaction function.

Tenreyro's summary on the signalling channel and QE more broadly is as follows:

Overall, it is conceivable that QE could work to some extent via signalling channels, but those effects should also be modest in size ... the key question is how much QE reduces long-term bond yields. The evidence is supportive of stronger effects on yields during times of stress via broad liquidity channels, while there may be some evidence for small and temporary effects on yields through portfolio-balancing and signalling channels.

Quantitative easing is ultimately presented as a tool that is best suited to supporting the pursuit of price stability when markets are dysfunctional, although it is as least debatable whether QE is still a tool of monetary policy in this scenario (as opposed to macroprudential policy; see Section 4.16.3):

Market-wide liquidity can dry up in times of stress and QE can have material effects on yields in such times. There is ample evidence for a state-contingent market liquidity or market functioning channel from a large number of event studies ... even if its role in reducing yields is limited, QE can still play a role as an insurance device, helping to meet the inflation target in case of future episodes of financial stress.

4.14 Financial Stability QE

During the acute phase of the pandemic crisis and the so-called 'dash for cash', global central banks resumed QE. Not only were there significant increases in the quantum of asset purchases around the world, but those purchases were completed as fast as possible. The key point to note about the initial burst of Covid-QE is that it was not purely intended to deliver price stability, as a conventional monetary policy operation is designed to do, but to safeguard financial stability too, as Hauser (2021) observes:

> The huge asset purchase programmes unleashed in Spring 2020 had a dramatic and immediate calming effect, 'getting in all the cracks' of the liquidity shortage amongst non-banks, and taking duration risk off dealers' balance sheets. Central banks made it clear their operations were aimed, in part, and at least initially, at restoring market functioning . . . Central banks were 'buyers of last resort' more than 'market makers of last resort'.

The Bank was intimately familiar with the market maker of last resort (MMLR) function long before the dash for cash. Recall that the Bank was already purchasing private sector assets before the launch of QE in March 2009 (Fisher (2010)). Indeed, Paul Tucker's speech 'The Repertoire of Official Sector Interventions in the Financial System', which provides a detailed treatment of the MMLR function (among many other topics), including how such asset purchases for financial stability purposes sit alongside the objectives and implementation of monetary policy, was delivered in the immediate aftermath of the financial crisis in 2009 (Tucker (2009)):

> First, as with LOLR, central banks cannot engage in MMLR operations if to do so would interfere with monetary policy. Securities are purchased in exchange for cash, entailing an injection of reserves into the banking system. That has to be consistent with the target for the central bank's net supply of reserves. Second, a MMLR should aim to charge a penalty (eg buy at a discount) to the fundamental value of an asset. Put another way, any bid-ask spread should be unattractive relative to peacetime conditions in private markets. Third, any purchase (auction) mechanism should be designed to reveal information about the state of the market and the fairness of prices paid. Fourth, while the MMLR cannot avoid the risk inherent in outright purchases, it absolutely must not over reach its capital resources. Fifth, the MMLR should aim to be catalytic, helping ideally to kick-start the market rather than replace it. Sixth, the MMLR should avoid propping up markets that would not be fundamentally viable once peacetime returns.

Returning to the dash for cash, Cunliffe (2022a) is crystal clear on the thinking that underpinned BoE policy at this moment:

At the onset on the pandemic, in the second week of March 2020, the Bank of England cut interest rates to close to the effective lower bound. Only a week later we announced further action to purchase £200bn of gilts. The first decision was motivated by the need to support the economy through the pandemic and through the hit to demand that was on the horizon. However, the second, as the MPC made clear at the time, was motivated by the urgent need to reverse the increasing and unwarranted tightening of financial conditions driven by the disruption of the dash for cash. Though distinct, these two motivations – to keep demand and supply in line on the one hand and to restore market order on the other – clearly went in the same direction in the circumstance we faced at the time.

In the 'dash for cash' the monetary policy and financial stability policy objectives were aligned. But it was clear that the Bank would not always be able to rely on that coincidence; there might come a moment where the Bank would want to simultaneously tighten the stance of monetary policy and use an asset purchase tool to restore financial stability. Andrew Hauser of the Bank and Lorie Logan of the Federal Reserve led a Bank for International Settlements (BIS) working group to design a central bank tool that could be used in those circumstances, when conventional QE might be out of reach.

This moment arrived in 2022 when the Bank felt obliged to launch temporary and targeted asset purchase programme to restore calm in the liability driven investment (LDI) crisis during a period when the MPC wanted to tighten broad financial conditions, as Andrew Hauser, the then Executive Director for Markets, recounts (Kehoe (2024)):

> This was a tense and difficult period . . . You could even say that a G7 country had an emerging market crisis . . . We hoped that we could do it through means other than the ones we ended up doing, but the ones we ended up having to do was to buy gilts. Ultimately, the intervention was extremely successful. It brought yields down very quickly.

This type of operation is not designed to have a lasting macroeconomic impact, over and above managing the stress in markets which might otherwise have had a disinflationary impact. In other words, the objective is to restore the status quo ante where broad financial conditions are concerned. There is no intention of sending a signal about the future path of rates, although it is possible that the market could misconstrue the nature of the scheme and discern a signal that was not really there (Pill (2022)).

In fact, the Bank would have preferred to provide liquidity support by lending against collateral during the stress in the gilt market, but this proved not to be possible (Hauser (2022)). The Bank therefore began work on both designing a facility which would allow the possibility of lending funds to the insurance company and pension fund (ICPF) sector and reflecting on how to extend access to a wider set of non-bank financial institutions (Hauser (2023)). So, asset purchases may only be used as a last resort for financial stability purposes in future moments of crisis.

4.15 Stock Theory of QE

This review of Bank thinking on QE concludes with a discussion of one of the familiar talking points in the broader market discussion about QE: the stock versus flow debate. The conventional reference for the stock theory of QE is D'Amico and King (2013):

> 'Stock effects' are defined as persistent changes in prices that result from movements along Treasury demand curves. To estimate stock effects, we model the cumulative change in each CUSIP's price between March 17, 2009 and October 30, 2009 (i.e., the cross-section of Treasury returns) as a function of the total amount that the Fed purchased of that CUSIP and its potential substitutes . . . Meanwhile, 'flow effects' are defined as the response of prices to the ongoing purchase operations and could reflect, on top of portfolio rebalancing activity due to the outcome of the purchases, impairments in liquidity and functioning that lead to sluggish price discovery.

The stock theory is typically understood to be a hypothesis that asset purchases that were completed in the past continue to have an impact on asset prices today, and hence the current size of the asset portfolio that the central bank has acquired over the past (the stock) is part of the effective monetary stance today. In passing, this conventional treatment of the stock theory of QE is the one reflected in the model which features in the appendix of the Bailey and colleagues' (2020) working paper, and the paper on which it is based, written by one of Bailey's co-authors (Harrison (2017)) – that is, it is the current size of the bond portfolio enters the IS curve.

We can certainly find MPC members making stock-based arguments in the early years of the QE era. In his testimony to Parliament, Paul Tucker explained why there was a powerful countervailing mechanism that would continue to underpin the effectiveness of asset purchases as the stress in financial markets abated – because the Bank was holding more bonds (Tucker (2010)):

> My two points: that as the financial markets work better, the markets are more efficient and so the impact would be smaller. That's true ... On the other hand, the more gilts we take away from the long-term institutions the greater the effect would be because the marginal value to them of losing the duration, the interest rate exposure of long-term gilts gets greater. If you buy £1 million worth or £1 billion worth of gilts off the long-term institutions, you don't do very much. If you buy a vast amount you do more and that would continue ... do I believe that quantitative easing would still help to stimulate demand if we found ourselves wanting to do more? Yes.

It stands to reason that views on the stock theory should reflect views on the transmission mechanism of QE. Some channels of transmission are clearly easier to reconcile with the stock theory than others. The portfolio rebalancing channel is a natural bedfellow, although for the stock theory to hold we must believe that the adjustment in asset prices triggered by the initial shift in the private sector's asset holdings is highly persistent (presumably, the preferred habitats that exist in financial markets and the constraints on arbitrage are similarly persistent).

In principle, one could instead try to reconstruct a version of the stock theory based around the signalling channel, but this would require that the information that was released alongside past decision to purchase assets was somehow still 'news-worthy' to current market pricing and the asset purchases were still lending credibility to that signal. However, it seems likely that any signal that was released in the past about the state of the economy or the reaction function of the central bank has either been validated by subsequent events or not, so the signal itself would cease to have value.

As we have seen, the Committee has shifted to varying degrees away from the portfolio rebalancing channel towards the signalling channel. As a result, we should expect the Committee to have shifted away from the stock theory of QE, as conventionally defined. Indeed, Vlieghe (2016) explicitly argues there is no reason to believe that bonds purchases in the past influence (distort) current asset prices:

> There is nothing anomalous about the low level of long-term interest rates, nor is there any evidence that government bond yields are 'distorted' by

> central banks' asset purchases .... if one thought that asset purchases work primarily through term premia, this might give credence to the idea that central bank bond purchases are 'distorting' long-term interest rates. But, as the data show, most of the fall in long-term interest rates was not due to risk premia, but due to expectations of the future path of policy rates.

Broadbent (2018) also touches on the stock theory in the footnote of a speech, albeit in a slightly more equivocal tone, acknowledging some uncertainty around the impact of the existing stock:

> There's an important distinction here between the effects of existing stock, such as they are, and those of future changes in the APF. If the there's material uncertainty about the impact of the existing stock, even many years after it was purchased, there's an argument for beginning the unwind that much earlier (i.e. for having a lower interest-rate threshold).

Interestingly, the Bank has increasingly framed the debate around the stock theory in a forward- rather than a backward-looking sense, focusing on the impact of purchases that are expected to take place in the future (that will add to the stock in the future) as opposed to those that were executed in the past. This *expected* stock versus flow framework is described in a footnote of the 2020 Working Paper published by the Governor and co-authors (Bailey et al. (2020)):

> By definition, the total stock of assets purchased is equal to the sum of the flows of purchases over time. Stock effects are generated by changes in the current and future expected stock of assets to be purchased by the central bank. Flow effects are those which occur as a result the central bank being an active participant in the market and the act of purchasing the assets.

The emphasis on *expected* stock is important. Investors may not be certain that all of the purchases that are scheduled to take place in an elongated ('go slow') programme will ultimately be delivered, as Haldane's vote in June 2021 (to reduce the target for the stock of purchases from £875 billion to £825 billion) underlines. A 'go fast' programme may have more impact on asset prices simply because investors will be more confident that the entire programme will be delivered (and, implicitly, if they believe that bonds acquired under a 'go fast' programme will not be rapidly sold back to the market if the macroeconomic outlook improves to the point where a 'go slow' programme would stop early).

4.16 Reflections

It is worth repeating that we should have expected 'the Bank view' on the transmission mechanism of QE to have evolved over time, thanks to the arrival of new information and the arrival of new policymakers (and particularly those in senior positions). There is nothing wrong with the QE narrative changing.

Nonetheless, this review of Bank thinking raises at least three interesting questions. First, given that more importance is now attached to the signalling channel outside moments of market dysfunction, how does the Bank think the signalling channel works? Second, how do Bank policymakers manage to align around decisions to increase asset purchases if they disagree on the mechanism? Third, given an emerging consensus on the state contingent nature of QE, what is the appropriate status of QE as a policy instrument – is it as much a macroprudential policy tool, best suited to deal with episodes of market dysfunction, as a monetary policy tool?

4.16.1 The Signalling Mechanism

There are several plausible mechanisms through which the signalling channel of QE could work. We will consider five mechanisms here: revealing that the central bank is unconstrained at the lower bound on the policy rate; revealing a change in the reaction function that will guide the future path of the short rate that is a direct result of the decision to purchases assets; an unspoken commitment to mimic a 'low for too long' strategy; revealing private information that shifts rate expectations; and, ruling out rate hikes over the period in which purchases are made. One interesting feature of the comments and decisions of policymakers is that they appear to confront and to varying degrees dismiss the relevance of these mechanisms to BoE QE (Barwell (2024)).

To begin with, the Bank's description of the signalling channel captured the idea that by buying bonds a central bank was reassuring the outside world that it was not 'out of monetary ammunition'. If people believed that the central bank was impotent once it reached the lower bound on the policy rate (and they were not confident that fiscal policy would be activist) then the economy would have effectively shifted to a new constrained policy regime, with a weaker central case path for the economy and an increase in the risk of very bad outcomes (further downside shocks would not be met by an effective policy response). That shift in beliefs could then have had a further counter-productive impact on behaviour – with increased precautionary saving by households and a collapse in any investment that is partially irreversible. The signal that policy is not constrained, that an unconventional policy instrument exists, could then influence expectations about the most likely path for the economy and lower the perceived probability of very bad outcomes (because future downside shocks would now be met with additional monetary stimulus). In theory, that signal could have a powerful effect, by cutting off the left tail of the distribution of future outcomes (Blanchard (2009)). Consistent with that, this signal should actually bring forward expectations of the timing of the first increase in Bank Rate (raise forward rates), not push them back (down) as with the usual QE signalling narrative.

In theory, this signal mechanism should be particularly powerful when QE is first announced. Beliefs shift from an outlook in which monetary policy is constrained to one in which it is once again unconstrained. However, it is less obvious why from that point onwards beliefs about the prevailing macro regime would become fragile again (shifting back to the constrained monetary policy regime). If they do not, then this mechanism is no longer relevant in future QE episodes. Perhaps one can make the argument that investors constantly worry about the existence of a (perceived) upper bound on the stock of asset purchases, and therefore every fresh QE announcement brings fresh reassurance that there is scope to do more (the upper bound on QE is not close). However, it is possible in this world that additional bond buying could be viewed as counter-productive, bringing that QE ceiling closer wherever it is. In short, this signalling mechanism should probably only have been present at the start of QE1. From this perspective, perhaps the narrative about the waning transmission mechanism of QE should focus more on the signalling channel and less on the portfolio balance channel.

Furthermore, this expectations argument relies on bond buying being an effective monetary policy tool in its own right and being perceived as such by the outside world. It is hard to see how the central bank taking actions that (are perceived to) have no significant macroeconomic impact would have a stabilising impact on expectations; indeed, such actions could prove counterproductive, cementing beliefs in the constrained monetary policy regime. This brings us back to the debate within the Bank about whether there is a meaningful portfolio balance channel when markets are not dysfunctional, and hence whether that might even have had a potentially counterproductive impact on beliefs about the extent to which the central bank is constrained.

The signalling mechanism favoured by many academics focuses on the actions of the central bank once the time approaches to leave the lower bound on the policy rate. It is argued that the accumulation of assets changes the reaction function of an independent central bank by introducing a concern to manage the profit and loss on the asset portfolio (Bhattarai, Eggertsson, and Gafarov (2023)). Rates are now expected to remain at the lower bound 'for too long'. This argument is a novel twist on the familiar expression 'put your money where your mouth is' – by putting their money where their mouth is and buying assets, central bankers credibly change the words that will come out of their mouth in the future. But the Bank has been crystal clear on this mechanism: the fact that the APF is fully indemnified means that the MPC is *not* influenced by such considerations – see, for example, Ramsden (2023):

> The APF is fully indemnified by HM Treasury, which ensures that monetary policy decisions are not constrained by the potential implications for the Bank's balance sheet.

In passing, it is not even clear that this mechanism delivers the 'low for too long' message when the central bank is buying ultra long-term bonds. A low 'for too long' message can push down expectations of the likely path of Bank Rate over the near-term, but there ought to be a pay-back in terms of the likely path further out, and an increase in the inflation risk premium implicit in long-term bond yields. In other words, a 'low for far too long' message could cause the price of long-term bonds to fall, not rise.

A related but distinct mechanism – referenced by Bailey and colleagues (2020) – is the idea that QE can *mimic* a commitment to hold rates low for too long, which then triggers a shift in expectations of the future path of policy. There are a couple of points to note here. First, as Woodford highlighted in his Jackson Hole speech, this mechanism would surely be more effective if it was 'accompanied by explicit forward guidance, rather than regarded as a substitute for it'

(Woodford (2012)). Second, this unspoken commitment to low for too long would surely be more convincing if the people making the argument could point to the institutional 'bees wax and rope' that will bind future policymakers to the strategy of keeping interest rates low at the point when the conventional reaction function suggests rates should rise, especially for central banks like the BoE with an indemnity. Indeed, it is hard to see how the bees wax and rope could be implemented given the turnover in the composition of policy committees, and in the UK context the instruction to vote your view and not search for consensus (Broadbent (2022a)). Third, even if this unspoken commitment without bees wax and rope was effective in the past, it seems likely that it will be less effective in the future given the path of policy in the aftermath of asset purchases during the pandemic, when rates stayed anything but low (Schnabel (2024)). Even if we believe that QE could send a credible unspoken 'low for too long' signal about the future rate path it is worth asking whether policymakers wanted to send that signal during this period – that is, whether this mechanism is relevant. In the case of the BoE, we have the answer. The BoE has made clear that it has not tried to give such a commitment. Indeed, Deputy Governor Broadbent has argued that such commitments have been extremely rare across the global central banking community (Broadbent (2022a)). Indeed, it is unclear that the Committee tried to send *any* signal about the rate path alongside QE announcements during this period (Joyce et al. (2011)). Consistent with this, Cassar (2023) argues that forward guidance of this kind was excluded from consideration as a policy option in order to 'insulate the Bank from the credibility costs of committing itself to a policy path and then reneging on it'.

An alternative view of the signalling mechanism is that QE releases private information to the outside world, which then triggers a shift in expectations, including about the path of the policy rate. The Bank's QE narrative has touched on this channel. Haldane and colleagues (2016) emphasise the role of 'information frictions' in the transmission of QE. From this perspective, the information embedded in, or released alongside a QE announcement represents news to the market (unless we are going to appeal to arguments about coordinating on public signals (Morris and Shin (2002)). A couple of points should be noted about this mechanism. First, calibrating the net impact of the signal may not be straightforward, and the shift in the expected policy path cannot be taken as a summary statistic of the impact of the signal. For example, if the central bank reveals that it has a more pessimistic assessment of the outlook than the private sector then that ought to lead to a lower expected path for the policy rate if agents revise their priors somewhat. Bond yields would fall. But the revised view of the outlook might also lead to an adjustment in risk premia embedded in many asset prices, so the overall impact of the signal on broad financial condition is less clear. But even if financial conditions loosen, the impact on spending is less clear cut. If households and companies revise their expectations of the outlook – if they are spooked by downbeat central bank communication – then they may save more and spend less, despite looser financial conditions. Second, the power of this signalling mechanism should be inversely proportional to the effectiveness of the central bank's communication to that point. That is, the more that past communications have helped the market to understand central bank's assessment of the economy and its reaction function, the smaller the stock of private information about the outlook or the reaction function that is available to release. One can find examples of MPC members referencing this mechanism. Vlieghe (2016) argued that additional QE might have been a signal that the economy was weaker than expected or that low interest rates were less stimulatory than expected (because the neutral rate was lower). In passing, it is interesting to reflect on the relative merits of communicating this information implicitly via QE versus communicating it explicitly, say, via the publication of a comprehensive analysis of the macroeconomic outlook or the likely level of the neutral rate. However, as noted earlier, Deputy Governor Broadbent has argued (in the context of a debate about sending explicit messages about the future path of rates) that the Bank does not have *any* additional private information to reveal over and above what is already in the public domain, and it would be very hard to agree any additional message to send.

Finally, a more pragmatic interpretation of the QE signal is that a long, slow asset purchase programme can push-back expectations of the next rate hike because the market would not expect the central bank to simultaneously raise rates and buy bonds (Busetto et al. (2022)). However, even this commitment mechanism may not be effective in the future given the voting record during 2021. This was a period where the Bank was executing the plan agreed in November 2020 to buy bonds throughout 2021. However, one member of the MPC voted at the June 2021 meeting to scale back that agreed purchase plan, potentially bringing forward the timing of the first hike, and then at the November meeting, three members voted to reduce the target stock of purchases, two of whom voted to raise rates *before* the final phase of the purchase programme was completed (BoE (2021b)):

> In light of this, while agreeing with the majority on maintaining Bank Rate, this member judged that it would be appropriate to remove some of the monetary stimulus to asset prices by terminating the existing asset purchase programme at this meeting, ahead of any subsequent increase in Bank Rate
>
> For two members of the Committee, the economic outlook warranted a tightening in the monetary policy stance at this meeting. These members preferred an immediate end to the existing asset purchase programme, as well as an immediate increase in Bank Rate to 0.25%.

4.16.2 *Groupvote Not Groupthink*

As is hopefully very clear from the content of this chapter, there is no Groupthink about how QE works at the Bank of England. From the outset, the Bank flagged the uncertainty around the transmission mechanism of QE and over time clear differences of view have emerged, in particular around the quantitative significance of the portfolio balance channel outside moments of market dysfunction. But despite that diversity of view over how much good a given amount of QE does, there is a fair degree of conformity around how much QE to do. A detailed analysis of the voting record on QE is beyond the scope of this chapter, and some care needs to be taken about extrapolating from a relatively small number of meetings where there was a live vote on the target stock, but a couple of points stand out from the voting record. There is clearly dissent over QE – the Committee does not always unanimously agree on the target stock – and sometimes dissenting views are persistent. However, there is a tendency for policymakers to coalesce on a particular number for the target stock, and there have been several instances where dissenting votes on the stock last for only one meeting, with the minority validating the decision of the majority once the purchase programme has begun.

At first glance, this looks like a puzzle. One might have expected those differences in view on the effectiveness of QE (or perhaps more precisely the cost-benefit of more QE) to have translated into more material differences in the votes on how much QE to do. However, a casual check of the voting record on Bank Rate decisions reveals that there is no specific puzzle relating to QE decisions. *Groupvote* is the norm (Barwell (2019)). Major dissent on Bank Rate is extremely rare. Dissenting votes on Bank Rate are typically of the order of ±25 basis points, which suggests that MPC members are in the habit of voting the direction but not the extent of their dissent of their view on policy. If MPC members have systematically chosen to self-censor dissenting votes on monetary policy that reflect differences of opinion on the macroeconomic outlook, then it should come as no surprise that they would have chosen to self-censor votes on monetary policy that reflect differences of opinion on the effectiveness of monetary policy instruments.

It is certainly possible that a 'portfolio balance sceptic' on the Committee might have reached the conclusion that additional bond purchases would have done little to no lasting good (outside of a moment of financial stress) at least relative to the costs involved. However, that sceptic might have concluded that to vote against a majority decision to carry out additional bond purchases, with an associated paragraph in the minutes that justified the dissent with arguments challenging the effectiveness of the QE, would have attracted considerable attention in the markets, in the media and the political sphere. It is therefore possible that such a sceptic might have decided to go along with the majority view on additional asset purchases rather than risk being accused of undermining confidence in the power of monetary policy to support the economy, or in the Bank of England itself. The problem with this argument is that it cannot explain why that 'portfolio balance sceptic' would then be happy to write speeches explaining why he or she was a sceptic, or even pointing out that QE is likely to be ineffective in certain circumstances.

This train of thought underlines the value in an oral history of the MPC, along the lines conducted by Cassar (2023). An unexpurgated insiders' account of BoE QE would be of interest to those within the central bank watching community who want to understand the inside story of an unconventional policy tool that Bernanke famously observed works in practice but not in theory. That information will not present itself to the Bank watchers: we will have to collect it. In fact, the creation of an oral history would be a worthwhile exercise even if the finished product never saw the light of day and remained locked in a safe in the Parlours of Threadneedle Street. An incoming Governor or Deputy Governor would surely be interested to learn from his or her predecessors about the true nature of the internal policy debate around QE: about the extent of the differences of view about the effectiveness of asset purchases in different states of nature; the relative merits of purchases of public and private assets; the perceived costs attached to dissent about the efficacy of QE; whether key design choices at inception created precedent that had a lasting impact on the conduct of policy; and so on.

4.16.3 Monetary QE versus Macroprudential MMLR

The final topic worth reflecting on is around the fate of QE as a monetary policy tool given the questions that some policymakers have raised around the state contingent nature of the portfolio balance channel and the issue highlighted earlier concerning the ambiguous nature of the mechanism that underpins the signalling channel. This might sound like a strange question to ask given that the official Bank narrative on QE continues to stress the effectiveness of asset purchases in fair market conditions as well as foul, and that part of the rationale for the Bank's Quantitative Tightening programme is to create additional headroom for further rounds of asset purchases. However, the implicit challenges to the efficacy of QE in certain states of the world and the uncertain nature of the signalling mechanism remain, and it is unclear how future shifts in the composition of the Committee and the senior management of the Bank will impact the 'house view'. It is unclear how keen a future Committee might be to relaunch QE, particularly in moments when markets are not dysfunctional, and more so if rate expectations have already concertinaed onto the lower bound. At this point, that future cohort of policymakers may have to confront the challenge posed by Vlieghe, as to whether whatever benefits additional QE might deliver would exceed the costs.

In contrast, there does appear to be a consensus that asset purchases can move asset prices in dysfunctional markets. There is correspondingly broad support for the idea that QE is an effective tool for restoring financial stability in febrile markets, which can then indirectly support the pursuit of price stability. But there is a reasonable argument to label such interventions as macroprudential MMLR and not monetary QE – and to treat those interventions accordingly, including both the governance around who pulls the trigger and the default strategy for unwinding the purchases (fast in the case of macroprudential and typically slow in the case of monetary).

Restoring order to core financial markets is certainly conducive to the pursuit of price stability. The people who set monetary policy cannot afford to be indifferent about the state of financial markets. Dysfunctional financial markets mean a dysfunctional monetary transmission mechanism, with an unwanted tightening in financial conditions transmitted to the real economy. As the minutes of the February 2009 policy meeting make clear, the Committee appreciated that while the purchases of commercial paper and corporate bonds that took place in early 2009 were a financial stability operation, there might still be an indirect impact on the macroeconomic outlook (BoE (2009a)):

> Those purchases were aimed at improving conditions in the specific credit markets rather than achieving the inflation target. Nevertheless, these measures might help to change banks' behaviour and boost the broad supply of money, which could provide a material stimulus to nominal spending.

Nonetheless, restoring order to financial markets is not a core responsibility of the MPC. The responsibility instead sits with the custodians (plural) of financial stability who, in the case of the UK, also reside at the Bank of England. Responsibility for the design and approval of asset purchase programmes that are intended to restore financial stability should presumably be placed accordingly. Indeed, the fact that the FPC, and not the MPC, recommended that action be taken in response to the stress in the gilt market in 2022 was a welcome step in that direction (Aikman and Barwell (2022), Barwell (2022)), although it was the Bank's Executive that was ultimately calling the shots (Cunliffe (2022b)):

> in line with the Bank's governance, the Bank's Executive took the necessary decisions on the planning, design and implementation of the operation, which was taken in pursuit of the Bank's statutory financial stability objective to protect and enhance the UK financial system. The FPC was engaged ahead of its launch, recognising the risks to UK financial stability from dysfunction in the gilt market. The FPC recommended that the Bank take action, and welcomed the Bank's plans for temporary and targeted purchases in the gilt market on financial stability grounds at an urgent pace.

4.17 Conclusions

This chapter has tried to document the evolving view at the Bank on the transmission mechanism of asset purchases, based on the speeches, papers, and comments of policymakers and the staff.

There does appear to have been a shift in thinking on the relative importance of the different transmission channels across the Committee. To begin with, the portfolio balance channel was *primus inter pares*. But over time and to varying degrees, policymakers appear to have become less convinced that this channel can deliver a significant and persistent impact on bond yields via compressed term premia in moments when markets are tranquil. That is not to say that the Bank has given up on the portfolio balance channel. The official Bank narrative still includes it. But there have been a number of interventions by individual policymakers – and not all external members – questioning its efficacy outside moments of market dysfunction.

The focus has shifted towards the signalling channel, in which bond purchases influence bond prices by shifting expectations of the future path of the policy rate. The key question that this chapter has not resolved is precisely how MPC members believe that the signalling channel of QE works: that is, the precise nature of the information that was released and how the decision to buy bonds alongside the release of that information provides added credibility to, and therefore amplifies the impact of, that signal. The question here is not whether it is possible for a central bank to shift expectations of the future path of policy through the release of private information (it can) nor whether the literature can provide mechanisms through which asset purchases could embed a signal (it has). The question is how the MPC believes that signalling mechanism works in the context of QE.

There have clearly been differences of opinion on the quantitative significance of the portfolio balance channel across the Committee over recent years and, given the uncertainty over the mechanism that underpins the signalling channel, there may well have been differences of opinion over the quantitative significance of the signalling channel too. There is an interesting question – beyond the scope of this chapter – about how members of the Committee with divergent views on the transmission mechanism of bond buying managed to reach a consensus on how many bonds to buy.

References

Aikman, D. and Barwell, R. (2022), 'Reactions to the Bank of England's gilt market operation', Macroprudential Matters, Blog, 11 October.

Bailey, A. (2020), 'The central bank balance sheet as a policy tool', speech, 28 August.

Bailey, A., Bridges, J., Harrison, R., Jones, J., and Mankodi, A. (2020), 'The central bank balance sheet as a policy tool: past, present and future', *Bank of England Staff Working Paper* 899.

Bank of England (2009a), Minutes of the Monetary Policy Committee meeting of 4–5 February.

Bank of England (2009b), Minutes of the Monetary Policy Committee meeting of 4–5 March.

Bank of England (2009c), Markets and operations, *Bank of England Quarterly Bulletin*, Q3.

Bank of England (2011), Minutes of the Monetary Policy Committee meeting of 5–6 October.

Bank of England (2012), Minutes of the Monetary Policy Committee meeting of 4–5 July.

Bank of England (2016a), Minutes of the Monetary Policy Committee meeting of 3 August.

Bank of England (2016b), Markets and operations, *Bank of England Quarterly Bulletin*, Q3.

Bank of England (2021a), Minutes of the Monetary Policy Committee meeting ending 22 June.

Bank of England (2021b), Minutes of the Monetary Policy Committee meeting ending 2 November.

Barwell, R. (2019), 'Inertial Groupvote', in Barwell, R. and Chadha, J. (eds.), *Renewing our monetary vows*. NIESR Occasional Paper 58. National Institute of Economic and Social Research.

Barwell, R. (2022), 'The risk taker of last resort', Macroprudential Matters, blog, 5 April.

Barwell, R. (2024), 'Revisiting the signalling channel of quantitative easing', *VoxEU* column, 2 October.

Bean, C., Paustian, M., Penalver, A., and Taylor, T. (2010), 'Monetary policy after the Fall', speech, 28 August.

Benford, J., Berry, S., Nikolov, K., Young, C., and Robson, M. (2009), 'Quantitative easing', Bank of England Quarterly Bulletin, Q2, pp. 90–100.

Bernanke, B. (2010), 'The economic outlook and monetary policy', speech, 27 August.

Bhattarai, S., Eggertsson, G., and Gafarov, B. (2023), 'Time consistency and duration of government debt: A model of quantitative easing', *The Review of Economic Studies*, 90(4), pp. 1759–99.

Blanchard, O. (2009), '(Nearly) nothing to fear but fear itself', *The Economist*, 29 January.

Broadbent, B. (2018), 'The history and future of QE', speech, 23 July.

Broadbent, B. (2022a), 'Reliable partners', speech, 30 March.

Broadbent, B. (2022b), Q&A at 'The MPC at 25' conference, 30 March.

Busetto, F., Chavaz, M., Froemel, M., Joyce, M., Kaminska, I., and Worlidge, J. (2022), 'QE at the Bank of England: A perspective on its functioning and effectiveness', *Bank of England Quarterly Bulletin*, Q1.

Butt, N., Churm, R., McMahon, M., Morotz, A., and Schanz, J. (2014), 'QE and the bank lending channel in the United Kingdom', *Bank of England Staff Working Paper* 511.

Carney, M. (2016), Letter to the Chancellor, 4 August.

Carney, M. (2020), 'A framework for all seasons', speech, 9 January.

Cassar, D. (2023), 'Economics as intervention', *Socio-Economic Review*, 22(3), pp. 1–30.

Clouse, J., Henderson, D., Orphanides, A., Small, D., and Tinsley, P. (2003), 'Monetary policy when the nominal short-term interest rate is zero', *Topics in Macroeconomics*, 3(1), pp. 1088–22.

Cunliffe, J. (2022a), 'Learning from the dash for cash', speech, 9 February.

Cunliffe, J. (2022b), Letter to the Chair of the Treasury Committee, 5 October.

D'Amico, S. and Kaminska, I. (2019), 'Credit easing versus quantitative easing', *Bank of England Working Paper* 825.

D'Amico, S. and King, T. (2013), 'Flow and stock effects of large-scale treasury purchases: Evidence on the importance of local supply', *Journal of Financial Economics*, 108(2), pp. 425–48.

Dale, S. (2010), 'QE – one year on', speech, 12 March.

Darling, A. (2009), Letter from the Chancellor to the Governor, 3 March.

Eggertsson, G. and Woodford, M. (2003), 'The zero bound on interest rates and optimal monetary policy', *Brookings Papers on Economic Activity*, 34(1), pp. 139–235.

Fisher, P. (2010), 'The corporate sector and the Bank of England's asset purchases', speech, 18 February.

Haldane, A., Roberts-Sklar, M., Wieladek, T., and Young, C. (2016), 'QE: The story so far', *Bank of England Staff Working Paper* 624.

Harrison, R. (2017), 'Optimal quantitative easing', *Bank of England Working Paper* 678.

Hauser, A. (2021), 'From lender of last resort to market maker of last resort via the dash for cash: Why central banks need new tools for dealing with market dysfunction', speech, 7 January.

Hauser, A. (2022), 'Thirteen days in October: How central bank balance sheets can support monetary and financial stability', speech, 4 November.

Hauser, A. (2023), 'A journey of 1000 miles begins with a single step: Filling gaps in the central bank liquidity toolkit', speech, 28 September.

IEO (2021), IEO evaluation of the Bank of England's approach to quantitative easing, 13 January.

Joyce, M., Lasaosa, A., Stevens, I., and Tong, M. (2011), 'The financial market impact of quantitative easing in the United Kingdom', *International Journal of Central Banking*, 7(3), pp. 113–61.

Joyce, M., Miles, D., Scott, A., and Vayanos, D. (2012), 'Quantitative easing and unconventional monetary policy: An introduction', *Economic Journal*, 122(564), pp. F271–F288.

Joyce, M. and Spaltro, M. (2014), 'Quantitative easing and bank lending: A panel data approach', *Bank of England Working Paper* 504.

Joyce, M., Tong, M., and Woods, R. (2011), 'The United Kingdom's quantitative easing policy: Design, operation and impact', *Bank of England Quarterly Bulletin*, 51(3), pp. 200–12.

Kehoe, J. (2024), 'The heated phone calls that landed Andrew Hauser at the RBA', *Financial Review*, 4 June.

King, M. (1999), 'Challenges for monetary policy: New and old', speech, 27 August.

King, M. (2004), 'The institutions of monetary policy', speech, 12 January.

King, M. (2009), 'Speech to the CBI Dinner', speech, 20 January.

King, M. (2012a), Remarks in the Inflation Report press conference, 16 May.

King, M. (2012b), Remarks in the Inflation Report press conference, 8 August.

McLaren, N., Banerjee, R., and Latto, D. (2014), 'Using Changes in auction maturity sectors to help identify the impact of QE on gilt yields', *Economic Journal*, 124, pp. 453–79.

Miles, D. (2014), 'The transition to a new normal for monetary policy', speech, 27 February.

Miles, D. and Schanz, J. (2014), 'The relevance or otherwise of the central bank's balance sheet', *CESifo Working Paper* 4615.

Morris, H. and Shin, S. (2002), 'Social value of public information', *American Economic Review*, 92(5), pp. 1521–34.

Pill, H. (2022), 'Monetary policy and central bank asset purchases: Substitutes and complements', speech, 23 November.

Posen, A. (2010), Remarks to the Treasury Select Committee, 25 November.

Posen, A. (2011), 'How to do more', speech, 13 September.

Ramsden, D. (2023), 'Quantitative tightening', speech, 19 July.

Salmon, C. (2017), 'Market functioning', speech, 24 January.

Schnabel, I. (2024), 'The benefits and costs of asset purchases', speech, 28 May.

Tenreyro, S. (2023), 'Quantitative easing and quantitative tightening', speech, 4 April.

Tucker, P. (2004), 'Managing the central bank's balance sheet', speech, 28 July.

Tucker, P. (2009), 'The repertoire of official sector interventions in the financial system: Last resort lending, market-making, and capital', speech, 28 May.

Tucker, P. (2010), Remarks to the Treasury Select Committee, 25 November.

Vlieghe, G. (2016), 'Monetary policy expectations and long-term interest rates', speech, 19 May.

Vlieghe, G. (2018), 'The yield curve and QE', speech, 19 May.

Vlieghe, G. (2019), 'Monetary policy: Adapting to a changed world', speech, 15 October.

Vlieghe, G. (2021a), 'What are government bond yields telling us about the economic outlook?', speech, 27 May.

Vlieghe, G. (2021b), 'Running out of room: Revisiting the 3D perspective on low interest rates', speech, 26 July.

Weale, M. and Wieladek, T. (2014), 'What are the macroeconomic effects of asset purchases?', *External MPC Unit Discussion Paper* 42.

Woodford, M. (2012), 'Methods of policy accommodation at the interest-rate lower bound', paper presented at the Jackson Hole symposium on 'The Changing Policy Landscape', 31 August.

Yates, T. (2003), 'Monetary policy and the zero bound to nominal interest rates', *Bank of England Quarterly Bulletin*, Spring, pp. 27–37.

11

Quantitative Tightening

5 *The Effects of Quantitative Tightening on Financial Markets*

A Comparison with Quantitative Easing

SIMON LLOYD, DANIEL OSTRY AND FILIPPO BUSETTO

5.1 Introduction

Balance-sheet policies are no longer 'new' tools in central banks' arsenals, but their effects are still debated despite a vast literature assessing the impact of quantitative easing (QE) policies (surveyed in Bhattarai and Neely, 2022).[*] Early studies into QE focused on financial-market impacts,[1] while authors were able to analyse more QE's macroeconomic impacts as time wore on.[2] Event studies were typically used to analyse QE's financial-market impacts (Gürkaynak and Wright, 2013), assessing bond-yield moves around central-bank policy announcements and examining the factors explaining asset-prices moves – for example, risk-neutral expectations of future short-term interest rates or term premia. Authors agreed that QE announcements – especially those around new asset-purchase programmes – reduced bond yields, but different studies ascribed varying degrees of importance to the different factors explaining these changes.

As central banks have sought to tighten policy after more than a decade at, or close to, the effective lower bound (ELB) for short-term interest rates, discussions around whether and how to go about quantitative tightening (QT) have been brought to the fore (e.g., Jefferson, 2023; Ramsden, 2023; Schnabel, 2023; Tenreyro, 2023). However, unlike

* The views expressed here are solely those of the authors and so cannot be taken to represent those of the Bank of England or any of its committees, or to state Bank of England policy.

1 See, e.g., Gagnon et al., 2011; Joyce et al., 2011; Krishnamurthy and Vissing-Jorgensen, 2011; Breedon et al., 2012; Christensen and Rudebusch, 2012; Bauer and Rudebusch, 2014.

2 See, e.g., Gambacorta et al., 2014; Haldane et al., 2016; Weale and Wieladek, 2016; Lloyd, 2017, as well as Chapters 1 and 3 in this volume.

QE, the literature on QT is, necessarily, more nascent (some exceptions include, Bräuning, 2017; Kim et al., 2020; Smith and Valcarcel, 2023; D'Amico and Seida, 2024; Du et al., 2024; Lloyd and Ostry, 2024, as well as Chapter 2 in this volume). Therefore, understanding whether QT has equal and opposite effects to QE is a pressing question.

In this chapter, mirroring the approach in the early QE literature, we focus on the financial-market effects of QT. We first analyse how government bond yields changed on QE and QT announcement dates. This evidence allows us to compare the effects of QT announcements on the yield curve to the range of event studies into the yield effects of QE announcements.

The general picture from these event studies is that, compared to QE announcements, the magnitude of yield changes on QT announcement dates is muted. We reach this conclusion by analysing one-day changes in two- and ten-year government bond yields on QE and QT announcement dates in the US and UK. In isolation, our evidence suggests that QT announcements were associated with more limited impacts on interest-rate expectations and term premia.

However, the information content in QE/QT announcements has changed over time and, as noted by Smith and Valcarcel (2023), the comparatively limited QT announcement effects are likely by design, a result of policymaker's objectives. In both the US and UK, the Federal Open Market Committee (FOMC) and Monetary Policy Committee (MPC) have sought to carry out QT in a gradual and predictable manner to limit the financial-market impact of such announcements. The event-study evidence we present suggests that, to date, this has indeed been the case; QT announcements have not come as a 'surprise', that is, contained limited new information for market participants to react to.

However, even if these estimates reflect the 'modal' effects of QT announcements on financial markets, the past may not always be a good guide for the future. So, it is also important to understand the 'risks' associated with such policies. To address this, we analyse the sensitivity of government bond yields to 'surprise' moves in financial markets around QE and QT announcements, that is, reactions to unforeseen information in central-bank announcements. These surprises are backed out from intra-day asset-price changes around policy announcements. While such announcements may contain information about a range of monetary policies, we apply the assumptions of

Swanson (2021) to focus on US asset-price surprises that weigh on medium- and long-term expectations and, therefore, most closely reflect the maturities associated with QE and QT. Applying the empirical specification of Lloyd and Ostry (2024), we then document that these QT surprises post-2017 had larger and more persistent causal effects on US two-year treasury yields than equal-sized QE surprises. On the other hand, we do not find evidence of asymmetries at the ten-year horizon.

Finally, we seek to understand the mechanisms underpinning this, by using empirical decompositions of US treasury yields into expectations of future short-term interest rates and term premia (Kim and Wright, 2005; Adrian et al., 2013; Lloyd, 2020). Despite differences in these three decompositions, they all indicate that asymmetries at the two-year horizon arise because QT surprises have larger and more persistent effects on expected future rates than equal-sized QE surprises. We then show that this is consistent with a simple equation characterising the term structure of interest rates, with an effective lower bound (ELB) on future short-term rate expectations.

While our analysis of the daily-frequency effects of QE and QT announcements of financial markets does not provide a complete picture into the possible similarities and differences between the two, it does provide an initial indication about the potentially asymmetric effects of QT (vs. QE) on the real economy. To the extent that policymakers wish to minimise the economic costs of QT, as our event-study evidence suggests, our yield-sensitivity analysis indicates that continued and concerted efforts to conduct QT 'gradually' and 'predictably' are likely to be important factors in limiting financial-market responses.

The remainder of the chapter has the following structure. Section 5.2 presents our event-study evidence, before Section 5.3 documents our yield-sensitivity analysis. Section 5.4 concludes.

5.2 Event-Study Evidence

To provide some initial indication as to whether QE and QT announcements had differential effects, we begin by assessing how bond yields responded to policy announcements. 'Event studies' of this form were common in the early QE literature (e.g., Gagnon et al., 2011; Joyce et al., 2011; Krishnamurthy and Vissing-Jorgensen, 2011; Breedon et al., 2012; Christensen and Rudebusch, 2012; Bauer and Rudebusch, 2014).

Such event studies rely on the lumpy nature of monetary-policy announcements. As is the norm, we evaluate the change in interest rates within a narrow (one-day) event window on event dates where notable announcements pertaining to QE or QT occurred. To gauge the effects of policy announcements across the yield curve, we report one-day changes in the two- and ten-year zero-coupon government bond yields.

Table 5.1 reports QE and QT event dates for the US. The nine QE dates, presented in the left-hand columns, correspond with those studied in Krishnamurthy and Vissing-Jorgensen (2011, 2013). As is well documented in the literature, the one-day changes in government bond yields demonstrate that QE announcements led to significant reductions in US treasury yields. On average across the nine announcement dates, ten-year yields fell by nearly 15 bps, while two-year yields declined by 6.5 bps. The earliest announcements had some of the most pronounced effects on yields. However, even within this set of nine events, the 'surprise' content of announcements varies; for instance, while early QE announcements resulted in sizeable declines in yields, even the fourth announcement on 28 January 2009 was met with a small increase in yields, as market participants anticipated more information about the possibility and timing of purchases of longer-dates US treasuries.

In contrast, US yields did not *increase* in the same magnitude on QT announcement days. The right-hand columns in Table 5.1 report eleven US QT event dates, which correspond to those used by Smith and Valcarcel (2023). Of those dates, the first two events (22 May 2013 and 19 June 2013) were tapering announcements, where the FOMC revealed intentions to slow the pace of asset purchases. Compared to the subsequent nine dates – events where the FOMC communicated plans to reduce their balance-sheet size, either in statements, minutes or speeches – these tapering announcements stand out. On these two dates, ten-year yields rose by 10 bps and 14 bps, respectively – similar in magnitude to some QE dates. But on the nine balance-sheet reduction dates, US yields increased only marginally in comparison to the magnitude of changes seen on QE announcement dates. On average, two-year yields increased by a little under 1.5 bps, while ten-year yields rose by just over 2 bps only.

Table 5.1 *US QE and QT event-study evidence.*

QE event date, description	Δ2Y yield	Δ10Y yield	QT event date, description	Δ2Y yield	Δ10Y yield
25/11/08, QE1 announced	-14.15	-21.91	22/05/13, taper announced	1.19	9.96
01/12/08, QE1 T-bill announced in Fed chair speech	-11.64	-22.07	19/06/13, taper pushed back	3.93	14.13
16/12/08, QE1 T-bill announced	-10.58	-17.92	21/05/14, normalisation signal	1.44	3.11
28/01/09, QE1 LSAPs continued	4.63	11.73	09/06/14, gradualism signal	2.24	1.25
18/03/09, QE1 LSAPs continued	-25.76	-53.87	20/08/14, unwind planning	3.97	2.17
10/08/10, QE2 reinvest assets	-2.54	-7.28	17/09/14, unwind announced	3.20	1.88
21/09/10, QE2 reinvest assets	-3.58	-11.05	12/01/17, speeches on unwind	-0.84	-1.29
21/09/11, MEP 'Operation Twist'	6.58	-8.63	05/04/17, reinvest.-end signal	-1.68	-1.93
13/09/12, QE3 announced	-0.68	-3.53	24/05/17, reinvestment-end plan	-1.56	-2.99
			14/06/17, asset-runoff plan	-1.45	-6.61
			20/09/17, runoff next month	4.87	3.69
QE average	-6.41	-14.95	QT average	1.39	2.12

In isolation, this comparison of yield changes suggests that – except for tapering dates – announcements of balance-sheet reductions were associated with limited changes in US financial markets. However, these results could also reflect variation in the surprise-content of announcements, rather than a fundamental distinction between QE and QT. Indeed, as Smith and Valcarcel (2023) note, the comparatively small effects of QT announcements on US financial markets may have been by design. Indeed, Yellen (2017) emphasises that, in contrast to QE, a key aim of FOMC communications around QT was to mitigate market reaction:

> the plan is one that is consciously intended to avoid creating market strains and to allow the market to adjust to a very gradual and predictable plan. My hope and expectation is that when we decide to go forward with this plan, that there will be very little reaction to it, that it's clear how we intend to proceed, and that this is something that will just run quietly in the background over a number of years, leading to a reduction in the size of our balance sheet and in the outstanding stock of reserves . . . as one of my colleagues, President Harker, described it, it will be like watching paint dry, that this will just be something that runs quietly in the background. (Yellen, 2017)

The UK reactions display a similar picture, as Table 5.2 documents. QE announcements in the UK, listed in the left-hand columns, were associated with significant reductions in interest rates across the yield curve, albeit with variation across different rounds of QE (Busetto et al., 2022). The largest reductions in yields were associated with the first £200 billion QE programme. Joyce and colleagues (2011) estimate that this led to a fall in medium- to long-term gilts of around 100 bps – starting with the near-32 bp reduction in ten-year yields on the first announcement dates (5 March 2009).

Despite occurring during a period of short-term policy rate tightening, QT announcements – outside of the September 2022 'LDI crisis' period, a time of marked financial-market volatility – have generally had limited effects on government bond yields. As the right-hand columns of Table 5.2 show, two- and ten-year yields have, on average risen by less than 1 bp and 2 bps, respectively, on such dates.

As in the US, these limited financial-market effects from QT announcements are largely by design, in line with the objectives set out by the MPC. Indeed, MPC minutes have explicitly noted that the impact of a reduction in the stock of purchased assets 'is likely to be smaller than that of asset purchases on average over the past' provided that such a reduction takes place 'in a gradual and predictable manner and when markets are functioning normally' (MPC, 2021).

Table 5.2 *UK QE and QT event-study evidence.*

QE event date, description	Δ2Y yield	Δ10Y yield	QT event date, description	Δ2Y yield	Δ10Y yield
05/03/09, QE1 announced	-2.0	-31.7	05/08/21, QT announced	0.8	-0.9
07/05/09, QE1 extended	1.2	5.7	03/02/22, passive QT begins	12.8	12.3
06/08/09, QE1 extended	-3.4	-7.3	19/07/22, QT size specified	1.6	-5.7
05/11/09, QE1 extended	0.6	6.9	22/09/22, active QT begins	14.0	18.2
06/10/11, QE2 announced	4.1	4.5	28/09/22, LDI crisis: QT paused	-25.1	-38.2
09/02/12, QE2 extended	0.9	5.4	19/10/22, QT skews short end	-2.7	-5.8
05/07/12, QE3 announced	-7.1	-6.0	03/08/23, QT assessment	-3.5	7.3
04/08/16, QE4 announced	-8.3	-16.8	20/09/23, QT pace announced	-14.7	-10.4
19/03/20, QE5 announced	-13.0	-30.5	01/08/24, QT assessment	-2.8	-2.2
18/06/20, QE5 extended	1.9	4.5			
05/11/20, QE5 extended	2.3	3.0			
QE average	-2.1	-5.7	QT average (Ex. LDI crisis)	0.7	1.6

5.3 The Sensitivity of Yields to Surprises: Asymmetries and Risks

Overall, the evidence from raw event studies suggests that announcement *effects* from QT have been less pronounced in magnitude relative to QE announcements, especially in the US. This is, to a large extent, by design; central banks have sought to clarify that QT is not an 'active' tool for policy in stabilising inflation. In this sense, past evidence suggests that future QT announcements could continue to have limited effects on financial markets.

However, the past may not always be a good guide to the future. So, to understand the *risks* around QT, it is insightful to analyse the sensitivities of bond yields to 'surprises'. Doing so can indicate how 'news' about QT transmits through financial markets. To do this, we draw on the empirical framework of Lloyd and Ostry (2024), who investigate the sensitivity of US yields to QE and QT surprises. We focus on the US, where QT initially occurred while short-term interest rates were at (or close to) their ELB – as the dates in the right-hand column of Table 5.1 evidence.[3]

5.3.1 Empirical Specification

The setup of Lloyd and Ostry (2024) focuses on the effects of US QE and QT surprises on US treasury yields at a daily frequency. Since changes in treasury yields in turn drive the transmission of monetary policy to real activity, the response of these asset prices in the weeks following the FOMC announcements provide an indication of the (potentially distinct) effects of QE and QT, albeit not a complete picture.

To identify QT and QE shocks, Lloyd and Ostry (2024) leverage the high-frequency LSAP surprises proposed and constructed by Swanson (2021). These shocks are estimated by decomposing monetary-policy surprises, extracted as common factors in asset-price movements in thirty-minute windows around FOMC announcements, into three distinct components: shocks to the level of the effective federal funds rate, forward-guidance shocks to its expected path and LSAP shocks to the Fed's balance-sheet size. More specifically, Swanson (2021) constructs these shocks by rotating three factors that underlie a panel of asset-price movements, which together explain 94% of variation in asset-price changes around FOMC announcements from July 1991 to June 2019, using the following restrictions:

- both forward-guidance and LSAP shocks have no contemporaneous influence on the federal funds rate; and,
- the variance of LSAP shocks is minimised from 1991 to 2008.

3 By the same reasoning, we do not extend our analysis to cover UK QT, since that occurred during a short-rate tightening cycle, making it more challenging to disentangle the effects of multiple concurrent policies from asset-price surprises alone.

A narrative check of the rotated factors supports the interpretation that they reflect surprises to the three types of interest-rate policies used by central banks. As such, the Swanson (2021) surprises – in particular the LSAP factor – are well suited for our investigation into the asymmetric effects of QE and QT.

Figure 5.1 plots the Federal Reserve LSAP surprises from December 2008 (when LSAPs began) to June 2019 (the end of the available sample) in units of standard deviations. The announcement of the Fed's first LSAP programme (QE1, which included the purchase of treasuries and mortgage-backed securities), on 18 March 2009, marks the largest surprise in the sample. On that date, the Fed announced the purchase of over $1.1 trillion of long-term bonds – around 16% of the outstanding US treasury market at the time. This substantial easing is captured as a nearly six standard-deviation expansionary (negative) surprise (policy looser than expected). Given the large size of this shock, alongside evidence in Swanson (2021) and Lloyd and Ostry (2024), who find that the effects of LSAP surprises on yields are even more persistent when excluding QE1, we henceforth omit the QE1 surprise from our baseline results – although our headline conclusions are robust to their inclusion.

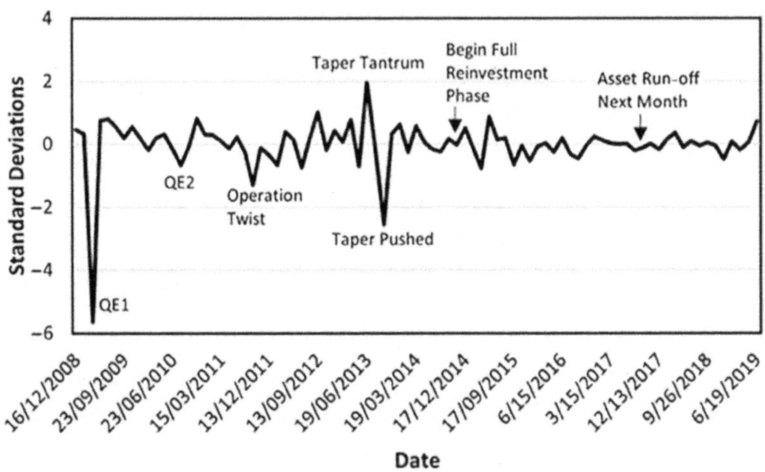

Figure 5.1 Federal Reserve LSAP surprises.

The 'QE2' announcement surprise (focused solely on the purchase of US treasuries) on 10 August 2010 and the MEP1 'Operation Twist' surprise on 21 September 2011 are also visible and, reassuringly, show up as negative shocks. The largest contractionary (positive) surprise (policy tighter than expected), of around two standard deviations, occurred on 5 May 2013 around the 'Taper Tantrum' – an event that was not associated with any actual tightening *ex post*. This policy reversal ('Taper pushed') shows up as the large expansionary (negative) surprise in the subsequent FOMC meeting on 19 June 2013.

Following Smith and Valcarcel (2023), as in Lloyd and Ostry (2024), we focus on two noteworthy periods of Fed QT policy, which we highlight in Figure 5.1 as well. First, an 'Asset-Runoff' (AR) phase from October 2017 to the end of our sample. In this period, the Fed actively purchased fewer assets than were maturing, such that bank reserves and Fed assets declined. Second, a 'Full-Reinvestment' (FR) phase from October 2014 to September 2017, when reserves passively declined, but the Fed reinvested proceeds of maturing securities to keep asset holdings constant. The surprises in Figure 5.1 during these periods are somewhat more muted – consistent with the fact that QT-related events generally lacked the large announcement effects that characterised QE. Nevertheless, over the two phases, there were some significant surprises, for instance, the 0.7 standard-deviation tightening on 19 June 2019.

Combining the LSAP surprises and the time-period classification, Lloyd and Ostry (2024) assess the distinct effects of QE, QT in the AR and QT in the FR phases on financial markets using the following local-projection setup:

$$y_{M,t+h} - y_{M,t-1} = \alpha^h + \beta^h \varepsilon_t^{lsap} + \delta_{FR}^h(\varepsilon_t^{lsap} \times 1_t^{FR}) + \delta_{AR}^h(\varepsilon_t^{lsap} \times 1_t^{AR}) + \theta_{FR}^h 1_t^{FR} + \theta_{AR}^h 1_t^{AR} + \gamma^h \boldsymbol{x}_t + u_t^h \quad (1)$$

where ε_t^{lsap} is the LSAP-surprise observed on the 85 FOMC announcement days between December 2008 and June 2019, and $h = 0, 1, \ldots, 50$ is the number of business days over which the dynamic response of the dependent variable $y_{M,t+h}$ is estimated. 1_t^{FR} and 1_t^{AR} are dummy variables which are set to 1 (0 otherwise) if the surprise occurred during the FR (October 2014 to September 2017) or AR (October 2017 to June 2019) phases, respectively.

The dependent variables are the ten- or two-year zero-coupon US treasury yields (Gürkaynak et al., 2007), such that $y_{M,t+h} - y_{M,t-1}$ for $M = 10, 2$ measures the yield change, in basis points, from the day prior to the FOMC announcement $(t-1)$ to the h-th day after $(t+h)$. The ten-year yield provides a natural focus, having been a key object of interest in the literature studying the financial-market effects of QE. But the two-year tenor is also of interest, having also been shown to move in response to QE announcements (Gagnon et al., 2011; Christensen and Rudebusch, 2012; Lloyd, 2017; Lloyd, 2020) and capturing central banks' broad focus on managing expectations of the short-rate path roughly two years into the future (Bernanke et al., 2004; Gürkaynak et al., 2005; Swanson and Williams, 2014; Gertler and Karadi, 2015; Hanson and Stein, 2015).

In regression (1), the coefficient β^h captures the marginal effect of QE LSAP surprises, which are implicitly defined to occur during the period 2008:12–2014:09 when $1_t^{FR} = 1_t^{AR} = 0$. $\beta^h + \delta_i^h$ captures the marginal effect of surprises in the FR and AR phases of QT for $i = FR, AR$, respectively. We focus on the magnitudes of overall marginal effects (β^h and $\beta^h + \delta_i^h$), which reflect the overall economic significance of our results (for a given sized surprise), but we also discuss the statistical significance of the difference in magnitudes (δ_i^h).

x_t denotes the set of controls, which include the level and forward-guidance surprises from Swanson (2021), along with their own interactions between the QT dummy-variable indicators, to account for other contemporaneous monetary-policy events. The controls also include five daily lags of the dependent variable to captures macroeconomic conditions prior to the announcement and five lags of the one-year treasury yield to capture the pre-announcement stance of monetary policy – where the lag choices are informed by information criterion.

5.3.2 *Asymmetric Sensitivities*

Figures 5.2a and 5.2b present results from regression (1) for the ten- and two-year tenors, respectively. While the effects of LSAP surprises in the QE and AR-QT periods are not significantly different at the ten-year maturity, the most striking differences arise at the two-year tenor. Here, QE surprises have no clear significant effect, while the results in Figure 5.2b highlight that surprises in the AR-QT period did move two-year yields, with the effects statistically different to those in the QE

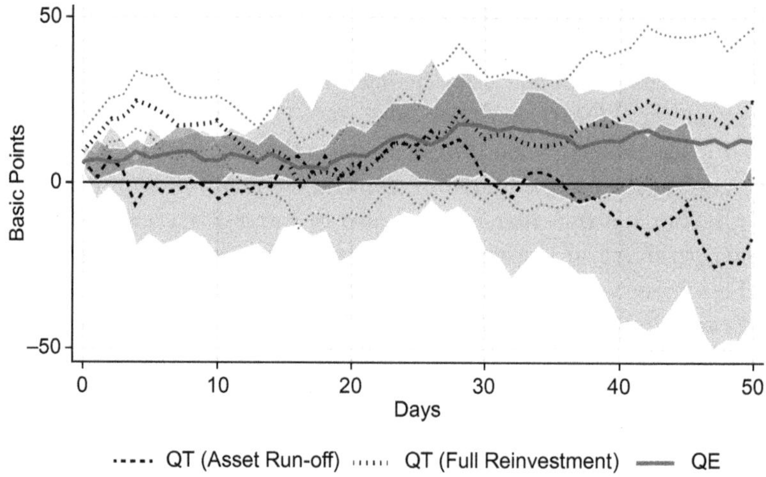

Figure 5.2a Asymmetric response of ten- and two-year treasury yields to LSAP surprises in QE and QT periods: 10-year yields.

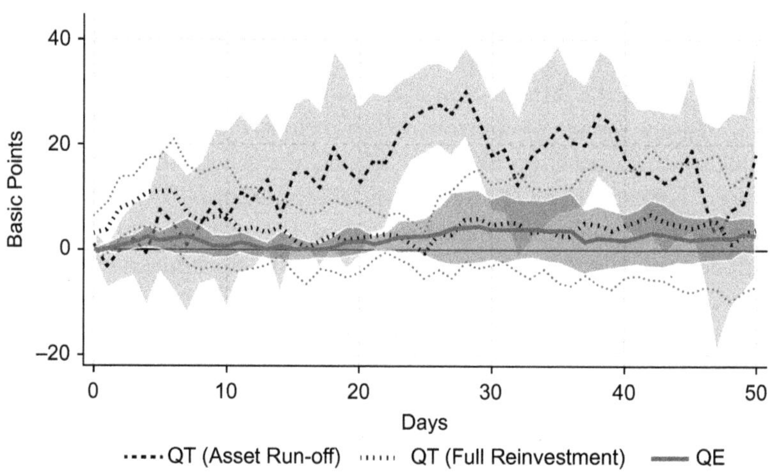

Figure 5.2b Asymmetric response of ten- and two-year treasury yields to LSAP surprises in QE and QT periods: two-year yields.

period. Our findings suggest that, one month after the announcement, a one standard-deviation QT surprise in the AR period pushed two-year yields up by around 30 bp. In contrast, a one standard-deviation

QE surprise generated an insignificant response in the two-year yield of around 5 bp. These differences, however, are less economically meaningful when accounting for the fact that the surprises themselves were around four times more volatile in the QE period versus QT, as highlighted in Figure 5.1.

In contrast, there are no significant differences between the effects of LSAP surprises in the FR-QT and QE phases on yields at either tenor. This is in line with the findings of others who find that the majority of QT's effects occurred when the Fed actively reduced its asset holdings – that is, in the AR phase (Smith and Valcarcel, 2023; D'Amico and Seida, 2024). Nevertheless, that our results indicate that QT surprises from late 2017 to mid 2019 had larger and more persistent effects on two-year treasury yields as compared to equal-sized QE shocks suggests that QT announcement surprises could potentially have stronger and more persistent effects on financial markets than previously envisioned.

5.3.3 Understanding Risks by Decomposing Drivers

To dig deeper into the economic mechanisms underpinning these differences, we consider a decomposition of *M*-period government bond yields $y_{M,t}$ into two components: (i) expectations of future short-term rates $exp_{M,t}$; and (ii) term premia $tp_{M,t}$:

$$y_{M,t} = \underbrace{\frac{1}{M}\sum_{m=0}^{M-1} y^{e}_{1,t+m}}_{exp_{M,t}} + tp_{M,t} \tag{2}$$

This decomposition has been widely used by academics and policymakers to ascertain the channels through which LSAPs can influence the real economy (Bernanke, 2010). Changes in the expectations component have been linked to a 'signalling channel', through which LSAP announcements influence expected future short-term rates, and changes in term premia have been linked to a 'portfolio rebalancing channel', whereby LSAPs influence the compensation investors require for holding treasuries.

Although this decomposition is used widely, there exist a wide array of alternative empirical estimates of this decomposition from dynamic term-structure models (DTSM), which often yield different results

(Lloyd, 2017). Given this, we use three daily-frequency decomposition estimates: (i) Adrian et al. (2013), which applies a linear-regression approach to decompose yields; (ii) Kim and Wright (2005), which augments a DTSM with survey expectations of interest rates to discipline the decomposition; and (iii) Lloyd (2020), which augments a similar DTSM with short-maturity overnight indexed swap rates. Using these estimated decompositions, we re-estimate regression (1) using changes in each component of the treasury yield as the dependent variable. Based on the asymmetries documented in Section 5.3.1, we present results for the two-year tenor only and focus on the AR phase.

While the term-premium responses are statistically indistinguishable for all three decompositions (Figures 5.3b, 5.3d, 5.3f), there are significant asymmetries in the response of expectations (Figures 5.3a, 5.3c, 5.3e). Like the two-year yield itself, the response of the expectation component of two-year treasury yields is larger and more persistent to LSAP surprises during the AR phase of QT than equal-sized QE events. The differences are particularly striking when comparing QE and AR-phase QT estimates using the expectations components from the

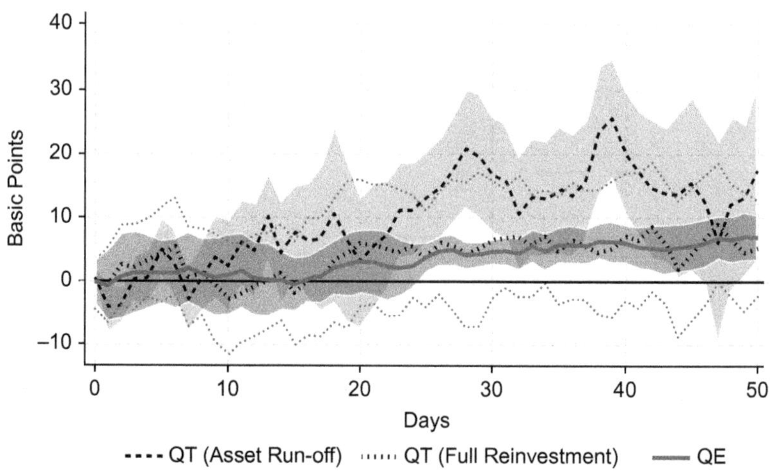

Figure 5.3a Asymmetric response of two-year treasury-yield components to LSAP surprises in QE and QT periods: expected future short-term interest rates.

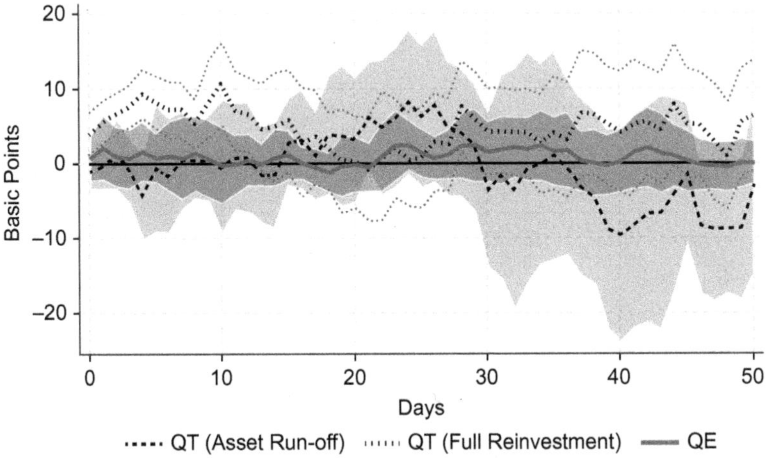

Figure 5.3b Asymmetric response of two-year treasury-yield components to LSAP surprises in QE and QT periods: term premium.
Figures 5.3a and 5.3b: Adrian et al. (2013) decomposition

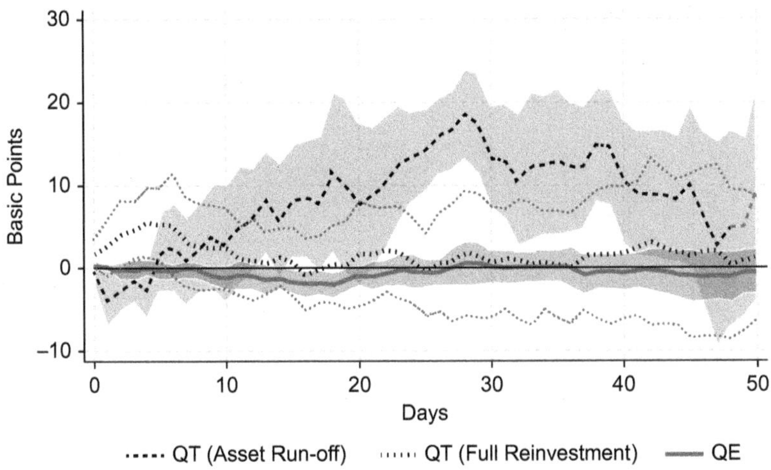

Figure 5.3c Asymmetric response of two-year treasury-yield components to LSAP surprises in QE and QT periods: expected future short-term interest rates.
Source: Lloyd and Ostry (2024). Notes: Estimated average marginal effect of one standard-deviation LSAP surprise on h-day-ahead US treasury yields during QE (December 2008 to September 2014), QT FR (October 2014 to September 2017) and QT AR (October 2017 to June 2019) periods from regression (1) (h=0,1,...,50). Sample: December 2008 to June 2019 (excl. QE1 announcement). Shadings/thin-dashed lines represent 95% confidence bands, constructed from Newey-West standard errors with twelve lags.

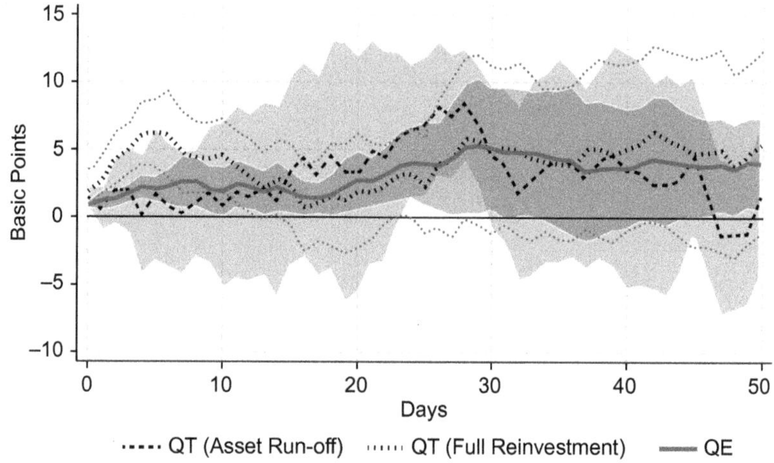

Figure 5.3d Asymmetric response of two-year treasury-yield components to LSAP surprises in QE and QT periods: term premium.
Figures 5.3c and 5.3d Kim and Wright (2005) decomposition

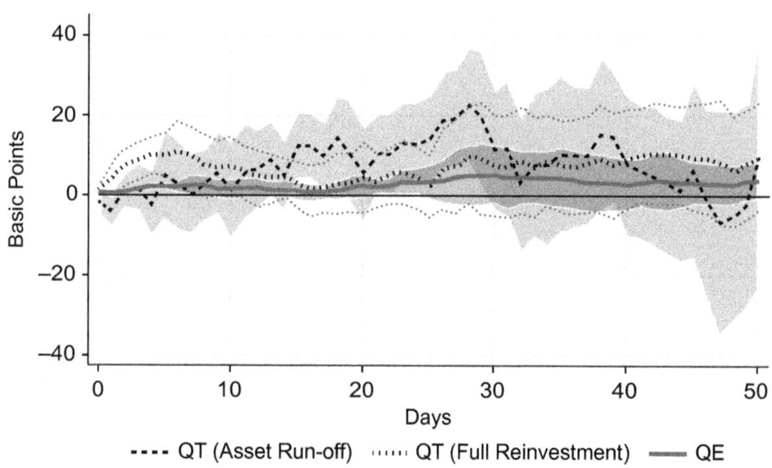

Figure 5.3e Asymmetric response of two-year treasury-yield components to LSAP surprises in QE and QT periods: expected future short-term interest rates.

Adrian and colleagues (2013) and Kim and Wright (2005) decompositions, but remain statistically significant at some horizons with the Lloyd (2020) decomposition as well.

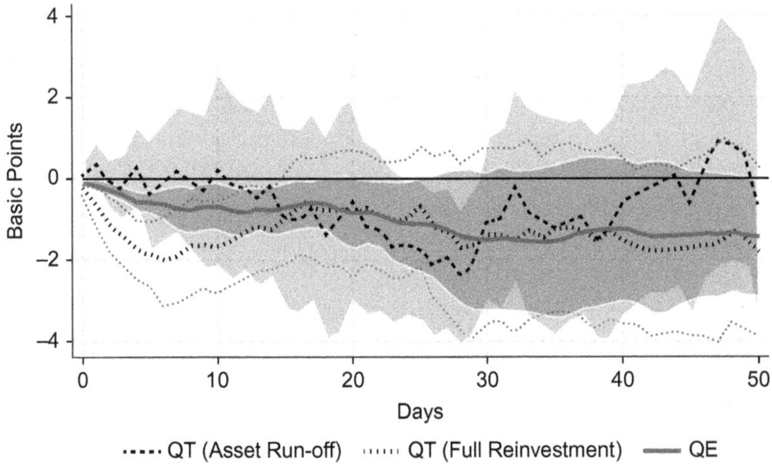

Figure 5.3f Asymmetric response of two-year treasury-yield components to LSAP surprises in QE and QT periods: term premium.
Figures 5.3d and 5.3f Lloyd (2020) decomposition

We interpret this result through the lens of the term-structure equation (2). Given an ELB on short-term policy rates ($y_{1,t+m} \geq \underline{y}$ for all t, m), this implies an ELB on expected future short rates ($\text{exp}_{M,t} \geq \underline{y}$ for all t, m) as well. To the extent that the ELB binds more at shorter maturities (for low M), it follows that, for a given maturity M, the ELB can limit the efficacy of the signalling channel in response to QE surprises, since policymakers are unable to signal a path for short term rates that goes below the ELB in any future period. So, although signalling can be an important channel through which QE announcements operate, the ELB constrains the relevance of changes in expectations at a given maturity by increasing the relevance of changes in longer-maturity expectations for the current stance of policy.

An implication of this result is that LSAP *surprises* during times of tightening can carry larger effects on expectations of future rates *at a given maturity* – as we document in Figure 5.3a–f. As a result, policymakers seeking to limit the real economic costs of QT may wish to guard against the risk that communications about the central bank balance sheet normalisations are misinterpreted by, or surprise, market participants.

5.4 Conclusions

In this chapter, we have compared the high-frequency effects of QT announcements and surprises on financial markets to those of QE. Although our analysis provides an incomplete picture about the overall transmission of QT policies, it does offer some initial indication about possible asymmetries and risks at an early stage of the transmission mechanism.

Our results have confirmed that the impact of US and UK QT announcements on financial markets has, thus far, been small compared to QE. This has, in large part, been by design, part of a concerted effort to carry out QT in a 'gradual and predictable' manner – in effect, limiting the extent to which QE 'surprises'.

Analysing the sensitivity of US bond yields to QT (vs. QE) surprises, suggests that this 'gradual and predictable' approach may have been the right thing to do too. Near-to-medium-term yields, as well as short-term interest rate expectations over corresponding horizons, appear to have asymmetric sensitivity to QT 'surprises', versus QE. For a given magnitude of surprise, the responsiveness of two-year yields during the QT period is *larger* than the corresponding sensitivity during the QE period. Such asymmetry is also consistent with an ELB on short rates placing an ELB on expected future short rates. However, the volatility of QT surprises is smaller, rationalising the more limited impacts of QT announcements on financial markets to date.

Therefore, to limit the potential costs of QT, policymakers should continue to guard against the risk that communications of asset-purchase reversals are misinterpreted by, or 'surprise', financial markets.

References

Adrian, T., Crump, R. & Moench, E., 2013. Pricing the Term Structure with Linear Regression. *Journal of Financial Economics*, Volume 110, pp. 110–138.

Bauer, M. D. & Rudebusch, G. D., 2014. The Signaling Channel for Federal Reserve Bond Purchases. *International Journal of Central Banking*, Volume 10, pp. 233–289.

Bernanke, B. S., 2010. *Opening Remarks: The Economic Outlook and Monetary Policy*. Federal Reserve Bank of Kansas, pp. 1–16.

Bernanke, B. S., Reinhart, V. R. & Sack, B. P., 2004. Monetary Policy Alternatives at the Zero Bound: An Empirical Assessment. *Brookings Papers on Economic Activity*, Volume 35, pp. 1–100.

Bhattarai, S. & Neely, C. J., 2022. An Analysis of the Literature on International Unconventional Monetary Policy. *Journal of Economic Literature*, Volume 60, pp. 527–597.

Bräuning, F., 2017. *The Liquidity Effect of the Federal Reserve's Balance Sheet Reduction on Short-Term Interest Rates*. Federal Reserve Bank of Boston.

Breedon, F., Chadha, J. S. & Waters, A., 2012. The Financial Market Impact of UK Quantitative Easing. *Oxford Review of Economic Policy*, 28(4), pp. 702–729.

Busetto, F., Chavaz, M., Froemel, M., Joyce, M., Kaminska, I. & Worlidge, J., 2022. QE at the Bank of England: a perspective on its functioning and effectiveness. *Bank of England Quarterly Bulletin*, Volume Q1.

Christensen, J. H. E. & Rudebusch, G. D., 2012. The Response of Interest Rates to US and UK Quantitative Easing. *Economic Journal*, Volume 122, pp. 385–414.

D'Amico, S. & Seida, T., 2024. Unexpected Supply Effects of Quantitative Easing and Tightening. *Economic Journal*, Volume 134, pp. 579–613.

Du, W., Forbes, K. & Luzzetti, M. N., 2024. Quantitative Tightening Around the Globe: What Have We Learned? NBER Working Papers 32321.

Gagnon, J., Raskin, M., Remache, J. & Sack, B. P., 2011. The Financial Market Effects of the Federal Reserve's Large-Scale Asset Purchases. *International Journal of Central Banking*, Volume 7, pp. 3–43.

Gambacorta, L., Hofmann, B. & Peersman, G., 2014. The Effectiveness of Unconventional Monetary Policy at the Zero Lower Bound: A Cross-Country Analysis. *Journal of Money, Credit and Banking*, 46(4), pp. 615–642.

Gertler, M. & Karadi, P., 2015. Monetary Policy Surprises, Credit Costs, and Economic Activity. *American Economic Journal: Macroeconomics*, Volume 7, pp. 44–76.

Gürkaynak, R. S., Sack, B. P. & Swanson, E. T., 2005. Do Actions Speak Louder Than Words? The Response of Asset Prices to Monetary Policy Actions and Statements. *International Journal of Central Banking*, Volume 1, pp. 55–93.

Gürkaynak, R. S., Sack, B. P. & Wright, J. H., 2007. The US Treasury Yield Curve: 1961 to the Present. *Journal of Monetary Economics*, Volume 54, pp. 2291–2304.

Gürkaynak, R. S. & Wright, J. H., 2013. Identification and Inference Using Event Studies. *Manchester School*, Volume 81, pp. 48–65.

Haldane, A., Roberts-Sklar, M., Wieladek, M. & Young, C., 2016. *QE:* The Story So Far. Bank of England Staff Working Paper 624.

Hanson, S. & Stein, J., 2015. Monetary Policy and Long-Term Real Rates. *Journal of Financial Economics*, Volume 115, pp. 429–448.

Jefferson, P. N., 2023. 'Implementation and Transmission of Monetary Policy'. Washington and Less University, Lexington, Virginia, Speech at the H. Parker Willis Lecture.

Joyce, M. A. S., Lasaosa, A., Stevens, I. & Tong, M., 2011. The Financial Market Impact of Quantitative Easing in the United Kingdom. *International Journal of Central Banking*, Volume 7, pp. 113–161.

Kim, D. H. & Wright, J. H., 2005. *An Arbitrage-Free Three-Factor Term Structure Model and the Recent Behavior of Long-Term Yields and Distant-Horizon Forward Rates.* Board of Governors of the Federal Reserve System (US).

Kim, K., Laubach, T. & Wei, M., 2020. *Macroeconomic Effects of Large-Scale Asset Purchases: New Evidence.* Board of Governors of the Federal Reserve System (US).

Krishnamurthy, A. & Vissing-Jorgensen, A., 2011. The Effects of Quantitative Easing on Interest Rates: Channels and Implications for Policy. *Brookings Papers on Economic Activity*, 43(2), pp. 215–287.

Krishnamurthy, A. & Vissing-Jorgensen, A., 2013. The Ins and Outs of LSAPs. In: *Proceedings: Economic Policy Symposium.* Federal Reserve Bank of Kansas City, pp. 57–111.

Lloyd, S. P., 2017. Unconventional Monetary Policy and the Interest-Rate Channel: Signalling and Portfolio Rebalancing. Cambridge Working Papers in Economics 1735, University of Cambridge.

Lloyd, S. P., 2020. Estimating Nominal Interest Rate Expectations: Overnight Indexed Swaps and the Term Structure. *Journal of Banking and Finance*, Volume 119.

Lloyd, S. P. & Ostry, D. A., 2024. The Asymmetric Effects of Quantitative Tightening and Easing on Financial Markets. *Economics Letters*, Volume 238.

MPC, 2021. *Monetary Policy Committee Minutes – August 2021.* Bank of England.

Newey, W. & West, K., 1987. A Simple, Positive Semi-Definite, Heteroskedasticity and Autocorrelation Consistent Covariance Matrix. *Econometrica*, Volume 55, pp. 703–708.

Ramsden, D., 2023. 'Quantitative Tightening: The Story So Far'. London, Speech at the Money, Macro and Financial Society.

Schnabel, I., 2023. 'Quantitative Tightening: Rationale and Market Impact'. Frankfurt am Main, Speech at the Money Market Contact Group Meeting.

Smith, A. L. & Valcarcel, V. V., 2023. The Financial Market Effects of Unwinding the Federal Reserve's Balance Sheet. *Journal of Economic Dynamics and Control*, Volume 146.

Swanson, E. T., 2021. Measuring the Effects of Federal Reserve Forward Guidance and Asset Purchases on Financial Markets. *Journal of Monetary Economics*, Volume 118, pp. 32–53.

Swanson, E. T. & Williams, J., 2014. Measuring the Effect of the Zero Lower Bound on Medium- and Longer-Term Interest Rates. *American Economic Review*, Volume 104, pp. 3154–3185.

Tenreyro, S., 2023. 'Quantitative Easing and Quantitative Tightening'. Glasgow, Speech at the Scottish Economic Society Annual Conference.

Weale, M. & Wieladek, T., 2016. What Are the Macroeconomic Effects of Asset Purchases? *Journal of Monetary Economics*, 79(C), pp. 81–93.

Yellen, J., 2017. *June 2017 Post-FOMC Press Conference*. Federal Reserve.

6 *Quantitative Tightening*

How Fast and How Far

TIM YOUNG

6.1 Introduction

Quantitative easing (QE) was widely adopted in the wake of the financial crisis as an exceptional measure to provide supplementary monetary easing, at a time when economic activity was remaining subdued despite normal monetary easing, involving lowering short-term interest rates, being fully utilised. The interest rates most closely controlled by central banks, in terms of which normal monetary policy is specified and which influence a range of other short-term interest rates, had been set to about zero, considered to be as low as practicably possible. As will be discussed in more detail, QE involved large-scale central bank purchases of financial assets, comprising mostly bonds, paid for in new central bank money, created for the purpose, with the aim of delivering economic stimulus by expanding money supply and increasing asset prices.[1] Unfortunately, just as developed country economies seemed to be recovering more firmly by 2019, and an end to QE was envisaged, the SARS-CoV-2 pandemic began, causing government bond yields to spike higher on the prospect of heavy additional debt issuance to fund

[1] Conveniently for analysis, the Bank of England (BoE) did all its QE via a subsidiary called the Bank of England Asset Purchase Facility Fund Ltd (BEAPFF), a separate legal entity holding a portfolio comprising the assets purchased for QE purposes plus a funding liability in the form of a loan from the BoE. The BoE executed the asset purchases as, formally, an agent of the BEAPFF, paying for the purchases in central bank money, then assigned both the assets and a funding loan matching the central bank money paid out to the BEAPFF. The beneficial owner of the BEAPFF is the UK finance ministry, HM Treasury, a structure which insulates the BoE from any profit or loss arising from QE. Even if, in other monetary areas, the assets purchased for monetary policy purposes and the liabilities funding those purchases are not separately identified on the central bank's balance sheet, a QE sub-portfolio is present, and could be delineated if required, so the discussion here may be applied in principle to all central banks as if a separate QE portfolio does exist.

government spending on the medical response and income replacement programmes for laid-off or furloughed workers,[2] so QE was extended to absorb much of that government bond supply, thereby holding down bond market yields.

At the time of writing (mid 2024), however, the pandemic has been suppressed, while, despite real economic activity having still not fully recovered except in the USA, inflation over the past two years has risen far above most central banks' inflation targets, prompting central banks to lift their monetary policy interest rates well above zero. So, not only has the need for QE passed, but to the extent that it remains in place and continues to have an easing effect, it is desirable to withdraw QE, by liquidating assets and using the proceeds to eliminate money.

Notwithstanding the fact that the assets bought largely comprised fixed-term bonds which will self-liquidate as they mature, meaning that the QE holdings will naturally shrink over time, some asset sales may be preferable to accelerate the run-off process, especially because, given that QE bond purchases were typically spread over the range of maturities in the market, it may well be many years before the longest holdings mature.[3] The problem with reversing QE by asset sales, however, is that the asset holdings are too large to sell off quickly.[4] This chapter considers the principles involved in managing the contraction of the QE asset holdings, termed quantitative tightening (QT), with a particular focus on the approach taken to QE and QT by the Bank of England (BoE).

6.2 The Voluntary and Market-Terms Role of the Private Sector in QE and QT

Central banks doing QE generally bought bonds from a select group of commercial banks which were both recognised bond market-makers and counterparties in their central bank's normal monetary policy operations (as specified in Bank of England, n.d.a), known as 'open market operations' (OMOs). These banks hold current accounts at the

[2] An event popularly known as 'the dash for cash'.

[3] The longest maturity bond bought by the BoE does not mature until 22 October 2071.

[4] For example, at its peak size in December 2021, the BoE's QE portfolio held UK government bonds with a total nominal value of £760 bn, almost four times the total sales of new UK government bonds in that financial year.

central bank, in which positive balances are called 'reserves', and the central bank paid for each QE bond purchase by crediting the selling bank's reserves account, thereby creating additional reserves. The central bank's monetary policymakers would specify the quantity of additional reserves to be created by bond purchases, and its operational staff would buy enough bonds to create as close to the required quantity as practicable.

Besides settling asset trades between OMO counterparties and central banks,[5] reserves are also used to settle inter-bank payments routinely generated by bank customer transactions.[6] These transactions include the out-payments as bank loans are drawn down, and one of the initial intentions of QE was to at least remove any brake on the circulation of money caused by scarcity of reserves, if not to positively encourage banks to use the resulting abundance of reserves to make loans to customers.

However, central banks typically buy relatively liquid bonds issued by more creditworthy borrowers, and UK banks tend to hold only small amounts of these for specific purposes, so most QE purchases, while directly acquired from banks, were sourced indirectly from non-bank private sector (NBPS) holders, notably insurance companies, pension funds, fund management companies, family offices and foreign investors of various types.[7] And since reserves accounts are provided exclusively for banks, the banks could not pay NBPS sellers by transferring reserves to them, but instead retained reserves they received for sales to the central bank, and in turn paid for the bonds they bought from each NBPS seller

[5] The routine monetary policy operations involving central bank lending to and (occasionally) borrowing from commercial banks may be thought of as loan asset trades, with QE transactions a generalisation of this activity to other assets.

[6] Note that, although most governments use their central bank as their main (but not necessarily only) banker, government deposits are not formally counted as reserves. This means that transactions between private sector banks and the government, such as payments to the government, like tax, or from government, like benefits, can eliminate and create reserves respectively. Ideally, though, if the central bank has monetary policy independence, the balances in these government bank accounts are carefully managed to ensure little or no significant change in the balances from one day-end to the next, which would otherwise compromise monetary policy independence. To simplify the discussion here, all bank current account balances will be referred to as 'cash'.

[7] To be strictly correct, these sellers may well have included public sector entities, such as, in the BoE's case, UK public sector pension funds, and overseas foreign exchange reserves managers or sovereign wealth funds, so it is acknowledged that 'NBPS' is not perfectly accurate.

by crediting a bank account held by the seller. Thus, QE purchases also generated deposit money. Indeed, the BoE's QE programme was specifically designed to draw bonds from the NBPS, because that created additional deposit money as well as reserves (Fisher, 2010).[8]

A notable point of principle for the purposes of the present chapter is that the OMO counterparties' trading with their central banks is essentially voluntary and at market prices, typically achieved through competitive auctions. While some minimal level of participation is required of both OMO counterparties and bond market-makers, members of either group are free to drop out if they wish, so apart from a desire to maintain goodwill with the authorities, banks were under no pressure to accept the central bank's terms for QE trades if the banks considered those terms unsatisfactory.

Therefore, in order to buy suitable bonds in their QE reverse auctions, central banks had to be willing to accept offers tendered at prices high enough to allow commercial banks to, in turn, having extracted some mark-up for themselves, offer high enough prices to induce NBPS holders to sell those bonds to the banks. The terms of the exchange of bonds for reserves balances therefore reflected banks' understanding of the value to them of holding reserves, and NBPS holders' expectations of the utility of deposit money. The greater these benefits were believed to be, the lower the bond prices that central banks were obliged to pay to implement QE. The nature of these benefits is considered in Section 6.3. As in any market, trust between the participants, especially about the terms of trade, is vital.

6.3 The Importance of Paying Interest on Reserves (IoR)

The payment settlement function of reserves makes them like a book-entry version of banknotes, except held primarily for inter-bank transactions purposes. Together, reserves and banknotes are called 'base money', reflecting their role providing the base for the money system. When monetary policy is operating normally, the ultimate source of base money is commercial banks borrowing newly created reserves from their central bank, typically at or close to, its monetary policy

8 Note that even if a central bank did buy bonds directly from the NBPS, the fact that the NBPS cannot hold reserves means that the purchases would still create deposit money, as the central bank would credit the seller's bank's reserves account, with that bank in turn crediting its customer's bank account.

interest rate.[9] Like banknotes, reserves are perpetual assets, meaning that, collectively, banks cannot reduce their collective holding of reserves without buying assets from, or repaying debt owed to, the central bank. The implication is that additional reserves created by QE remain in the banking system until QT has eliminated them all.

Historically, in line with banknotes, reserves bore no interest, so banks would be inclined to hold no more reserves than necessary. Nevertheless, banks do like to have at least a minimal quantity of reserves, serving as a buffer stock to manage somewhat unpredictable settlement flows without going overdrawn at the end of any settlement period – typically meaning the close of each business day – because overdrafts generally are prohibitively penalised. Moreover, in some monetary regimes, banks are required by bank regulators to maintain larger reserves holdings than the banks might freely choose, with penalties for failing to maintain at least the set balance, which effectively raises the floor, to the level corresponding to the reserve requirement.[10] Regardless of the nature of the floor though, balances above that level are described as 'excess' reserves, and individual banks target a holding of excess reserves which minimises the expected cost of ending the day with either some zero-interest reserves balance on the one hand, or incurring some shortfall penalty on the other.

To avoid frequent transactions with many banks, central banks typically conduct OMOs to adjust the aggregate stock of reserves in bulk at fixed times only, and leave the banks to adjust towards their own preferred reserves balances by inter-bank lending and borrowing from the present day to the next, known as an 'overnight' interest rate, in the so-called 'money market'.

Conventional monetary policy aims to guide the money-market-clearing interest rate to some desired level, which influences interest rates set by banks for customer loans and deposits, and thereby affects the whole economy. Confusingly, the official monetary policy rate may refer either to (1) a rate fixed for OMOs, which typically involve lending for terms in the order of weeks, as in the case of the BoE and

[9] To be ready to serve retail customer demand at ATMs and branch counters, banks can obtain banknotes, on demand from the central bank, using their reserves to pay, the implications of which will be discussed further in Section 6.6.

[10] If regulatory reserve requirements must be strictly met at all times, reserves held for those purposes cannot be used by a commercial bank to settlement payments, though they still support the bank's creditworthiness.

European Central Bank (hereafter 'ECB') or (2) the market-clearing overnight interest rate, as in the case of the US Federal Reserve (henceforth 'Fed'), called the 'overnight Fed funds target rate'.

Whenever inter-bank trading, transferring reserves from banks which have unwanted excess reserves to those which would otherwise not have enough, does not proceed smoothly, money market interest rates are liable to spike above or below the central bank's target. On one side, if the aggregate supply implies at least one bank going overdrawn when all payments are settled, the market-clearing interest rate spikes towards an interest rate reflecting the shortfall penalty. On the other, if the aggregate level of reserves implies one or more banks holding more reserves than they want, the market-clearing interest rate plunges towards zero. Since monetary policymakers are trying to control money market interest rates, such spikes are considered to be undesirable, and to be minimised.

For this reason, the BoE began to pay interest on reserves from 18 May 2006 (Bank of England, 2006). By paying the monetary policy interest rate – which should be very close to money market interest rates – on reserves, the opportunity cost of holding excess reserves is largely eliminated, so banks held more reserves, and the spikes in money market interest rates were much attenuated. On the day of the change, when the BoE monetary policy interest rate, known as 'Bank Rate', and hence the IoR rate, stood at 4.5%, UK banks' freely chosen aggregate holding of reserves leapt from about £3 bn (0.2% of the stock of UK M4 broad money at the time) to about £24 bn (1.7%). These figures show that the pure (i.e. in the absence of IoR) transactions demand for reserves is tiny, because banks are skilled at managing payments activity with minimal settlement balances, but also that banks will readily increase their holdings of reserves if the return on them is acceptable.

When developed country central banks began QE after the financial crisis, they were all[11] paying close to their monetary policy interest rate on excess reserves.[12] Thus, what central banks doing QE were offering

[11] The Fed was already planning to begin paying interest on reserves before the financial crisis struck, but brought forward the implementation date, to allow its balance sheet to be expanded to respond to the financial crisis, while maintaining control of inflation (Federal Reserve, 2008).

[12] This abstracts from the existence of so-called 'standing' (i.e. available on demand) facilities at which banks can borrow or deposit practically unlimited quantities of reserves at interest rates respectively above and below the OMO rate, designed to prevent money market interest rates drifting unacceptably far

to the market in exchange for fixed-interest bonds was something similar to holdings of a perpetual floating-rate note (FRN) bearing overnight-floating interest at about the respective central bank's monetary policy rate.[13] Since central banks are state institutions, reserves are effectively credit-risk-free state debt, like government FRNs. From the point of view of the market, therefore, selling government, or government-guaranteed, bonds to the central bank was like switching from fixed-interest state debt into floating-interest state debt.

To inform remaining sections of this chapter, it is necessary to explain why, in order to do a significant amount of QE at acceptable prices, central banks needed the private sector to expect that, at least until the last of the reserves created by QE had been eliminated by QT, the central bank would continue to pay about their policy rate of interest on those reserves.

As described in Section 6.2, QE purchases left the private sector in an initial position of back-to-back holdings, of reserves in a commercial bank with a matching bank deposit owned by a NBPS institution. So, a necessary condition for the central bank to induce the private sector to accept that position was that both the bank had to be content to receive reserves, and the NBPS institution involved had to be content to receive deposit money. Naturally, payment of interest is a key component of the value of reserves to banks and deposit money to non-banks. If both the bank and the NBPS asset seller are considering holding their respective side of the trade indefinitely, until QT presents them with an attractive opportunity to reverse their position, they would each receive the interest paid on their side of the position during that holding period. And it is not just current interest rates that matter but also expectations of how those rates might change.

However, either of them is free to trade out of some or all of their side of the initial position. Unless constrained by a reserve requirement, an individual commercial bank may reduce their holding of reserves by

from the OMO interest rate. With a structural under or over supply of reserves, the loan or deposit rate respectively effectively determines the IoR rate, which then becomes the policy rate, as, due to the structural over-supply of reserves produced by QE, is presently the situation at the ECB. Standing facilities are discussed further in Section 6.10.

13 Naturally, the monetary policy interest rate is most likely to be reset following monetary policy meetings, so will often remain fixed for extended periods, but it can potentially be changed on any day, hence the IoR rate may be considered to be an overnight floating rate.

trading with another bank, while any bank deposit holder can use their deposit to make a payment transfer to another bank depositor. Indeed, central banks expected both that the additional reserves and deposit money created by QE would circulate to some degree between banks and between non-banks respectively. Naturally, bank deposits, even bearing interest, are not the type of asset normally held by the type of NBPS asset holders which sold into QE demand, typically institutional investors holding assets like fixed-interest bonds, equity, real estate, and so on. It was therefore envisaged, and, as will be explained in Section 6.4, actively hoped, that the NBPS institutions would soon use the deposit money created by the initial QE purchase to buy closer substitutes for the bonds they are sold, disbursing that deposit money, generally in pieces to a number of asset sellers. Moreover, some these asset sellers may have been businesses seeking funding for real economic activity, such as for construction projects, or selling consumer goods with credit or hire arrangements, paying their suppliers and workers, and so on, thereby diffusing the deposit money through the non-financial economy too, typically through a potentially long and branching sequence of transactions.[14]

A necessary condition for such growing chains of transactions to proceed is that each potential next holder of reserves or deposit money has to accept them at face value, then the next, and so on. And again, expected interest payments are an essential reason why trade recipients of reserves or deposit money value them.

The basis for those expectations is a presumption that IoR will be paid at about the central bank's policy rate, because this is necessary for the central bank to hold inflation to its target. As noted earlier in this section, individual banks are free to reduce their holdings of reserves by trading with another bank. One way to do this is to buy something, typically a financial asset, either from another bank, or from a NBPS counterparty using a different bank. If many banks are doing this, though, say because they consider the IoR rate to be inadequate, that activity can be expected to be inflationary, so the central bank *must* pay a high enough IoR rate to restrain the circulation of reserves. That will

[14] The extent of that chain depends on how frequently recipients of deposit money have a bank loan which they use the deposit to pay down, thereby eliminating deposit money.

be an interest rate about the same as the monetary policy rate, assuming that monetary policy is set at the right level to hold inflation on target.

Similar logic applies to the deposit money, initially meaning, given the typical size of QE purchases, typically large 'wholesale' deposits. Deposit money is also a perpetual asset which individual NBPS holders can freely transfer to a different bank, either to take advantage of a higher interest rate, or in settlement of a purchase such as of an asset. Indeed, holders of wholesale deposits tend to actively manage them, and are likely to respond by shifting deposits to quite small differences in interest rates. Banks will wish to retain deposits as long as the interest spread between what the bank must pay and reserves is profitable, but in a competitive banking system, that will require banks to pass on to the NBPS much of the interest received from their central bank, albeit somewhat less after subtracting their operating costs and normal profits.

The conclusion is that, for central banks to be able to make QE asset purchases at acceptable prices, it was vital for interest to be paid on reserves at about the central bank's monetary policy rate and passed through to deposit money, with no expectation of that arrangement changing adversely for at least as long as the stocks of reserves and deposits created by QE remained. If any tapping of this through-flow of interest by the authorities, say by the introduction of a reserve requirement or a windfall withholding tax on deposits, had been anticipated, this would have reduced the value of reserves and deposits to potential holders, propagating through the chain of transactions and resulting in the relevant central bank having to pay higher prices for its QE purchases.

6.4 The Shifting Justification for QE

With economic activity remaining disappointingly subdued for years after the financial crisis had receded, QE was repeatedly expanded, resulting in banks accumulating far more reserves than they needed for payment settlement purposes. However, the 'flighty' nature of wholesale deposits discouraged the banks from using them, as it had been hoped, to make loans (Butt et al., 2014), although it remained the case that QE expanded the stocks of actively circulated reserves and deposit money beyond what was possible using conventional money market operations. Instead, the justification for QE shifted from monetary expansion to emphasising the effect of removing fixed-interest bonds from the private sector on longer-term interest rates. The idea was that the correspondingly increased prices of longer-term assets would stimulate economic activity either by wealth effects or by encouraging the creation of new assets to sell into those higher prices, ideally corporate bond or equity issuance funding business investment, hence increasing future potential output too. Or perhaps more accurately during the pandemic period, QE was holding bond yields down against a surge in government borrowing to fund responses to the pandemic including income replacement programmes and increased medical expenditure.

Asset purchases may influence long-term interest rates and stimulate economic activity through 'flow effects' as they happen, and/or through 'stock effects', from the lasting impact of the operations in the form of a sustained reduction of yields (see, for example, D'Amico and King, 2011), and analysts differ in their emphasis on each of these. Regardless of the central bank's view, however, the degree of easing was always specified by monetary policymakers in terms of the quantity of reserves created by asset purchases.

6.5 Passive versus Active QT

A QE portfolio comprising fixed-term bonds and funding liabilities in the form of central bank reserves will naturally shrink as its bonds mature and the bond issuers' banks pay reserves into the QE portfolio, thereby eliminating reserves and contracting the money supply.[15] Also, to the extent that the maturing bonds are replaced by new issuance which now remains in private sector hands, that will, other things equal, also raise long-term interest rates. This shrinkage therefore reverses some QE and represents monetary tightening. Allowing this natural run-off process to proceed is termed 'passive' QT.[16]

15 In the case of government bonds, typically but not always, payment via a government bank account at the central bank itself.

16 Even without maturities, a QE portfolio comprising coupon-bearing bonds will also produce some passive QT, or even passive additional QE, according to whether the aggregate coupon income produced by the bonds respectively exceeds or falls short of the interest paid on reserves. A helpful way to understand this is to realise that buying a coupon-bearing bond is like buying a bundle of cashflows, of which the redemption payment is only one, paid out regularly over the period corresponding to the remaining life of the bond.

If monetary policymakers prefer a faster rate of contraction for one or more of the reasons discussed in Section 6.7, implying more aggressive tightening, some of the bonds can be sold before maturity, while the rate of contraction can be slowed by reinvesting some maturity proceeds in new purchases of bonds, with purchases and sales being used to hold the quantity of reserves to any level or path specified. Accelerating the rate of contraction by selling bonds is termed 'active' QT.

6.6 QE Returns and Public Sector Finances

Albeit from a smaller range of types of assets and liabilities than a commercial bank would hold, a central bank does similarly generate net cashflow, and, to the extent that its assets and liabilities have variable market values, also creates mark-to-market gains or losses. The difference between them is that, because a central bank can always credit commercial banks' reserve accounts, it never lacks the liquidity to cover losses, and is not subject to closure by bank regulators if its equity becomes negative.

Normal monetary policy operations done to control money market interest rates generate negligible returns for the central bank. Even with IoR, reserves balances are balanced by assets bearing practically the same rate of interest.[17]

What does generate a substantial and steady positive cashflow and profit for central banks, though, known as 'seigniorage', is banknote issuance. That profit arises because, as noted in Section 6.3, banknotes bear no interest, but are paid for, via reserves, previously created by commercial banks selling interest-bearing loan assets to their central bank.

Generally, central banks' realised profits, mostly arising from seigniorage, net of their operating costs, are remitted to the monetary area's finance ministry.[18] In practical terms, this means that the central bank credits a government account which can be expected to be rapidly disbursed through government spending, hence seigniorage does not contract the base money supply. Any losses realised on central bank operations can be handled either by reducing seigniorage or by running

[17] Exceptions to this close match are the Fed and the Bank of Japan, which, apart from any foreign currency assets (foreign exchange operations are not considered here), hold mostly assets comprising not repo loans to commercial banks but government bonds issued by their respective governments.

[18] Various allocation arrangements for central bank returns are discussed by Long and Fisher (2024).

down the central bank's equity. Normally, no adjustment is made for mark-to-market losses, although occasionally, a government may recapitalise its central bank by gifting it assets, typically marketable government bonds.

In the absence of QE, a central bank's returns are so small and slowly changing in relation to other state incomes that hardly any members of the public are aware of them. For example, in the UK at present, the banknote circulation is about £89 bn (worth about 3% of GDP), meaning that, if Bank Rate averages 4% (around the level corresponding to a neutral stance of monetary policy), seigniorage contributes about £3.5 bn (just over 0.1% of GDP) annually to UK government revenue, compared with total government revenue of about £1,100 bn (almost 40% of GDP).

As QE portfolios expanded, however, the potential for them to generate much larger returns than central bank operations normally do increased greatly. Specifically, QE generates interest rate risk, because QE purchases of fixed-interest bonds lock in a yield-to-maturity on the bonds depending on the price and coupon rate, whereas, as noted in Section 6.3, the IoR rate is an overnight floating rate.

Unfortunately, that interest rate risk was realised when inflation accelerated as the pandemic receded. To make matters worse, the net interest outflow surged after Russia invaded Ukraine in February 2022 and natural gas and food prices stepped higher, prompting monetary policy interest rates to be increased sharply. As a result, nearly all of the central banks which did QE then faced big losses which, at the time of writing, look likely to exceed any gains made on QE before the pandemic. The net interest outflows from their QE portfolios look set to continue for the foreseeable future, of a size that will take many years of unremitted seigniorage income to pay off. In fact, depending on the size of the loss, and the future demand for banknotes (or perhaps zero-interest central bank digital currency instead), it is conceivable that the losses are too large for seigniorage to *ever* pay off, practically forcing government recapitalisation of the central bank. Whether realised in the form of net cashflows over the remaining life of the QE portfolio, or crystallised by liquidating the portfolio, realised QE losses are permanent real losses for the taxpayer.[19]

[19] The description of the Eurozone's QE losses as 'recoupable' from seigniorage, by the IMF's Belhocine, Bhatia and Frie (2023), is therefore misleading. For QE

The BoE's experience demonstrates starkly how interest rate risk has developed under QE. Over the period in which the BoE purchased bonds, 98% of which were UK government bonds, known as 'gilts', from 11 March 2009 to 15 December 2021, the proceeds-weighted average gilts yield locked in was roughly 1.5%. Moreover, about half the BoE's QE portfolio was acquired as QE was accelerated from 9 March 2020 in response to turmoil in the gilts market at the onset of the pandemic, and the proceeds-weighted yield on those gilts purchases was about 0.5%, compared with 2.25% in the preceding eleven years of QE. From the beginning of QE to 16 December 2021, when monetary policy began to be tightened in response to rising inflation, Bank Rate had averaged 0.45%, so that, by mid 2022, the BoE's QE portfolio had generated a cumulative cash flow of +£124 bn. By agreement (Bank of England, 2012), this was entirely remitted to the UK finance ministry, HM Treasury (HMT). However, as inflation surged, and Bank Rate rose steadily from 0.1% on 16 December 2021, rising above 2% in the second half of 2022, the BoE's QE portfolio began to generate a cash outflow, obliging, by the same agreement, HMT to return cash to the BoE QE portfolio.

By the end of March 2024, by which time Bank Rate had reached 5.25%, all but about £40 bn of the cumulative net cashflow received by the QE portfolio had had to be repaid by HMT. Altogether, at that time, the BoE QE portfolio had, over its lifetime, sustained a mark-to-market loss of about –£100 bn (worth roughly 4% of UK GDP).[20] This represents the return that would be crystallised if its remaining assets could be sold off immediately at market prices. The implication is that the cash raised from those asset sales would be insufficient to repay the funding liability, with the balance having to be covered by cash paid into the portfolio by HMT in order to complete its closedown.

6.7 Reasons to Accelerate Contraction of a QE Portfolio

A natural reason for active QT is that the exceptional nature of QE would suggest a default position of withdrawing QE when such extreme easing is no longer needed, and the policy interest rate is set

losses to begin to be genuinely recouped, short-term interest rates would have to fall back below the bond yields in the QE portfolio.

20 Calculations by Bill Allen.

well above zero. That recreates space to renew the use of QE if desired in future.

A second reason is that above-target inflation makes faster contraction of QE portfolios desirable for monetary policy tightening purposes (although most central banks have stated that raising the policy interest rate is considered to be the most effective and therefore their preferred way to tighten monetary policy). Indeed, monetary policymakers adhering to the stock view, under which merely retaining the QE portfolio represents loose monetary policy, should arguably consider it imperative to contract their QE portfolio to withdraw its easing as soon as possible by active bond sales. Ideally, there would be a method to express both QT and interest rate tightening effects in common terms, but, in practice, this is not straightforward because of the uncertainty about exactly how QE, and hence QT, works, so monetary policymakers do not formally allow for QT in setting their monetary policy interest rate.[21, 22]

A third reason for active QT is to reduce interest rate risk. Assuming that the bond market is 'efficiently' priced,[23] the mark-to-market value of a QE portfolio comprising government bonds is equal to the discounted terminal value of the portfolio assuming that (a) the portfolio is allowed to run off under passive QT, and (b) credit-risk-free short-term interest rates, as set by the central bank's monetary policy, follow the path implied by government bond yields.[24] That implied path of monetary policy rates determines both the expected reserves liability contributions to the cash balance generated by the QE portfolio (via IoR) and the interest rates at which those expected

21 Nevertheless, Bin Wei (2022) of the Atlanta Fed has suggested a translation method.

22 In practice, monetary policymakers have preferred to conduct QT in such a manner as to try to avoid tightening monetary conditions by raising longer-term interest rates anyway, presumably because that would increase the costs of active QT. Active QT has therefore been done gradually, with the aim of receiving prices for the bonds sold no worse than the bid side of the market. As a result, it seems that the effect of QT so far on long-term bond yields is small (Du, Forbes and Luzzetti, 2024).

23 In the sense of leaving no risk-arbitrage opportunities across the yield curve.

24 As the central bank is a state institution and typically conducts its monetary policy operations via secured repo lending and borrowing, it may be assumed that the central bank's policy rate is a credit-risk-free rate. Although that is not strictly true in the case of the Fed, as its policy rate is a target for unsecured money market transactions, the difference is negligible.

cashflows are discounted. These implied rates are not certain to occur but represent the bond market's central expectations of future interest rates, known as forward rates.[25] Although losses on QE programmes now appear inevitable, the implication of the uncertain nature of forward rates is that, under passive QT, the discounted loss is as likely to turn out larger than the current projection as it is to turn out smaller.[26] Therefore, if the central bank and/or the finance ministry is risk-averse, they should favour active QT to eliminate that risk at the earliest cost-effective opportunity.

A fourth reason, following from the third, for closing down the QE portfolio as soon as cost-effectively possible is that it can be imagined that the increase in net interest outlay on the QE portfolio caused by raising the monetary policy interest rate, and hence the IoR rate, may well make monetary policymakers hesitate to go through with raising their policy rate when inflation is projected to rise above its target, especially when practically all central banks remit their returns to their government and the net interest outlay on QE has fiscal policy implications. So early liquidation of the QE portfolio removes a potential conflict of interest for monetary policymakers and minimises the involvement of monetary policy with fiscal policy.[27]

Notwithstanding the previous arguments, it would be reasonable to vary the pace of QT, just as QE was generally expanded over a series of tranches, according to the stance of normal monetary policy, such as accelerating QT in support of a tightening stance – to coin a phrase, 'opportunistic QT'.

[25] Almost in the statistical sense – i.e. the mathematical expectation over the distribution of forward rates.

[26] In fact, given that the forward rates are positive, the market expectation of the cash loss on QE is larger than its current closeout value, as may be seen in the projections depicted in the quarterly reports published by the BoE – for example that for 2024Q1 (Bank of England, 2024). Whether a market or a social discount rate should be applied to a state project like QE raises a classic economic theory debate, but, to the extent that the social discount rate is the lower of the two, that is another argument for active QT. For a recent discussion of this issue, including an account of the development of the economic theory, see Chichilnisky, Hammond and Stern (2020).

[27] The extreme case, where the primary aim of monetary policy priority becomes alleviating the state debt burden, is called fiscal dominance.

6.8 Can Prospective Interest Rate Losses Be Reduced by Reducing the Run-off Rate?

The short answer to that question is 'not reliably, but maybe a little', but it is a question which has generated considerable confusion.

Naturally, realising losses sustained on QE is embarrassing for monetary policymakers, and ends any hope of market movements making the problem simply go away. So, despite the arguments put forward in Section 6.7 for beginning to contract QE as soon as monetary policy easing is no longer appropriate, some policymaker preference for realising the losses later, via net interest outflow, is understandable.

Indeed, of the major central banks which did QE, only the BoE has done active QT by selling bonds.[28] The Fed and the ECB have both tightened monetary policy by raising their policy interest rates, though both have not only not sold bonds but even braked the run-off rate of their QE portfolios by reinvesting some proceeds of maturing bonds to achieve a specified shrinkage rate of their portfolios for some time ahead. Moreover, while the Fed and the ECB have sustained large mark-to-market losses on their QE programmes, their losses have not been reported and publicly discussed as intensively as the BoE's losses.

Besides the fact that Fed and ECB have not done active QT, another reason why their QE losses have been less prominent is that the losses have been obscured by offsetting them against seigniorage, which is suspended for the time being, with any remaining loss retained and recorded in an entry on the central bank's balance sheet. In the Fed's case, since US dollar bills are used globally, its seigniorage revenue is large, so the Fed has chosen to record realised net QE losses on its balance sheet as a negative liability described as a 'deferred asset', to be pared down and eventually eliminated by future seigniorage, after which remittances to the US Treasury will resume.[29] In the ECB's case, the bulk of the Eurozone's QE programme has been distributed around the Eurozone member states' central banks, so the losses and the treatment of them vary between Eurozone central banks, but they will also suspend remitting seigniorage to their respective finance

[28] The Swedish Riksbank and the Reserve Bank of New Zealand have also sold down some of their QE portfolios.

[29] Faria-e-Castro and Jordan-Wood (2023) provide an explanation of the term 'deferred asset'.

ministries, formally recording that on their balance sheets as a reduction in some entry—like provisions, reserves, retained earnings or capital, and even potentially by 'revaluation of gold reserves', for as long as losses last. It seems unlikely that Eurozone member states will allow their respective national central bank's equity to become significantly negative, preferring, in that event, to recapitalise their central bank. Whichever way realised losses are presented, though, the effect on the taxpayer is the same.

The BoE is legally obliged to remit its seigniorage to HMT, meaning that the BoE's QE losses cannot be offset against seigniorage. Moreover, its losses are large in relation to the amount of QE done, because the BoE's QE portfolio includes longer bonds, with comparatively large exposure to interest rate risk. This reflects the fact that the gilts purchases were spread fairly evenly over the range of maturities in the gilts market, which has the greatest average maturity, at about fourteen years, of any major government bond market (Debt Management Office, 2024 – Annex A, Chart A.5).

The prominence of the BoE losses has led to some poorly informed criticism of the BoE by British politicians (Conservative Way Forward, 2024), under the illusion that holding the bonds to maturity would mean no loss being realised. Alas, to reiterate, if the bond market is priced efficiently, the discounted value of the return eventually realised on QE over its lifetime can be 'expected' to be the same whenever it is realised, regardless of whether QT is active or passive.[30]

Notwithstanding the previous discussion, there are two reasons to believe that passive QT just might deliver lower lifetime QE losses, though, in both cases, their effects are hard to quantify. First, if central banks initiate sales of QE bonds rather than waiting for them to mature, central banks can expect to at least have to accept the lower prices on the bid side of the market, but may even incur larger losses by moving the market against themselves. Indeed, the mere mention by the Fed Chairman on 22 May 2013 that 'we could . . . take a step down in the pace of our [QE asset] purchases' within a few months (Reuters, 2013) was enough to trigger a sharp rise in US treasury yields, popularly known as the 'taper

30 A complication is that braking the natural contraction of a QE portfolio by rolling over some maturing bonds may, if yields fall after roll-over, produce compensating profits. Ideally, any roll-over returns should be reported separately from the returns on the original QE purchases.

tantrum', suggesting that *sales* of QE assets could be expected to drive their prices substantially lower. Second, empirically, credit-risk-free yield curves do seem to slope upwards on average, suggesting that short-term interest rates do on average run lower than forward rates from government bond yield curves imply, but estimates of term premiums are not straightforward to derive, and have often been negative in recent years.

6.9 Can State QE Losses Be Avoided by Changing the Terms of the Deal Struck with the Private Sector?

Obviously, central bank ongoing interest rate losses on QE could be curtailed by paying no more interest on the stock of reserves created by QE than the return being generated by the bonds in the QE portfolio.

That could be engineered by adapting the reserve requirements widely used for monetary control purposes.[31] These reserve requirements work by compelling each bank to hold a tranche of reserves on which little or (most commonly) no remuneration is paid, with the size of that tranche typically set at some percentage of the bank's liabilities, structurally penalising banks' balance sheet expansion. As mentioned in Section 6.3, control of money market interest rates can then operate via the excess reserves banks will choose to hold above that lower tier of required reserves, of a size which can be expected to depend on the rate at which the upper tier is remunerated.

Given, however, that the purpose of reserve requirements in the present context is to reduce the central bank's net interest outlay arising from its QE portfolio, a typical unremunerated reserve requirement varying in proportion to a bank's liabilities would be unsuitable, not only because penalising banks' balance sheet expansion may not be desired but also because the resulting aggregate lower tier quantity of reserves could be a poor fit to the amount of unremunerated reserves required to eliminate the interest outlay arising from QE only. That amount will depend on the IoR rate that would otherwise be paid on all reserves, and the stock of reserves, originally created by QE, still remaining after some reduction by QT. For example, at the end of

[31] Reserve requirements are especially useful for monetary control when movements in the exchange rate driven by interest rate changes are undesirable. For a survey of the range of motivations for imposing reserve requirements and the structures applied in OECD countries, see Lepers (2018).

March 2024, when Bank Rate was 5.25% and the remaining stock of reserves created by QE stood at £744 bn, generating a locked-in yield of about 2%, the annual net interest outlay of about £24 bn could be eliminated by an unremunerated reserve requirement of £461 bn.[32, 33]

This aggregate reserve requirement could then be allocated to banks according to their share of the aggregate stock of bank deposits at some point in time or on average over the period of QE purchases, for example. To avoid distorting banks' incentives, their share would remain fixed until QT is complete. But it would be reasonable to reduce the aggregate requirement in line with QT, and also update it to reflect changes in the monetary policy interest rate, and by implication the interest rate paid on the upper tier of reserves.

So, it is technically feasible to use such a tiered remuneration approach to avoid net interest outlay on QE, but would it be advisable?[34] That is doubtful, in view of the trouble that introducing sizable unremunerated reserve requirements would cause.

One problem would be the impact on banks' profitability, and hence probably on the banks' customers too. In the UK, bank profitability has been low since a range of additional regulatory capital, leverage and liquidity requirements were imposed on banks in response to the financial crisis, along with various levies to recover the state's costs of bank support. In the three years before the pandemic disturbed the economy, UK banks collectively made taxable profits averaging £20 bn per year.[35] Even in FY2022–23, with the benefit of higher interest rates, UK banks only made £33 bn. At present interest rates, a £461 bn aggregate reserve requirement to save QE net interest outlay of £24 bn per year at the banks' expense would therefore wipe out much of UK banks' taxable profits.

32 From [744 x (0.0525–0.02)] / 0.0525 = 461. Note that there is practically no likelihood of this calculation implying such a large unremunerated reserve requirement that it would interfere with the central bank's ability to control short-term interest rates.

33 That is 16% of UK M4ex deposits, which would be bigger than the normal size of reserve requirement used for monetary control, but not unprecedentedly large.

34 Paul De Grauwe and Yuemei Ji have been notably prolific, though somewhat polemic, advocates of a two-tier approach to save on central banks' interest outlay on reserves created in QE, a campaign beginning with De Grauer and Ji (2023), although Paul Tucker (2022) provided an earlier, more objective and economically rigorous discussion.

35 Source: UK Finance (2017–19) annual reports on the total tax contribution of the UK banking sector.

As explained in Section 6.3, to the extent that the banking market is competitive (which seems likely to be the case in the UK at least),[36] IoR is largely passed on to banks' depositors. The implication is that lower returns on banks' reserves would reduce banks' profitability, but assuming that all banks were similarly affected, banks would be able to offset some of that on to banks' customers generally, such via a larger spread between loan and deposit rates, and higher bank charges. And given that banks derive much revenue from smaller retail customers, would be like a regressive tax increase. In the UK's case, assuming that the M4ex (M4 excluding intermediate other financial corporations) definition of broad money provides a reasonable indication of the size of UK banks' deposit-funded lending activity, recovering £24 bn from their customers could be achieved by widening the loan-deposit spread by 0.9%. But that would increase banks' vulnerability to losing more business to more lightly regulated 'non-bank financial intermediaries', also known as 'shadow banks', especially direct lenders, like peer-to-peer lenders and private credit funds, and money market funds buying commercial paper.

Another potential issue is the fact that reserves count, for liquidity coverage ratio (LCR) purposes, as a Level 1 (i.e. the most reliably liquid) asset available to meet a bank run, and will be many banks' main Level 1 asset given the present size of banks' reserves holdings.[37] By definition, required reserves could not be drawn down to meet liquidity needs, but one imagines that a bank run is a sufficient threat to financial stability, an arrangement could be readily agreed to allow for the emergency use of required reserves, such as using them as collateral to borrow from the central bank, which effectively already has possession of the reserves.

Arguably the greatest problem with tiered reserves remuneration is not immediately technical, though, but the fact that it would amount to an act of bad faith by the state.

As explained in Sections 6.2 and 6.3, the primary reason why banks ended up with large reserves holdings is that they were induced to participate, as payment settlement agents for non-banks and asset market intermediaries, in QE asset purchases, by the terms understood to be offered. This included the banks getting paid about the monetary policy

[36] A not unreasonable assumption, given that there are about 300 deposit-taking banks in the UK (Bank of England, n.d.b).

[37] The LCR is described in more detail in Section 6.10.

interest rate on the additional reserves they were taking onto their balance sheets. While those terms may not have been contractually specified, there was no hint that they might be changed adversely for the banks in the foreseeable future, and in central banks including the ECB and BoE, those terms were the established norm before QE began. Indeed, most central banks which had imposed bank liability-based reserve requirements prior to QE, abolished them when QE began, because reserve requirements of that nature would have conflicted with the monetary easing purpose of QE, and those central banks have generally not reintroduced them since.[38] It therefore seems reasonable to believe that those terms were reflected in the (lower than otherwise) prices paid by the central bank for QE asset purchases.

Moreover, in the UK's case, the fact that HMT withdrew the cash generated by net interest inflows when QE was working to the state's advantage suggests that the UK state was content with the terms.

It is also possible that, if banks had expected the interest rate paid on reserves to be capped, they might have hedged against that possibility in the market, which would have counteracted some of the QE effect on long-term interest rates.

Changing the terms now that the trade has turned against the state would be a breach of trust. Any central bank which does so may come to regret it if that central bank wanted to use QE again in future, in which case commercial banks might well be reluctant to participate, or demand either high prices for assets sold or legally enforceable guarantees of reserves remuneration. The banks could even try to establish private payment settlement arrangements cutting out their perfidious central bank.

6.10 Defining the Endpoint of QT

Although QE was originally conceived as an exceptional monetary policy measure, for various reasons it should not be assumed that QT must return the stock of reserves to its starting level, especially after fifteen years of changes in the money and banking system.

[38] An exception is the ECB, which did formally retain its statutory reserve requirement of 1% of specified bank liabilities, albeit paying interest on those required reserves at or close to its monetary policy rate. And the ECB did return to paying no interest on required reserves in July 2023, but that only affects about 5% of the present Eurosystem QE portfolio.

Naturally, nominal economic expansion could be expected to scale up monetary flows, and hence the stock of reserves needed when the baseline is reached and normal monetary policy resumes, even if practices like banks' uses of reserves, and the operation of monetary policy, return to how they were before QE began. For example, in the UK case, the stock of UK M4 broad money increased by a multiple of 2.2 times since interest began to be paid on reserves, meaning that, other things equal, the £24 bn reserves that banks chose to hold then would imply reserves demand now of £53 bn.[39]

In practice, however, banks' usage of reserves has changed greatly, not least as the result of their own, and bank-regulator-ordered, adjustments designed to make a recurrence of the financial crisis less likely, and these changes seem to have increased bank demand for reserves by several times as much as scale effects.

Foremost among those responses to the financial crisis is the more developed bank liquidity regulation introduced in 2013, with the aim of engineering at least short-term resilience of banks to withstand a stylised run-off of bank liabilities lasting thirty days scenario.[40] Each bank is required to hold a ratio, known as the LCR, equal to its total holding of high-quality liquid assets (HQLA), which must include minimum proportions of the assets classed as more liquid, divided by a weighted sum of likely outflows, weighted according to the proportion of each particular category of liability expected to be lost over the thirty days, of no less than 1:1. Naturally, reserves count as the most reliably liquid (Level 1) asset, which created a new source of demand from banks to hold reserves.

The fact that QE involving bond purchases from the NBPS creates wholesale deposits, which are assumed to entirely run off in the thirty-day period, makes the stock of HQLA required to meet the LCR particularly large. Moreover, the LCR represents what regulators consider to be a reasonable level of liquidity, but experience has shown that banks prefer more than this minimum during periods of market turbulence. All the more so since it became clear from recent stress events, notably

39 Also, in the UK, the number of participants in the Sterling Monetary Framework, which can hold reserves accounts, increased during QE, from 43 in 2008 to 223 in June 2024, which will have increased the demand for reserves if banks have a fixed demand for at least a base holding of reserves – like a reverse netting effect.

40 For a definitive account of the role of the LCR in bank liquidity regulation, see Bank for International Settlements (2013).

including the run on Silicon Valley Bank in March 2023, that the combination of rapid diffusion of news via social media and customers' online management of bank accounts has made bank runs faster. Also, derivatives collateralisation has become stricter, requiring banks to hold more reserves to cover variation margin payments and receipts, to and from derivatives clearers.[41]

This rising level of the baseline level of reserves presents the problem of how to identify when QT has reduced the stock of reserves to near that baseline. The idea is to then slow QT as that level is approached, until the baseline level is judged to be reached, at which point QT terminates and monetary policy operations return to normal, with monetary policymakers guiding the money market clearing rate in an actively trading money market, as explained in Section 6.3. Indeed, that explanation, of how reserves supply from the central bank, and reserves demand by commercial banks, affects the market-clearing money market interest rate, suggests one indicator of whether or not QT has reduced the stock of reserves to close to the baseline level. That is, the return of sizable departures in the money market clearing interest rates from the IoR rate.

When normal monetary policy as described in Section 6.3 is in operation, the central bank controls the supply of reserves, via its OMOs, to give reserves some scarcity value, represented by the interest rates that banks will pay to borrow reserves. In microeconomic terms, the central bank is operating with a classic downwardly sloping demand curve. Then, inadvertent tightness of reserves supply will produce upward spikes in the money-market-clearing interest rate above the IoR rate. By contrast, under QE, the supply of reserves in the money market is made so abundant that there is little need for banks to trade, and if any bank does have a shortfall of reserves, there are many willing lenders, so that the money market clearing interest rate is practically fixed at the level of interest paid on reserves, regardless of the quantity of reserves. In microeconomic terms, the interest rate elasticity of demand for reserves is infinite. It may be supposed that there is some transitional region, where the slope of the demand curve decreases with increasing supply of reserves, implying smaller spikes in money market interest rates. In

41 Derivatives clearers are typically holders of reserve accounts – one of the few types of holders of reserves which are not commercial banks.

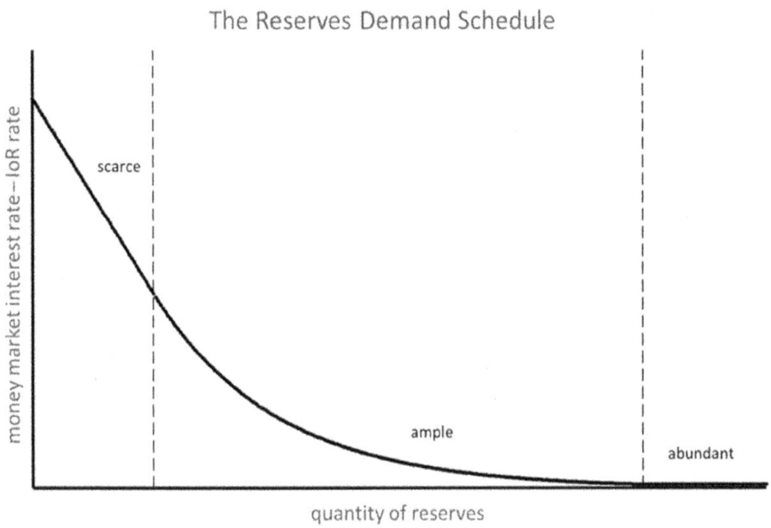

Figure 6.1 The reserves demand schedule.

the terms used by the Fed, reserves in this region are described as 'ample'. These three regions of the reserves demand curve are depicted in Figure 6.1. Hence as QT reduces the reserves from abundant to ample, the volatility of money market interest rates increases, revealing that the baseline is being approached.

Ideally, the money market demand curve could be constructed by plotting the changes in the differences between the money market clearing rate and the IoR rate, to identify the regions where reserves are scarce, ample and abundant. In practice, this raises several problems. First, some central banks, including the BoE, have few recent observations when reserves have not been abundant. Second, it appears that reserves demand is more complex than a simple function of money market interest rates. In particular because the demand for reserves also increases with the stock of transactions deposits held by banks' customers, the reserves demand function is better fitted by a surface. Unfortunately, estimating that surface presents the econometric problem that, because QE involving the NBPS created deposit money and reserves simultaneously, an instrumental variables estimation approach is required.[42]

[42] The seminal example of this method is Lopez-Salido and Vissing-Jorgensen (2021).

A related approach is to produce local estimates of the demand curve slope, expressed as the elasticity of reserves demand with respect to the money market interest rate departure from the IoR rate, rather than trying to model reserves demand. These local estimates are obtained from daily changes in the money-market-clearing interest rate and the stock of reserves.[43] The resulting 'swarm' of local elasticity estimates in the quantity-of-reserves, interest-rate-departure-from-IoR space can then be examined, and econometrically tested, for signs that reserves supply is no longer abundant, and becoming ample, with the local slope providing a measure of reserves 'ampleness', to use the Fed's term.

An alternative approach to assessing reserves ampleness is to measure specific aspects of banks' behaviour in the money market and payments activity.[44] For example, when the existing reserves supply is becoming a binding constraint, banks tend to try to process out-payments later than in-payments.

The Fed is relatively well placed to use such measures of reserves ampleness, because the US dollar money market is subject to more variations in reserves supply available to banks, partly because the US government is an active user of its bank account at the Fed (the Treasury General Account), and partly because the US money market includes some large holders of reserves which hold reserves on different terms to US commercial banks, including the Federal housing agencies and foreign banks. This ability to more clearly measure reserves ampleness makes it more feasible for the Fed to manage longer-term reserves supply by adjusting QT.

For other central banks like the BoE, reserves ampleness is more difficult to assess, creating a danger that they are surprised by the onset of reserves scarcity as QT proceeds, leading to undesirable spikes in money market interest rates. Those central banks can place more reliance on a 'standing' (i.e. available on demand) marginal lending facility, set up to provide practically an unlimited quantity of short-term loans to banks at some specified spread above the IoR rate, thereby capping the money market interest rate.[45] Usage of this standing facility provides another measure of reserves ampleness.

[43] See Afonso, Giannone, La Spada and Williams (2024) for details.

[44] As pioneered by Afonso et al. (2024).

[45] In the BoE's case, the short-term repo (STR) facility (Bank of England, 2022), providing one-week loans to banks at Bank Rate (i.e. no spread to the IoR rate). The Fed and ECB have similar standing facilities.

These alternative ways of dealing with approaching the baseline level of reserves have been dubbed as supply-driven and demand-driven respectively.[46]

Another approach is, initially, to simply ask banks what level of reserves they would like to hold, to produce an idea of the total reserves demand, which both the BoE and the Fed ask in regular bank surveys.[47] Naturally, to the extent that banks' individual desired holdings of reserves are driven by the LCR, the implied appropriate aggregate level of reserves over all the banks can be less than the total of banks' desired holdings, because, since (other than by transactions with the central bank) reserves exist within a closed circulation between banks, meaning that withdrawals from one bank must deliver reserves to another, which then has no shortage of reserves to meet any withdrawals it experiences.

An important consideration, however, is whether central banks should simply provide, whether by a supply-driven or a demand-driven approach, enough reserves to strongly suppress spikes in money market interest rates, accepting banks' usage of reserves after conditioning by years of QE. One issue is that, with reserves being abundant for so long, inter-bank lending and borrowing in the money market atrophied (Borio, 2023). Another issue is that, in an attempt to make use of the abundant reserves handed to them by QE, banks made commitments to customers involving potential drawdowns of reserves, notably credit lines, meaning that banks' demand for reserves has increased by more than might be expected, even given the increase in deposits mechanically created by QE (Acharya and Rajan, 2023). Arguably therefore, during this adjustment process, central banks should tolerate larger spikes in money market rates (meaning raising the spread between the monetary policy rate and any standing lending facility fixing the top of the band within which money market rates fluctuate), since it is these spikes that make inter-bank lending and borrowing worthwhile, thereby encouraging a return of pre-QE money market activity.

[46] Terms perhaps originated by the ECB's Isabel Schnabel (2023).

[47] To establish, respectively, the 'Preferred Minimum Range of Reserves' (PMRR; Hauser, 2019) and the 'Lowest Comfortable Level of Reserves' (LCLoR; Logan, 2019). For an introduction to the similar, but naturally more complex, issue in the Eurosystem of central banks, where the baseline level of reserves is called the floor required excess liquidity (FREL), see Aberg et al. (2021).

Also, banks' preferred holdings of reserves may be high at present because, with monetary policy rates generally above all but the shortest government bond yields, banks may well be relying on reserves to meet their LCRs, whereas with a more normal, upward sloping yield curve, banks would choose instead to hold more government bonds, which are also Level 1 assets for LCR purposes.[48]

Regardless of the method used to establish the baseline level of reserves, the final decision to be made is how to supply that baseline level for the indefinite future, after QT is deemed to be completed and monetary policy returns to normal. If the choice is for the central bank to continue to hold some of the bonds bought under QE as a structural reserves-supplying asset portfolio, the market value of the bonds at that point should be recorded so that the lifetime return, probably a loss, on QE can be calculated. The Fed in particular should be urged not to omit that final accounting, since the Fed has always used US treasuries, held in its system open market account (SOMA) portfolio, for the long-term backing for the bulk of its base money, so it would be especially easy for the Fed to turn seamlessly from QE to business-as-usual without formally marking an end to QT. In the case of the BoE, it looks likely that, unless QE is restarted for some reason, the BoE intends to sell all the gilts purchased under QE that have not already matured, and return to repo lending, perhaps with a base of longer-term loans, as the BoE's preferred method of supplying reserves (Saporta, 2024).

References

Aberg, P., Corsi, M., Grossmann-Wirth, V., Hudepohl, T., Mudde, Y., Rosolin, T. and Schobert, F. (2021). 'Demand for central bank reserves and monetary policy implementation frameworks: the case of the Eurosystem', European Central Bank Occasional Paper No.282; www.ecb.europa.eu/pub/pdf/scpops/ecb.op282~6017392312.en.pdf

Acharya, V. V. and Rajan, R. (2023). 'Liquidity, liquidity everywhere, not a drop to use: why flooding banks with central bank reserves may not expand liquidity', NBER Working Paper No.29680; www.nber.org/system/files/working_papers/w29680/w29680.pdf

Afonso, G., Giannone, D., La Spada, G. and Williams, J. C. (2024). 'Scarce, abundant, or ample? A time-varying model of the reserve demand curve', Federal Reserve Bank of New York Staff Reports

48 Conveniently adding to the demand in QT asset sales.

No.1019; www.newyorkfed.org/medialibrary/media/research/staff_reports/sr1019.pdf

Afonso, G., Clark, K., Gowen, B., La Spada, G., Martinez, J. C., Miu, J. and Riordan, W. (2024). 'A New set of indicators of reserve ampleness'. Federal Reserve Bank of New York Liberty Street Economics blog; https://libertystreeteconomics.newyorkfed.org/2024/08/a-new-set-of-indicators-of-reserve-ampleness/

Bank of England (n.d.a). 'Market operations guide'; www.bankofengland.co.uk/markets/bank-of-england-market-operations-guide/information-for-applicants

Bank of England (n.d.b). 'List of banks as compiled by the Bank of England'; www.bankofengland.co.uk/-/media/boe/files/prudential-regulation/authorisations/which-firms-does-the-pra-regulate/2024/list-of-banks/bank-list-2405.pdf

Bank of England (2006). 'New framework will modernise sterling money markets'; www.bankofengland.co.uk/-/media/boe/files/news/2006/april/new-framework-will-modernise-sterling-money-markets.pdf

Bank of England (2012). 'Transfer of excess cash from the Asset Purchase Facility to HM Treasury'; www.bankofengland.co.uk/-/media/boe/files/letter/2012/chancellor-letter-091112.pdf

Bank of England (2022). 'Short Term Repo Facility – Provisional Market Notice 4 August 2022'; www.bankofengland.co.uk/markets/market-notices/2022/august/short-term-repo-facility-provisional-market-notice-4-august-2022

Bank of England (2024). 'Asset Purchase Facility Quarterly Report – 2024 Q1'; www.bankofengland.co.uk/asset-purchase-facility/2024/2024-q1

Bank for International Settlements, Basel Committee on Banking Supervision (2013). 'Basel III: The Liquidity Coverage Ratio and liquidity risk monitoring tools'; www.bis.org/publ/bcbs238.pdf

Belhocine, N., Bhatia, A. V. and Frie, J. (2023). 'Raising rates with a large balance sheet: the Eurosystem's net income and its fiscal implications', IMF Working Paper WP/23/145; www.imf.org/-/media/Files/Publications/WP/2023/English/wpiea2023145-print-pdf.ashx

Borio, C. (2023). 'Getting up from the floor'; www.bis.org/speeches/sp230426.pdf

Butt, N., Churm, R., McMahon, M., Morotz, A. and Schanz, J. (2014). 'QE and the bank lending channel in the United Kingdom', Bank of England Working Paper No.511; www.bankofengland.co.uk/-/media/boe/files/working-paper/2014/qe-and-the-bank-lending-channel-in-the-uk.pdf

Chichilnisky, G., Hammond, P. J. and Stern, N. (2020). 'Fundamental utilitarianism and intergenerational equity with extinction discounting', *Social Choice and Welfare*; www.lse.ac.uk/granthaminsti

tute/publication/fundamental-utilitarianism-and-intergenerational-equity-with-extinction-discounting/

Conservative Way Forward (2024). 'The Bank of England: an international outlier'; www.conservativewayforward.com/_files/ugd/acef4a_7aeb03fce8484dd2a48c318abf3e7594.pdf

D'Amico, S. and King, T. B. (2011). 'Flow and stock effects of large-scale treasury purchases'; https://files.stlouisfed.org/files/htdocs/conferences/qe/damico_king_Apr11.pdf

Debt Management Office, UK (2024). 'Debt and Reserves Management Report 2024–25'; www.dmo.gov.uk/media/4kihuxsy/drmr2425.pdf

De Grauer, P. and Ji, Y. (2023). 'Monetary policies that do not subsidise banks', VoxEU; https://cepr.org/voxeu/columns/monetary-policies-do-not-subsidise-banks

Du, W., Forbes, K. and Luzzetti, M. (2024). 'Quantitative tightening around the globe: what have we learned?'; www.chicagobooth.edu/-/media/research/igm/docs/quantitative_tightening_around_the_globe_usmpf_2024_02_12.pdf

Faria-e-Castro, M. and Jordan-Wood, S. (2023). 'The Fed's remittances to the treasury: explaining the "deferred asset"', Federal Reserve Bank of St Louis On the Economy blog; www.stlouisfed.org/on-the-economy/2023/nov/fed-remittances-treasury-explaining-deferred-asset

Federal Reserve (2008). Press release, 6 October; www.federalreserve.gov/monetarypolicy/20081006a.htm

Fisher, P. (2010). 'An unconventional journey: the Bank of England's Asset Purchase Programme'; www.bankofengland.co.uk/-/media/boe/files/speech/2010/the-bank-of-englands-asset-purchase-programme.pdf

Hauser, A. (2019). 'Waiting for the exit: QT and the Bank of England's long-term balance sheet'; www.bankofengland.co.uk/speech/2019/andrew-hauser-speech-hosted-by-the-afme-isda-icma-london

Lepers, E. (2018). 'Reserve requirements: current use, motivations and practical considerations'; https://elischolar.library.yale.edu/cgi/viewcontent.cgi?article=15523&context=ypfs-documents

Logan, L. (2019). 'Observations on implementing monetary policy in an ample-reserves regime'; www.newyorkfed.org/newsevents/speeches/2019/log190417

Long, J. and Fisher, P. (2024). 'Central bank profit distribution and recapitalisation', Bank of England Staff Working Paper No.1069; www.bankofengland.co.uk/-/media/boe/files/working-paper/2024/central-bank-profit-distribution-and-recapitalisation.pdf

Lopez-Salido, D. and Vissing-Jorgensen, A. (2021). 'Reserve demand and balance sheet run-off'; https://drive.google.com/file/d/1W6qQLvCq0SzpiQk3XWnRYhC86AFZaOaT/view

Reuters (2013). News report, 22 May. 'Bernanke's Q&A testimony to Congressional panel'; www.reuters.com/article/us-usa-fed-bernanke-highlights/bernankes-qa-testimony-to-congressional-panel-idUSBRE94L0O720130522/

Saporta, V. (2024). 'Let's get ready to repo!'; www.bankofengland.co.uk/speech/2024/july/victoria-saporta-speech-at-afme-seminar

Schnabel, I. (2023). 'Back to normal? Balance sheet size and interest rate control'; www.bis.org/review/r230328c.pdf

Tucker, P. (2022). 'Quantitative easing, monetary policy implementation and the public finances', IFS Green Budget 2022, Chapter 7; https://ifs.org.uk/sites/default/files/2022-10/Quantitative-easing-monetary-policy-implementation-and-the-public-finances-Green-Budget-2022.pdf

UK Finance (2017–19). Annual reports on the total tax contribution of the UK banking sector; www.ukfinance.org.uk/policy-and-guidance/type/reports-and-publications

Wei, B. (2022). 'Quantifying "quantitative tightening" (QT): how many rate hikes is QT equivalent to?'; http://dx.doi.org/10.2139/ssrn.4103824

III

Fiscal and Governance Aspects of QE

7 *Fiscal Channels of QE and QT in the United Kingdom*

JACK MEANING

7.1 Introduction

That monetary policy innovations have consequences for fiscal aggregates, and fiscal policy more generally, is nothing new.[1] In many ways (but not all) the government can be thought of as similar to any other borrower in the economy and so when the central bank raises or lowers interest rates, the government's incentives and costs of borrowing also change. However, the programmes of large-scale purchases of government bonds by central banks since the global financial crisis of 2008 known as quantitative easing (QE), in the UK and beyond, have brought this interaction into starker focus. They have also introduced new channels through which monetary policy can impact its fiscal counterpart. In this chapter I outline three key fiscal channels of QE and quantitative tightening (QT) that operate through their impact on fiscal policy. One is the well-understood direct effect on government bond yields and the fiscal budget constraint. The other two are features of the QE asset swap on the consolidated public balance sheet debt interest cost and the profit and loss dynamics of a central bank bond portfolio. We show that these channels have had material consequences for fiscal policy in the UK since 2009. They can also lead to conflicts in times of QT. Finally, we look to international precedent for lessons on how to manage these fiscal interactions and propose a series of institutional changes which could minimise the conflicts.

7.2 The UK's Monetary-Fiscal Arrangements around QE and QT

Before beginning a discussion of the impact of central bank balance sheet policies on fiscal policy, it is worth giving a summary of the

[1] The views expressed here are solely those of the author and so cannot be taken to represent those of Barclays or any other institutions with which the author is affiliated.

specific institutional arrangements around UK monetary and fiscal policy. When the Bank of England began quantitative easing, it created an off-balance sheet special purpose vehicle (SPV) known as the Asset Purchase Facility (APF).[2] The Bank of England then made a loan to the APF funded by the creation of new central bank reserves. These reserves paid Bank Rate, as did the loan owed by the APF to the Bank of England, meaning the two sides of the Bank of England's balance sheet (the APF loan and the reserves) were matched. The loaned money was then used by the APF, at the behest of the Monetary Policy Committee (MPC), to buy assets, predominantly gilts, from the private sector with the seller's bank's account at the Bank of England being credited with the newly created reserves. Crucially, the SPV was indemnified against losses by the government.[3] The motivation for this was to insulate the Monetary Policy Committee (MPC) from considerations of profit and loss so that it could focus solely on the price stability objective when deciding the appropriate scale of asset purchases and reserve creation. This set-up was specific to the UK, with other jurisdictions, such as the Federal Reserve and the European Central Bank, opting to buy assets directly onto the balance sheet of the central bank itself.

Initially the positive carry of the APF's portfolio meant that money accrued to the APF. This money was retained in the APF. However, on 9 November 2012 the Chancellor of the Exchequer announced that this arrangement would change and surplus money would be transferred to HM Treasury on a quarterly basis. Between 2013 and 2022, around £126 bn was transferred to the Treasury, or 6% of nominal GDP. Since 2022, money has begun to flow back the other way, due to negative carry and valuation losses.[4] These dynamics and their implications are what we will consider in the remainder of this chapter.

[2] The APF was actually created before QE was begun, in January 2009 as a vehicle for other market interventions designed to ease credit conditions. However, these were temporary and quantitatively much smaller than QE, which quickly became the primary purpose of the APF after its inception in March 2009.

[3] A redacted version of the agreed indemnity document has been released at https://assets.publishing.service.gov.uk/media/673b2204a804531e2f499a9d/Asset_Purchase_Facility_deed_of_indemnity.pdf.

[4] For more detail on the institutional arrangements around the APF, HM Treasury and cash flows, see Dolan et al. (2022).

7.3 Three Fiscal Channels of QE and QT

The nature of QE and QT provides (at least) three channels of direct interaction between monetary policy and fiscal policy. There are, of course, more indirect, general equilibrium interactions that come from boosting overall growth and therefore tax receipts. These are beyond the scope of this chapter to discuss in detail, but the interested reader should see Adrian and colleagues (2024).

7.3.1 The Direct Yield Channel

The first channel we discuss is the most well documented, tested and understood. It is simply that if QE lowers (QT raises) government bond yields then it directly affects the cost and incentives for the government to borrow. Put another way, if long-term government bond yields are a positive function of the amount of debt outstanding to the private sector, implying that the elasticity of the demand curve for government debt held outside of the public sector is imperfectly elastic and upward sloping in yields, then QE will have consequences for the fiscal budget constraint.

This proposition has been explored theoretically, with an open discussion remaining about the precise channels through which this can be motivated. They include: theories on imperfect substitutability of assets and limits to arbitrage which give rise to preferred habitat investors and local supply effects (Modigliani and Sutch 1966; Tobin 1969; Giese et al. 2024); a signalling channel stemming from commitment or asymmetric information (Bernanke 2020; Bhattari et al. 2022); or liquidity premia.[5] From the point of view of the direct yield channel, the underlying mechanism does not matter. Rather, the fact that QE can reduce government bond rates, however it happens, is the key. This is an empirical question that has been tested by many and found to be true, although to varying degrees, both across studies and across states of the world. A comprehensive summary of the empirical literature can be found in Chapter 1 of this volume. They present a range of multipliers for £100 bn of gilt purchases on ten-year government bond yields of between -0.2 and -0.5. We take this range and follow the empirical exercise of Chadha and Meaning (2013) to get a sense of the scale of the direct yield channel resulting from UK QE. We look at gross issuance of

[5] For a summary of the vagaries of the theoretical debate on QE, see Busetto et al. (2022).

conventional government bonds over the period 2009–2022, up to the point that QT started. We abstract from the index-linked bond market, which accounted for between 7% and 25% of gross issuance over this period. This is because the Bank of England's QE programme never purchased index-linked bonds, and because the calculations inherent in our exercise for index-linked bonds would require additional assumptions on QE's impact on inflation and premia. The results in the rest of this chapter are therefore likely to be an underestimate of the true fiscal impact through this channel.

Table 7.1 shows that, gross issuance of conventional gilts was on average £147 bn per year between 2009 and 2022. Taking the bottom of the range of QE impact estimates and mapping it into the quantity of bonds purchased through QE implies that government bond yields were between 0.4 pp and 1.8 pp lower over this period, as the scale of QE rose from £200 bn to almost £900 bn. Using the modified duration of the

Table 7.1 ***Impact of QE and QT direct yield channel on nominal fiscal issuance.***

Fiscal year	Gross issuance (£bn)	QE impact on yields (pp)	Modified duration of gilts	Price impact (%)	Fiscal saving (£bn)
2009–10	198.3	-0.4	8.6	-3.4	6.8
2010–11	132.4	-0.4	8.2	-3.3	4.4
2011–12	140.4	-0.4	8.3	-3.3	4.7
2012–13	129.2	-0.7	9.2	-6.4	8.3
2013–14	114.4	-0.7	9.2	-6.4	7.4
2014–15	94.1	-0.7	9.0	-6.3	5.9
2015–16	94.9	-0.7	10.2	-7.1	6.7
2016–17	111.4	-0.9	10.2	-9.2	10.3
2017–18	87	-0.9	11.1	-10.0	8.7
2018–19	77.2	-0.9	11.4	-10.2	7.9
2019–20	114.8	-0.9	11.6	-10.4	12.0
2020–21	452.4	-1.8	12.6	-22.8	102.9
2021–22	168.4	-1.8	11.9	-21.4	36.0
2022–23	151.8	-1.7	11.5	-19.5	29.6
2023–24	210.4	-1.5	9.2	-13.8	28.9

Source: DMO, Bank of England and author's calculations.

government bond portfolio we than then calculate how much lower the price of that debt would have been to issue without QE holding rates down and prices up. Finally, we end up with how much more in terms of par/nominal debt the government would have had to issue to raise the same cash amount if QE had not been depressing yields. It shows that the government made a significant saving of between £4 bn and £12 bn per year up until the Covid-19 pandemic, at which point both significantly larger issuance and additional QE both increased the saving substantially. These savings reduce the overall debt burden for the government by reducing public sector net debt (PSND). What is more, for a given coupon rate, these savings are then locked in for the lifetime of the bonds issued over this period, presenting an ongoing saving.

Turning focus to QT, the empirical literature suggests an asymmetry that leads to a lower multiplier on to bond yields.[6] We therefore repeat the previous exercise for the period since 2022 but using a multiplier half as large (–0.1) to map into the change in yields and then to the nominal supply. This suggests that QT has increased yields cumulatively by around 20–30 bp, in line with estimates outlined by Ramsden (2023), and caused the government to have to issue £7.5 bn more nominal debt than it would have without QT, as of the start of fiscal year 24–25. However, while this amounts to a fiscal drag relative to the state of the world in which QT was not happening, the remaining APF portfolio continues to compress yields and therefore keep government borrowing costs lower than they would otherwise have been in the absence of the APF, currently amounting to just under £30 bn.

7.3.2 *The Interest Differential Channel*

The second fiscal channel of QE relates to the fact that QE is an asset swap in which the consolidated government balance sheet switches a fixed rate, term asset – a government bond – for a floating, short-term rate asset – central bank reserves. This amounts to a fraction of government debt now being financed at, in the case of the UK, Bank Rate, rather than the government bond rate. The saving can be shown as:

$$S_t = \theta_t[Y_t^A - r_t]$$

[6] See for example Du, Forbes and Luzzetti (2024) or Chapter 5 in this volume.

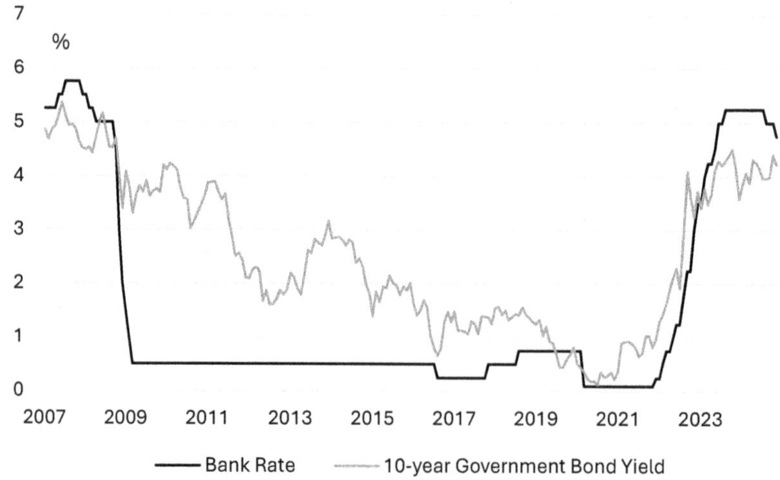

Figure 7.1 Bank Rate and ten-year nominal government bond yield.
Source: Bank of England.

Where the fiscal saving/costs S_t is a function of the quantity of government bonds held, θ_t, and the spread between the average yield on the central bank's government bond portfolio, Y_t^A and the policy rate, r_t.

This gives rise to a number of salient features. First, the asset swap makes the consolidated government balance sheet more interest rate sensitive, so swings in the policy rate will have more of an effect on the government interest rate cost. In this way, the interest differential channel is an amplifier of the direct yield channel. This increased rate sensitivity is discussed by the Office for Budget Responsibility (2021) and Allen and colleagues (2021), but is subtly different to the interest differential channel. The former focuses solely on the amplified impact of changes in the policy rate on the fiscal cost, as the central bank takes on more interest rate risk (which is one of the ways in which QE can be thought to reduce term bond yields; Vayanos and Vila 2021), effectively shortening the maturity of the government debt stock. The latter encompasses a level effect, changing the fiscal position by changing the quantity of debt paying the floating rate, rather than the fixed rate, regardless of whether or not either rate changes. In essence, it is the public sector exchanging the term premium for interest rate risk.

Second, if asset purchase policies are enacted only when the short-term interest hits the lower bound, then the interest rate differential channel will always begin as a positive flow to the fiscal authority, as term premia and upward-sloping rate expectations will keep the yield on bonds purchased higher than the short-term interest rate, which is at its lowest point, by definition. This was particularly true in the UK for the first round of asset purchases where the average yield was around 3 pp above Bank Rate (Figure 7.1).

Third, and in a similar vein, this channel is subject to diminishing returns as previous episodes of QE reduce term premia without lowering the policy rate, compressing the fiscal gain of moving from one form of funding to another. This can again be seen in the UK data where the spread for later QE programmes fell from over 3 pp to less than 2 pp for bonds purchased as part of QE2 and QE3, around 1 pp for bonds bought in QE4 and almost nothing for bonds bought in 2020 as part of the most recent QE programme.

Fourth is a point particularly pertinent for QT. At the point monetary policy needs to tighten, if the central bank tightens through raising the policy rate before it unwinds the portfolio of gilts held, this will reduce the benefits of the interest differential channel further. In the extreme, if the policy rate increases to above the average yield of the bond portfolio, the interest rate differential channel can actually reverse and act as a fiscal drag.

Finally, as with the debt-sensitivity point, the wider elements of the interest differential channel mean that it is complementary to the objectives of monetary policy, tightening the fiscal budget constraint at the point monetary policy wants to tighten and dampen demand and loosening it at the point the central bank wants to stimulate the economy.

All of the features previously described can be seen in the UK data. Between 2009 and 2022, the APF had received £175 bn in interest on its assets and paid £22 bn in interest on the reserves issued to finance those assets. This amounted to a fiscal boon of £153 bn for the public sector as a whole from the interest differential channel, more than 7% of nominal GDP, or 0.5% per year.[7] Since interest rates began rising in 2021–2022, this pattern has slowed and then reversed. The Office for Budget Responsibility now forecast that the net interest rate differential

[7] The cash transfers to HM Treasury were less than this (£126 bn) due to costs of administration and reinvesting the principals from maturing assets at higher prices.

will add around £5 bn to the government's fiscal cost each year until at least 2031 (OBR 2026).

7.3.3 The Profit and Loss Channel

As with any other portfolio of assets, the APF will make a profit or a loss. In the case of the UK, the indemnity agreed with the government means that these losses are borne by the government, and so have a direct fiscal consequence. The original motivation for the indemnity was to remove considerations of any eventual losses from the decision-making process of the MPC, allowing it to focus on setting monetary policy in pursuit of the inflation-targeting objective. However, as QT has begun and losses have crystallised, this fiscal drag has created a tension between a fiscal policy that is already constrained by high levels of debt and a requirement for substantial flows from the government to the central bank, coming at the expense of other spending, or lower taxation or borrowing.[8]

Looking at the individual bonds purchased across QE programmes (Table 7.2), we can see that most were bought at a price above par. In UK fiscal accounting this gap to par adds immediately to the level of public sector net debt, as government bonds are recorded at their par value, but the reserves which are replacing them as the net liability of the public sector vis-à-vis the private sector are recorded at their cash value. This piece of accountancy does not actually affect government issuance of bonds to the market though, until the bond matures and the gap between the price paid and the par value needs to be made good, pushing up the government's cash requirement. If the bond is sold, rather than held to maturity, then the difference between the price paid and the price received is what determines the fiscal impulse, which could be more or less than the gap to par, or even, in theory, positive. However, the nature of QE means that bonds are often bought when rates are low and prices high and then sold when rates have risen and

[8] This tension has been reduced somewhat by the recent changes to the fiscal rules in the October 2024 Budget. Prior to this, the fiscal rule based on Public Sector Net Debt excluding the Bank of England meant that losses reduced space against the fiscal rule by adding to debt. However, the metric now used in the fiscal rule, Public Sector Net Financial Liabilities, is not affect so directly by APF losses, although they do still affect the extent of gilt issuance as cash needs to be raised in the market to make the payment.

Table 7.2 ***Profit and loss position of QE programmes if held to maturity.***

	Proceeds amount purchased (£bn)	Par value of purchases (£bn)	Gross return to maturity (£bn)	Net return to maturity (£bn)
QE1	200	178	90	29
QE2	125	106	45	-2
QE3	50	42	8	-7
QE4	60	49	–	-18
QE5	440	387	-5	-160

Note: Net return assumes the loan from the APF continues to pay Bank Rate and that this averages 2% over the life of the portfolio as it matures. Source: Bank of England, author's calculations.

prices fallen. This has led to some to question whether QE programmes will inherently make a loss and therefore the profit and loss channel will always amount to a fiscal cost.

To test this, we again build on the work of Chadha and Meaning (2013) and look at the individual gilts purchased and held in the APF, separating them by QE programme. In each case, the ratio of the proceeds (cash amount paid) and par value of the bonds purchased is greater than one. Using an assumption that the bonds are held to maturity and the coupon flows retained shows that the gross return on four out of the five QE programmes in the UK would have been positive. However, taking into account the fact that the APF has a variable rate loan to pay to the Bank of England, which is aligned to Bank Rate as the rate of interest paid on reserve balances, and assuming simplistically that the average of Bank rate over the life of the portfolio is 2%, we can see that only the bonds bought under QE1 would have turned a profit, with the first four QE programmes collectively broadly breaking even. However, the final programme, begun in 2020, would have made a considerable loss given the prices paid and the associated coupon flows, if held to maturity. This shows that there is not an inherent reason that QE programmes must lose money. However, the reasons for the increasingly large losses in progressive programmes speaks to one of the features mentioned earlier in this chapter: the diminishing returns of interest rate differentials. The bonds bought under QE1 were purchased at a higher spread and had higher coupon payments as term premia had not, at that point been compressed. The central bank was therefore able to collect this term premium and, for a given path of the policy rate, these bonds would yield a higher return. Later programmes had less of a term premium to extract. Put another way, the average yield on the APF portfolio is around 2%. This would imply that, if Bank Rate averaged 2% over the portfolio's lifetime, then average loss would be simply the difference between the par and proceeds values, with coupons covering the interest on reserves cost. However, the average yield on bonds bought under QE1, given the term premia at the time of purchase, was significantly higher than 2%, and the average yield on bonds bought in 2020 was significantly lower.

The exercise above neglects two key elements. First, the assumption that the APF bond portfolio will be held to maturity is unrealistic. We have already seen active selling of bonds by the Bank of England amounting to around £100 bn in the original proceeds terms. Selling of bonds means that a view on the future profit and loss of the APF is a function of assumptions on, among other things, the pace of sales and the future path of bond prices. However, the Bank of England's own analysis suggests that, under plausible assumptions, the ultimate net position of the APF could be losses of between £55 and £115 bn, which is between 2–4% of GDP (Bank of England 2026). Second, the dynamic profile means that, even for a given final profit and loss position, losses will crystallise in a way that is dependent on the path of sales. The Office for Budget Responsibility quantifies the flows from HM Treasury to the Bank of England to average around £20 bn per year over the next five years. This is around 0.7% of GDP and, if the same amount of fiscal money were used to fund investment or spending, this could boost economic growth by around 0.3–0.7%, based on the fiscal dynamics from a large-scale semi-structural model (Carreras et al. 2016) and multipliers used by the OBR itself (OBR 2020). For further context, this amounts to roughly the same amount spent each year on the entire mental health services budget in the UK.

Any eventual fiscal cost must be weighed against the benefits of the policy. A simple heuristic can be derived using the estimates of the impact of QE on GDP from the meta-study of Fabo and colleagues (2021). They find a mean peak impact of QE on to the level of real GDP of 0.12% for each 1% of GDP spent for the UK specifically and 0.24%

across the wider, international sample of estimates. This diminishes by around half when calculating the cumulative impact over a longer horizon. The cumulative increases in QE at its peak in the UK amounted to around one-third of GDP, and so the implied cumulative impact would be between 1.7% and 4.6% of GDP. Not only is such a boost likely to be welfare-enhancing if it helps stabilise the economy in a downturn, but it will also lead to increased tax revenues, which reduces the fiscal cost it is weighed against (Adrian et al. 2024).

7.4 Implications for Sequencing of QT and Interest Rate Normalisation

A number of papers have looked at the optimal sequencing of unwinding asset purchase programmes and normalising policy rates. Harrison (2024) uses a structural general equilibrium model in which optimal policy implies beginning to unwind the asset portfolio before raising the policy rate, a result also found by Benigno and Benigno (2022) in a model whose dynamics centre on liquidity provision. Conversely, Cantore and Meichtry (2024) find the opposite result in a model that implicitly has a cost of being at the effective lower bound, and so points to raising the policy rate before unwinding the asset portfolio (which would prolong the time spent at the ELB). Our insights into the fiscal channels of QT can add to this debate. Both the interest differential channel and the profit and loss channel create a greater fiscal drag if QT begins after the policy rate has begun to be increased. This is because the spread between the return on the bond portfolio and the policy rate is reduced, or even reversed in the former case, and because the losses on bonds sold is higher in the latter case.

7.5 International Comparisons and an Alternative Framework

The UK's institutional framework is not the only way to have approached the monetary–fiscal interaction inherent in large-scale purchases of government debt by the central bank. In the United States, the Federal Reserve purchased bonds via the System Open Market Account (SOMA) portfolio, managed by the Federal Reserve Bank of New York (FRBNY), which amounts to holding them directly on the Fed's balance sheet. Like the Bank of England, the Federal Reserve transfers excess returns on its portfolio to the federal government, in the form of remittances. These peaked at $116 bn in 2016 as the interest differential channel was at its strongest. However, unlike the Bank of England, the Federal Reserve treats losses on its QE portfolio differently. Once losses are crystallised, rather than requiring an immediate fiscal transfer that tightens the fiscal position, the Federal Reserve can register a deferred asset on its balance sheet, a claim on future income from seigniorage, and then not pay remittances until that loss has been covered (Faria-e-Castro and Jordan-Wood 2023). The ECB follows a similar structure, with losses carried forward on the ECB's balance sheet to be offset against future profits (ECB 2024).

For the UK to move to such a system would require three step-changes, as outlined in Islam, Khan and Meaning (2024). The first would be that the APF's holdings of gilts would need to be moved onto the Bank of England's own balance sheet, with the bonds no longer receiving a fiscal indemnity. Given the Bank of England is likely to want to back some portion of future steady-state reserves with outright holdings of gilts, then this transfer could serve a double purpose, with the Bank of England being able to generate gilt holdings to back steady-state reserve balances and unwinding the APF without having to simultaneously buy bonds from the market for one purpose and sell bonds to the market for the other. As outlined by Bailey (2024) and Saporta (2024), a large part of the future steady-state of reserves is likely to be met by lending facilities, rather than outright gilt holdings, but even in this world there remains significant scope for a transfer from the APF.

The second step is that the Bank of England would need to change its institutional arrangements such that it could retain seigniorage, in the same way that the Federal Reserve and the ECB can. This would give it a future income stream to draw on which it could then use to allow the final piece of the puzzle: covering losses with a deferred asset.

What impact would this have on the fiscal channels of QE and QT? The standard direct yield channel would not be affected. The privately held supply of gilts would still evolve in the same way and therefore the impact on yields would be the same. However, both the interest differential channel and the profit and loss channel would be nullified, or at least significantly reduced. Starting from a phase of the economic cycle when the interest differential is acting as a headwind, the Bank of England would build up a larger deferred asset, rather than making a claim on the fiscal authority, freeing up fiscal space. When the differential returned to positive, this would be used to pay down the deferred asset, rather than as a fiscal boon to the Treasury. Positive term premia suggest that, over a long horizon, the interest differential should be positive on average, as more traditionally thought of with seigniorage income, and this will help with the change to the profit and loss channel. In the updated arrangement, rather than losses being an immediate fiscal cost, tightening the budget constraint at the point asset sales occur, the losses would be borne by the central bank and spread over a much longer time horizon. The government would lose the fiscal space it had previously earned through transferred seigniorage income but this would be a smaller loss each year than the current larger payments as bonds are sold or mature in a lumpy fashion. The spread of the ten-year government bond rate averaged 0.3 pp in the fifteen years before the global financial crisis in 2008. A return to this spread, on a steady-state holding of bonds of around £300 bn would provide seigniorage of just under £1 bn per year. This makes one risk of the proposal above apparent: whether the required timeframe would be sufficiently long that the deferred asset is never paid down, or could even be explosive in some states of the world. That will ultimately be determined by the average spread of government bond rates over the policy rate, term premia. The larger the term premia the central bank can extract, the less likely an unsustainable dynamic is.

Taken together, Islam, Khan and Meaning (2024) show that these changes could save the Exchequer around £20 bn per year over the next five years, although ultimately these costs are not eradicated, but rather spread out over a much longer horizon through forgone seigniorage transfers, as described previously.

7.6 Conclusions

Large-scale purchases of government bonds by central banks have brought the interactions of monetary and fiscal policy into focus. Most modelling of these interactions has looked at how QE and QT affect government bond yields narrowly. This chapter expands that view to encompass two more channels through which QE and QT have fiscal consequences and show that all three channels have had economically significant impacts on the UK's fiscal position since 2009. We think it is crucial that both policymakers and academic modelling take account of these channels in order to fully assess the impact of these policies, so they can be calibrated appropriately. Lastly, an alternative to the UK's institutional framework around QE/QT could have the effect of reducing the impact of these additional channels, and with that, reducing some of the conflicts currently facing policy in the UK.

References

Adrian, T., Erceg, C., Kolasa, M. and Linde, J., 2024. *Macroeconomic and fiscal consequences of quantitative easing*. Mimeo.

Allen, W., Chadha, J. S. and Turner, P., 2021. *Quantitative tightening: protecting monetary policy from fiscal encroachment*. National Institute Economic Review, 1–8.

Bailey, A., 2024. The importance of central bank reserves. Lecture in honour of Charles Goodhart, London School of Economics, May 2024.

Bank of England, 2026. *Asset Purchase Facility Quarterly Report – 2025 Q4*.

Benigno, G. and Benigno, P., 2022. *Managing monetary policy normalization*. Federal Reserve Bank of New York Staff Report 1,015.

Bernanke, B., 2020. 'The New Tools of Monetary Policy'. *American Economic Review*, 110(4), 943–83.

Bhattarai, S., Eggertsson, G. and Gafarov, B., 2022. 'Time consistency and duration of government debt: a model of quantitative easing'. *The Review of Economic Studies*, 90(4), 1759–99.

Busetto, F., Chavaz, M., Froemel, M., Joyce, M., Kaminska, I. and Worlidge, J., 2022. QE at the Bank of England: a perspective on its functioning and effectiveness. Bank of England Quarterly Bulletin, 1.

Cantore, C. and Meichtry, A., 2024. *Unwinding quantitative easing: state dependency and household heterogeneity*. Bank of England Staff Working Paper 1,030.

Carreras, O., Kirby, S., Liadze, I. and Piggott, R., 2016. *Quantifying fiscal multipliers*. NIESR Discussion Paper No. 469.

Chadha, J. S. and Meaning, J., 2013. *The direct fiscal boon from QE*. Written evidence to the Treasury Select Committee.

Dolan, P., Horn, T., Kant, S. and Phillips, R., 2022. *Box D: cash flow arrangements between the APF and HM Treasury*. Bank of England Quarterly Bulletin, 1.

Du, W., Forbes, K. and Luzzetti, M., 2024. *Quantitative tightening around the globe: what have we learned?* NBER Working Paper 32321.

European Central Bank, 2024. *Annual consolidated balance sheet of the Eurosystem*. Annual accounts.

Fabo, B., Jancokova, M., Kempf, E. and Pastor, L., 2021. 'Fifty shades of QE: comparing findings of central bankers and academics'. *Journal of Monetary Economics*, 120, May.

Faria-e-Castro, M. and Jordan-Wood, R., 2023. The Fed's remittances to the Treasury: explaining the 'deferred asset'. Federal Reserve Bank of St. Louis blog, November.

Giese, J., Joyce, M., Meaning, J. and Worlidge, J., 2024. 'Do preferred habitat investors exist? Evidence from the UK government bond market'. *Economic Letters*, 234(C).

Harison, R., 2024. Optimal quantitative easing and tightening. Bank of England Staff Working Paper 1,063.

Islam, M., Khan, A. and Meaning, J., 2024. APF shift: Reducing the fiscal burden of QE without tiering. Barclays UK Themes, July.

Modigliani, F. and Sutch, R., 1966. 'Innovations in interest rate policy'. *American Economic Review*, 56(1/2), 178–97.

Office for Budget Responsibility(OBR), 2020. *Box 2.1: t*he impact of fiscal policy on GDP growth and unemployment. Economic and Fiscal Outlook, November.

Office for Budget Responsibility(OBR), 2021. Box 4.1: Debt maturity, quantitative easing and interest rate sensitivity. Economic and Fiscal Outlook, March.

Office for Budget Responsibility(OBR), 2026. Economic and Fiscal Outlook, March.

Ramsden, D., 2023. *Quantitative tightening: The story so far*. Speech given at the Money, Macro and Finance Society, July.

Saporta, V., 2024. Let's get ready to repo! Speech given at the Association for Financial Markets in Europe (AFME), London, July.

Tobin, J., 1969. 'A general equilibrium approach to monetary theory'. *Journal of Money, Credit and Banking*, 1(1), 1529.

Vayanos, D. and Vila, J.-L., 2021. 'A preferred-habitat model of the term structure of interest rates'. *Econometrica*, 89(1), 77112.

8 The Parable of the Fiscal-Military State

The Napoleonic Bank of England

JAGJIT CHADHA

8.1 Alea Iacta Est

From around the seventeenth century, central 'bank-like' institutions started being born (Bordo, 2007 and Capie et al. 1991).[1] The Swedish Riksbank was established in 1668 as a joint stock bank and was chartered to lend the government funds. Shortly afterwards, the Bank of England was founded as a joint stock company to purchase government debt. Later Europeans cottoned on that these 'new-fangled beasts' could help with financial crises. The Banque de France, 1800, was established by Napoleon to stabilise the currency after the 1790s hyperinflation of paper money during the French Revolution, as well as to support the provision of finance. Such central banks issued private notes, which served as currency, and typically had a monopoly over note issue. And in the Bank of England's case, it also held a geographical monopoly.

British public debt rose rapidly during the Revolutionary and Napoleonic wars, ultimately to a level, in terms of national output, which remains the highest in British history. In this chapter we outline, using data from Parliamentary Papers, the extent to which the Bank of England bought government liabilities and expanded its balance sheet (in particular by buying government bonds, Exchequer Bills and other assets, such as East India bonds; see Barker et al. 2017). We interpret the operations according to contemporary practice of central bank bond purchases and relate that to the impact on the public balance sheet to and beyond Waterloo. Throughout the eighteenth century, the Bank of England operated as 'an engine of the state' by providing

[1] For this chapter, I am grateful for conversations with and comments from Francis Breedon, Elisa Newby, Patrick O'Brien, Issam Samiri and Ryland Thomas. I acknowledge funding from the British Academy/Leverhulme Grant SG150907.

finance during wartime. These extra resources formed a critical part of wartime strategy and supported a sequence of martial and maritime victories. The main reason for Napoleonic balance sheet operation was to provide extra fiscal resources. Our contemporary commentary on QE has largely avoided that explanation, focussing on QE as a monetary intervention. This is odd given the original rationale for central banks. It is like ignoring the basic rules of the game.

The heady mix of public debt, war and monetary policy has been of repeated interest to economists who have systematically worried about the loss of price and fiscal stability (Chabot and Herman, 2014). And at a deeper level, economists worry whether economic policy will become dominated by political will. What appears to be the early deployment of monetary-fiscal interventions did not have an inflationary objective; they did not seek to signal looser monetary policy nor provide subsidies to bond holders. Simply put, central bank loans allowed the government to bring forward the deployment of resources, Indeed, Dickson (1967) (see also Evans, 2024) argued that providing such resources were the primary *raison d'être* of eighteenth- and nineteenth-century central banks. Zooming to today, since around 2009/10, the British state has increased public indebtedness by some £2 trillion, of which the Bank of England has bought some 30%. We shall compare this to the Bank's purchases of public indebtedness we find in the Napoleonic period. Contemporary officials have though been very careful to state that recent purchases following the financial crisis were in no way designed to support fiscal policy and were primarily part of the monetary policy strategy.

The annual Parliamentary Papers (Figure 8.1), give us the value of central bank purchases in and around the Revolutionary and Napoleonic Wars. Indeed, Britain had just lost the American wars of Independence in 1783, at which point the Bank of England held £22.4 million of public debt. The Revolutionary Wars posed an existential threat from the start, in April 1792. As a result, debt held rose quickly to around £30 million. So, it is no surprise to note that, by the time the Revolutionary Wars ended in April 1802, public debt held had risen to over £40 million. There was a short hiatus during the Peace of Amiens in 1802. But the Napoleonic Wars kicked off in 1803 and ran to Waterloo's 1815 conclusion. By which time the Bank held well over £60 million and by its peak, a year or so later, over £80 million. Shortly thereafter, the value of public debt held fell rapidly.

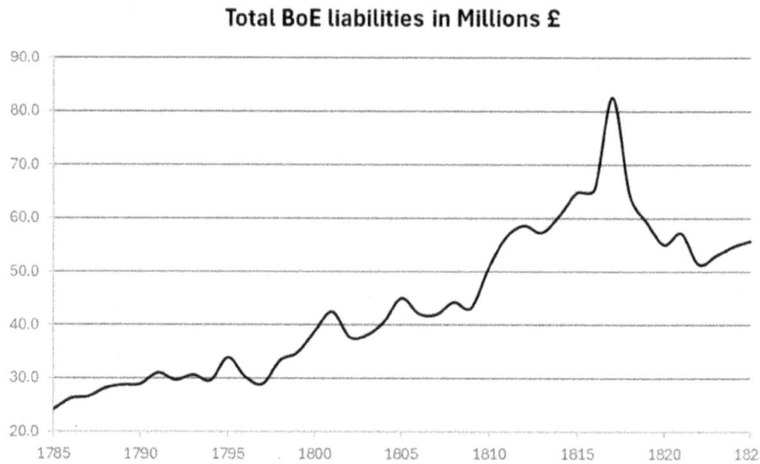

Figure 8.1 Total BoE liabilities in million £.
Source: Bank of England (1967) and Bank of England Millennium Database.

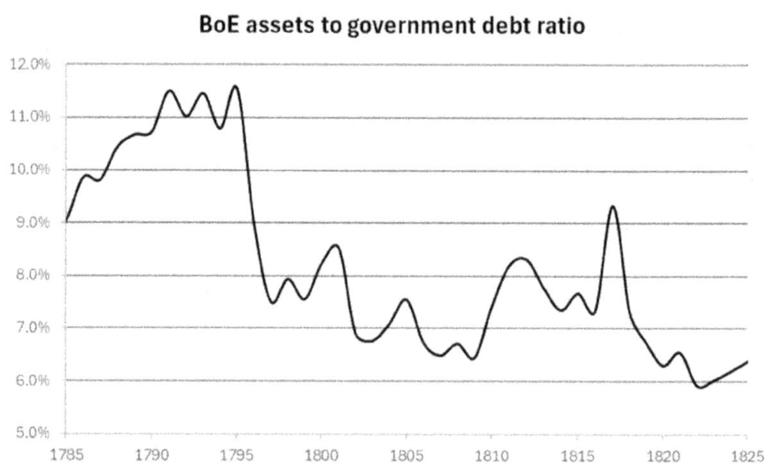

Figure 8.2 BoE assets to government debt ratio.
Source: Bank of England (1967) and Bank of England Millennium Database.

In Figure 8.2, we note that the fraction of public debt held by the Bank of England at the end of the American wars was higher than at the start of the French Revolutionary and Napoleonic wars, at around 11% of public debt. At these wars ended, the fraction stood at around

7%. Indeed, even though volatile, that was approximately where we found ourselves in 1815, with a peak of 9%. While the eighteenth-century peak of some 10% is far below today's peak of 30%, we do now have a broad-based democracy with a significantly greater elasticity of spending in response to shocks and hence, to public debt. And given the so-called separation of powers between monetary policy and fiscal obligations, should we not be surprised by the scale of fiscal support under a regime of central bank independence?

Before firming up our view, from for example Figure 8.3, on the Bank, let us examine two other exhibits. Rather than fiscal resources (see Figure 8.4), it has often been argued that the Bank of England was providing inflationary finance with an expansion of its liabilities. Technically, it was thought that a gold standard simply could not allow an increase in the value of Bank liabilities, as they were limited by the stock of monetary gold and its domestic price. And this was the norm. But in February 1797, the quantity of domestic monetary gold, as a result on an internal drain – what we might call a shock to the demand for gold in exchange for Sterling – started to dwindle and the gold standard was left. But we can also note that the Bank of England did not follow the gold standard 'rule', which implied fixing paper

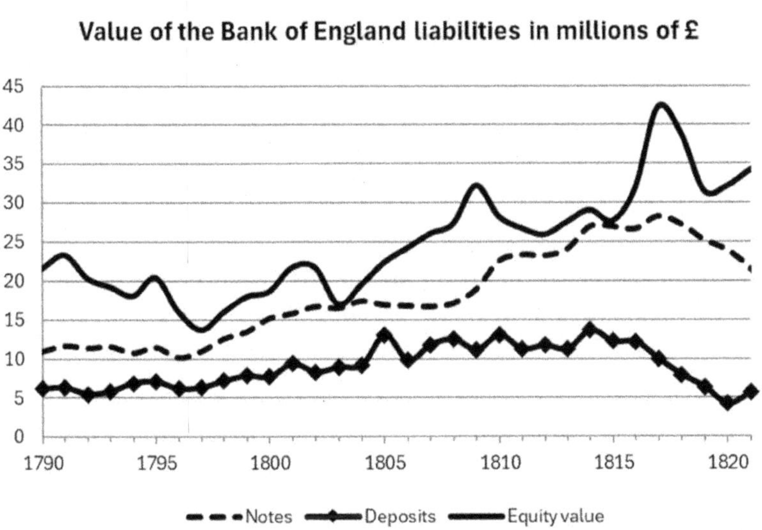

Figure 8.3 Value of the Bank of England liabilities in million £.
Source: Chadha and Newby (2013).

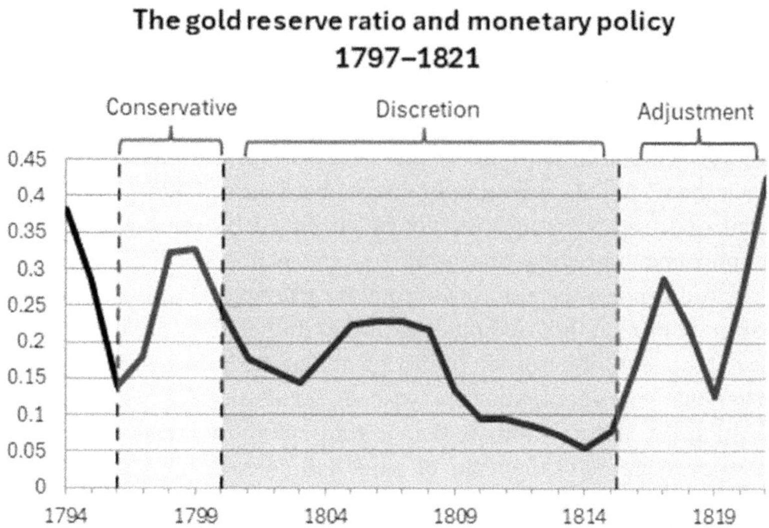

Figure 8.4 The gold reserve ratio and monetary policy 1797–1821.
Notes: Ratio of the Bank's unfunded debt holdings to the total unfunded debt, Gayer et al. (1953), tables 157 and 231.

liabilities as a constant multiple of monetary gold, and actually swayed with economic and market conditions, as Figure 8.4 shows.

Many have argued, for example Ricardo, that this gave the Bank of England an incentive to behave in an irresponsible manner with monetary issuance during the suspension period, which ran from 1797 to 1821. He was particularly concerned with the fall in the exchange rate on the Hamburg exchange and the premium (agio) on the gold prices. And thus triggered a notable debate between the Bullionists, who held this view, and those who thought the Bank acted responsibly, temporarily, to maintain economic stability in the face, for example, of bad harvests and trade shocks (see Report, 1810, Ricardo, 1810, and Thornton, 1802). There were other complications, as the Bank of England did not control the money supply. The total monetary stock comprised liabilities formed the base of a variable pyramid for an increasing yet known number of private Country Banks, servicing the ongoing industrial revolution around the country (Silberling, 1924). We thus cannot be sure but if the Bank had wanted to 'debase' the currency it did not have any instrument to do so. Finally, the stock of Bank of England notes seemed to move in line with the demands of industry, in what was called the Real Bill Doctrine, and we do not observe any attempt to increase leverage by expanding the means of payment beyond measures of output (Chadha and Newby, 2013, and O'Brien and Palma, 2023).

8.2 In Sum

Let us examine a final analysis in Figure 8.5. Despite a huge increase in this period of some of 80 percentage points in the price level, prior to Waterloo. By around 1820 the price level was back to where it started. We can comfortably argue that this formed a remarkable piece of price stability. The evolution of the Bank of England monetary gold stock depicts the same pattern, with a large temporary rise, albeit with a nominal peak of some 40%. The exchange rate with Hamburg sends the same message (see Figure 8.5). The price level is falling by 1820 and does eventually get back to its initial level. But the likely cause of delay is the post slump in the British economy, which led to slower

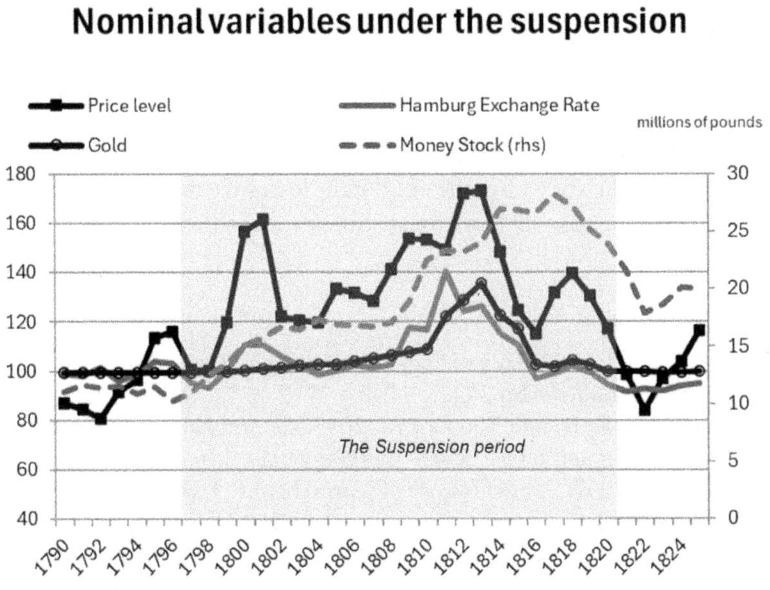

Figure 8.5 Nominal variables under the suspension.
Source: Chadha and Newby (2013) and Gayer, Rostow and Schwartz (1953).

adjustment in the price level (Chadha and Perlman, 2014), possibly implying a state contingent change in inflation-output preferences outlined in Figure 8.4.

8.3 Concluding Remarks

It is ironic that the original impetus in establishing the first government-sponsored banks in Europe, the Riksbank in 1668 and the Bank of England in 1694, was exactly for governments to obtain financial benefits. And despite three centuries of developing the functions of central banking, asset purchase programmes seem to be harking directly back to these base origins. The proximate given reason for the modern spate of central bank bond purchases emanates from the wish to offset the impact of the zero, or effective, lower bound for policy rates after the global financial crisis. The immediate asset purchase response, after the financial crisis, involved an attempt to stabilise falling bond prices as an increased issuance of public debt fuelled concerns about underlying advanced country sovereign risk. And these early operations turned out to be profitable at first, as bonds were bought at a low price and the support scheme drove prices higher. The monetary intervention thus had a positive fiscal implication and led to the remittance of profits to fiscal authorities. Perhaps unsurprisingly, given the size and duration of the operations, fiscal authorities, also known as our political leaders, were quick learners, and the purchases seem to have become once again an 'engine of the state'. But the exorbitant losses we now see on central bank balance sheets will leave fiscal scars for a generation,

References

Bank of England, 1967. Bank of England liabilities and assets 1696 onwards. *Quarterly Bulletin 1967 Q2.*

Barker, J., Bholat, D. and Thomas, R., 2017. Central bank balance sheets: past, present and future. *SSRN Working Paper.*

Bordo, M. D., 2007. 'A brief history of central banks'. Federal Reserve Bank of Cleveland, Economic Commentary 12/1/2007.

Capie, F., Goodhart, C. and Schnadt, N., 1991. The development of central banking in Capie, F., Fischer, S., Goodhart, C. and Schnadt, N. (eds), *The future of central banking: the tercentenary symposium of the Bank of England.* Cambridge: Cambridge University Press,

Chabot, B. R. and Herman, G., 2014. A history of large-scale asset purchases before the Federal Reserve. *Economic Perspectives*, *37*(4).

Chadha, J. S. and Newby, E., 2013. 'Midas, transmuting all, into paper': the Bank of England and the Banque de France during the Napoleonic Wars, CWPE1330

Chadha, J. S. and Perlman, M., 2014. Was the Gibson Paradox for real? A Wicksellian study of the relationship between interest rates and prices. *Financial History Review*, 21, pp.139–163.

Dickson, P. G. M., 1967. *The financial revolution in England: a study in the development of public credit 1688–1756*. London: Macmillan.

Evans, R. J. W., 2024. Peter Dickson. *Biographical Memoirs of Fellows of the British Academy*, 21, pp.541–571.

Gayer, A. D, Rostow, W. W. and A. J. Schwartz, 1953. *The growth and fluctuation of the British economy, 1790–1850*. Oxford: Clarendon Press.

O'Brien, P. K. and Palma, N., 2023. Not an ordinary bank but a great engine of state: the Bank of England and the British economy, 1694–1844. *The Economic History Review*, *76*(1), pp.305–329.

Officer, L. H., 2006. Purchasing power parity: from ancient times to World War II. *Economic History Services, EH.*

Report, further with, minutes of evidence and accounts, from the select committee on The High Price of Billion, (1810), The Bullion Report.

Ricardo, D., 1810. *The high price of bullion: a proof of the depreciation of bank notes*. London: John Murray.

Silberling, N. J., 1924. Financial and monetary policy of Great Britain during the Napoleonic Wars. *The Quarterly Journal of Economics*, *38*(3), pp.397–439.

Thornton, H. (1802). *An enquiry into the nature and effects of the paper credit of Great Britain*. London: J. Hatchard.

9 Post-crisis Monetary Policy in Britain and Its Governance

WILLIAM ALLEN

9.1 Introduction

This chapter examines British monetary policy in the period since the financial crisis and describes how quantitative easing was adopted as the main policy instrument.[1] It shows that many important issues were addressed not by the Monetary Policy Committee (MPC) of the Bank of England, which was set up by the statute which gave the Bank autonomy in monetary policy, but by the executive managers of the Bank of England. It also discusses accountability for the probably huge budgetary costs of the QE programme.

9.2 The Bank of England before the Financial Crisis

After the general decline of inflation in the 1980s, a new model of central banking emerged. The new model central bank was publicly owned, and its leading executives were appointed by the government, but it could act independently in managing monetary policy in pursuit of price stability. This model, born in New Zealand, was embodied in the Bank of England Act 1998. The Bank of England at that time carried out a number of functions which were regarded as largely separate.

[1] This chapter owes a great deal to discussions at NIESR events: the symposium on 'The MPC at 25' held on 30 March 2022, the QE to QT Workshop on 30 September 2022 and the workshop on central banking on 16 February 2024. I am indebted for useful conversations to Dylan Cassar, Jennifer Castle, Jagjit Chadha, Martin Ellison, Stephen Millard, Richhild Moessner, Duncan Needham, Bill Nelson, the late Philip Turner, Anders Vredin, Bill White and Tim Young, and for an enlightening discussion of Australia's experience with yield curve control to Andrew Gaffney. I am particularly grateful to Francis Breedon, Paula Bejarano Carbo, Dylan Cassar and Tim Young for helpful and stimulating comments on earlier versions of the chapter, and to Richhild Moessner for fruitful collaborations on earlier related papers. None of these people are to blame for errors of fact or interpretation in the chapter.

Of these functions, it was monetary policy which captured the most resources. Its overriding objective of price stability was, and is, defined by an inflation target determined annually by the government. The main instrument was the level of short-term interest rates; intervention in foreign exchange markets was allowed but rarely if ever used. The central bank determined short-term interest rates in the money market by supplying or withdrawing cash, in the form of deposits in the central bank, using primarily open-market operations in government security repos. The MPC decided the level of short-term interest rates independently of the government: a Treasury representative attended the relevant meetings but could not vote. The minutes of the meetings are published, so that the reasons for the decisions can be made clear.

Financial stability was, and is, the central bank's other main responsibility. It is less clearly defined than monetary stability, there being no quantified objectives analogous to inflation targets. However, the objectives clearly include the avoidance if possible and management if necessary of financial crises, and the available policy instruments for crisis management include the power to lend against good collateral.

Government debt management has been prominent in the history of central banking. However, in the 1980s and 1990s, it became possible for governments to finance themselves without the close collaboration of their central banks. This reflected both the liberalisation of financial markets, and the reduction of tail risks in government securities, owing to the recognition by governments of the merits of financial prudence and the prospect of enduring peace after the end of the Cold War. In the UK, the Treasury set up a Debt Management Office (DMO) in 1998, which took over the function of debt management from the Bank of England.

The global financial crisis demonstrated that the earlier arrangements for maintaining financial stability had been inadequate. Commercial and investment banks, many of which were too big to fail, had been managed recklessly, notwithstanding official supervision. This had made the financial system unstable. The latent instability had not been much noticed by central banks or governments and had not been addressed. The Bank of England, concerned about the moral hazard of lending even to a bank which was thought to be solvent, failed to act as lender of last resort to Northern Rock until a panic had developed and turned into a bank run, thereby provoking general uncertainty about central banks' intentions.[2] It thus failed to protect financial stability.[3]

The crisis exposed a glaring weakness in the financial system that could not be left unattended. Consequently, bank regulation and supervision became much more intensive and intrusive.

9.3 Monetary Policy during and after the Financial Crisis

9.3.1 How QE Was Negotiated

The Bank of England MPC cut Bank rate from 5% to 4.5% on 8 October 2008, at a special meeting, as part of an internationally co-ordinated interest rate reduction after the Lehman failure the previous month. It cut further in stages, reaching 1% on 5 February 2009.[4]

It was clear that monetary policy might need to be eased even after short-term interest rates could be cut no further. Early in 2009, the Bank of England and the Treasury had discussed the possibility of an asset purchase programme as a means of improving the availability of corporate credit, and on 19 January 2009, the Chancellor announced to Parliament a scheme for the Bank of England to buy privately issued securities. He said that 'the Bank of England will ensure that the total amount of money in the economy does not increase'.[5] The latter statement meant that the asset purchases were to be financed by the issue of Treasury bills, or by other operations by the DMO. The Bank of England Asset Purchase Facility Fund Ltd (APF), a subsidiary company of the Bank of England which was set up for this purpose, accordingly bought about £1 billion of commercial paper in

[2] The official press release of 14 September 2007 said that the Financial Services Authority 'judges that Northern Rock is solvent, exceeds its regulatory capital requirement and has a good quality loan book' (HM Treasury, Bank of England and Financial Services Authority 2007).

[3] Darling (2011, ch. 1). James (2020, p. 451) suggests delicately that if the Bank of England had not been independent, 'it is conceivable that the Treasury might have handled the initial response to the global financial crisis in 2007 more skilfully than the Bank, and in particular pressed the Bank to undertake the extensive liquidity provision undertaken by both the Fed and the ECB'.

[4] In 2007, Martin Feldstein criticised the Federal Reserve, and by implication other central banks also, for failing to cut interest rates promptly when credit markets were drying up (Feldstein 2007).

[5] Hansard, vol. 486 part 15, cols 483–486, 19 January 2009, Bank of England (2009b).

February–March 2009.[6] The Treasury agreed to indemnify the APF against financial losses; equally it was to benefit from profits. The Bank thus had 'no economic interest' in the APF.[7] Operations were to be subject to the Treasury's approval.

The Bank of England executive managers had it in mind that the APF could subsequently be used to buy gilts in exchange for central bank money, for monetary policy purposes, and the Chancellor had mentioned this in his January statement to Parliament.[8] In an important and fascinating paper based on interviews with people who had been involved at the Bank of England, Cassar (2023) describes how the MPC finally decided to implement monetary policy using this form of quantitative easing.[9] The Bank staff had been asked to devise possible new ways of easing monetary policy, and identified various possibilities, including, for example, official forward guidance about future short-term interest rates. In the end, however, the only option presented to the MPC was purchases of government securities in exchange for reserve balances in the Bank of England (some privately issued securities were also eligible for purchase).[10] The MPC agreed at its February 2009 meeting to ask for the Treasury's agreement to purchases of government and other securities. The mention of other securities suggests that some MPC members thought that the purchases should include privately issued assets, though no debate is recorded in the minutes.[11] The Chancellor consented to asset purchases of £150 billion, up to £50 billion of which could be private sector assets.[12]

The effectiveness of gilt purchases depended on the co-operation of the DMO, and the Chancellor concurred when he wrote in his letter to the Governor of 3 March 2009, 'I recognise the importance of ensuring

6 Source: Bank of England interactive database, variable YWWB98O.

7 Bean (2009). The indemnity is described in the Asset Purchase Facility Annual Reports (e.g. Bank of England 2021a), though it has not been published.

8 Hansard, vol. 486 part 15, cols 483–486, 19 January 2009, Letter from Governor to Chancellor, 29 January 2009.

9 Cassar had eighteen interviews which 'include interviews with current or former Bank of England personnel who occupied key positions and were directly or indirectly involved in monetary policymaking. This includes eleven interviews (including two repeat interviews) with seven former members of the MPC . . . and two former members of the top-level Executive team (made up of a Governor and two Deputy Governors prior to the 2012 and 2014 restructuring)'. There were an additional seven interviews involving six former Bank economist staff.

10 Cassar (2023, p. 12). 11 Bank of England (2009a, paragraphs 36–39).

12 Bank of England (2009a, paragraph 39), Darling (2009).

that debt management policy is consistent with the aims of monetary policy'.[13] This statement meant that the objectives of debt management policy, namely 'minimising [the government's] financing cost over the long-term taking account of risk', were subordinated to the objectives of monetary policy.[14]

At its March 2009 meeting, the MPC eased policy further. It cut Bank rate to 0.5%, and, wishing to go further than that, agreed to an initial purchase of up to £75 billion of assets on the newly agreed basis.[15] The minutes record that 'The Committee noted that, in so far as purchases of private sector assets fell short of the £75 billion target, the Bank of England would buy gilts to fulfil the overall quantity of purchases'.[16] The use of the word 'noted' implies that this decision was taken not by the MPC but by the Bank executives. In practice, nearly all of the Bank's bond purchases during the ensuing dozen years were of government securities. There was some dissent about asset choice: MPC member Adam Posen argued powerfully in a speech in October 2009 that gilts-only QE was too narrowly focused to meet the needs of the moment, and one former MPC member later described the gilts-only policy as 'purist'.[17]

Cassar (2023, p. 12) interprets the design of the asset purchase programme as an assertion of monetarism over the previously dominant new Keynesian model. Certainly some of the Bank's rhetoric emphasised money supply.[18] However, the nature of the assets purchased by the Bank of England did not determine the effect on the money supply: purchases of government securities would affect the money aggregates no more powerfully than purchases of, or loans against, privately issued debts; and other central banks, notably the Fed and the European Central Bank, bought large amounts of privately issued assets in their QE programmes.[19]

[13] Darling (2009). [14] Debt Management Office (2005).
[15] Bank of England (2009c, paragraphs 27, 44 and 45).
[16] Bank of England (2009c, paragraph 45).
[17] Posen (2009), private correspondence with Dylan Cassar. [18] See Chapter 4.
[19] In addition, it is by no means obvious that supplying additional reserve balances to the commercial banks would affect broad money any more powerfully than supplying them with additional Treasury bills, as in the original formulation of the programme: both reserve balances and Treasury bills were high-quality liquid assets (HQLA) and they were equally powerful in enabling banks to meet their liquidity requirements. Governor Mervyn King considered reserve balances more liquid than Treasury bills, as he made clear in a letter to the

In preferring government securities to privately issued ones, the executive managers of the Bank adhered to the doctrine promoted by the late Marvin Goodfriend: acquiring private securities would constitute an act of fiscal policy, for which a central bank lacked the necessary legitimacy.[20] Governor Mervyn King also claimed that gilts were 'the only asset available in sufficient quantity such that the Bank can rapidly inject large amounts of money into the economy'.[21] It is true that gilts were available in large amounts, but so were commercial debts, which could be used as collateral for loans.

Successive QE programmes drastically shortened the maturity structure of the public sector's debt. The fixed-interest gilts that the Bank of England bought from the market were replaced by reserve balances of the commercial banks, on which interest was paid at Bank rate. Thus very large interest rate risks were put onto the public sector's balance sheet, contrary to the normal objective of debt management policy.[22] The risks were the responsibility of the Treasury under the terms of the indemnity that it provided to the Bank, and they were quantified in the notes to the APF's published annual reports (Figure 9.4).[23] Nevertheless, the leading officials of the Bank appear, astonishingly, not to have understood for some time after they initiated QE that there was any interest rate risk to the public sector at all. At a hearing of the House of Commons Treasury Committee in November 2011, Andrea Leadsom MP presciently expressed concern that interest rates would increase and that the QE programme would incur losses. Governor Mervyn King reassured her that 'if the central government had the same accounting conventions as the asset purchase fund, mark to market, you would find . . . that the gain to one would be offset by the loss to another, because what is an asset to one party is a liability to another'. Ms Leadsom pointed out that 'if I sell you something more cheaply than I bought it from you, you have made a profit and therefore I have to have made a loss', and that 'there is the

Chairman of the House of Commons Treasury Committee dated 27 October 2011.

20 Bean (2009), Goodfriend (2011). 21 King (2011).

22 Office for Budget Responsibility (2021, ch. 4). See also Deutsche Bundesbank (2021) for a perspective from another country. A National Audit Office report of 2023 examined 'how government manages the risks of borrowing' but did not explore QE.

23 The interest rate risk can be measured by calculating the effect of a 1 basis point move in the yield curve on the value of the APF's portfolio. House of Commons Treasury Committee (2024, paragraph 59).

potential for a whacking great loss to the taxpayer', but the Governor could only reply 'Let's just beg to differ on that'.[24]

Decisions about which maturities of gilts should be purchased were both logically related to the purposes of QE and the main determinant of the APF's interest rate risk exposure. However, the MPC's reported discussion of maturity decisions was limited in scope, and included nothing about financial risks. The minutes of the March 2009 meeting record an aversion to buying short gilts, because they were more likely to be held by banks and overseas central banks, so that purchasing them would have less effect on money supply. The Bank initially also avoided very long maturities, so as to avoid disturbing the hedging of liabilities by pension funds.[25] Thus purchases were initially confined to five- to twenty-five-year maturities, but from August 2009, when the size of the programme was increased, the Bank was willing to buy gilts with any maturity longer than three years.[26]

Had the Bank of England instead confined its purchases to gilts that would mature in the period during which it expected to keep short-term interest rates low (or repos maturing in that period), as the Reserve Bank of Australia did during the Covid-19 pandemic, it would have given a much clearer signal of its intentions as regards short-term interest rates, and would have taken much less interest rate risk. Its decision to avoid short gilts was thus a strong expression of monetarist motivation.[27] Purchases of long gilts will have stimulated monetary growth, but they also constituted a bet on interest rate levels well beyond the MPC's time horizon.

The design of the reverse auctions at which the Bank of England bought gilts, which was not discussed by the MPC, was suboptimal, because the Bank's decision on which offers to accept was determined by market prices as observed at the end of the auction, and was exposed to manipulation by the market, which appears to have happened. A small army of commercial dealers made a healthy living buying from the DMO and selling to the Bank of England.[28]

24 Evidence to House of Commons Treasury Committee, 28 November 2011, QQ 56–58. House of Commons Treasury Committee (2012).

25 Bank of England (2009c, paragraph 42).

26 Bank of England (2009d, p. 82, 2009e, p. 168).

27 The Reserve Bank of Australia targeted the yield on a specific short-dated bond for a period. See Reserve Bank of Australia (2022).

28 Breedon and Turner (2016).

The MPC thus decided the amount of quantitative easing but was not a party to other important decisions about market operations.[29] This exclusion seems to have been based on the Bank of England Act 1998, according to which the MPC is responsible for 'formulating monetary policy', while the Court of Directors shall manage the Bank's affairs, other than the formulation of monetary policy, and in particular the risk management policies adopted by the Bank.[30] The Bank of England's executives espoused a very narrow interpretation of the phrase 'formulating monetary policy', confining it to setting the level of short term interest rates and the amount of quantitative easing.[31] A former MPC member interviewed by Cassar said

> [where] ... the MPC says do QE, this amount of QE, then the operationalisation of that is not for the MPC. It's for the Bank. And so then, by definition, the question of whether you bought corporate assets, private assets, mortgage-backed securities, whatever you name, would have become an operational decision, not an MPC decision. For sure the MPC had discussions around the merits of different asset purchase schemes. But that doesn't mean the MPC thought it was going to determine that ... There was a bit of vagueness between whose decision that will be.[32]

Later, in October 2012, a review commissioned by the Bank of England from the distinguished commercial banker Bill Winters of its framework for providing liquidity to the banking system noted that there was 'some lack of clarity over the precise roles of the [MPC and FPC] as regards the Bank's liquidity operations'. It recommended that the Bank, in discussion with the two committees, should set out a framework to establish their roles and responsibilities more clearly, and that the MPC should have an opportunity to give a view on liquidity operations.[33] In 2017, the MPC's powers as regards operations in financial markets were accordingly documented in a 'concordat' agreed between the Bank executives and the MPC, which was revised in June 2018:

[29] In 2008, some MPC members were not even told of the emergency liquidity assistance that was then being provided to Halifax Bank of Scotland and the Royal Bank of Scotland.

[30] Plenderleith (2012, paragraph 225).

[31] It should be noted that the Bank's executive management is not a body defined in statute. In other words, it includes anyone whom the Governor chooses.

[32] Cassar (2023, p. 17). [33] Winters (2012, p. 113).

the MPC has decision-making authority, at the margin, in respect of the deployment of all instruments and facilities that are varied over time with the primary intention of affecting overall monetary conditions in order to achieve the inflation target. At the present juncture [June 2018], that includes variations in Bank Rate, the volume of asset purchases financed by the issue of bank reserves and foreign exchange intervention. In the event that some key parameters of the SMF [Sterling Monetary Framework: the catalogue of market operations that the Bank undertook] are varied with the primary intent of affecting monetary conditions, then their control will pass to the MPC. The MPC will also approve the selection of schemes and structures primarily designed to deliver monetary policy aims.

The MPC has no responsibility in respect of the risk profile of the Bank's balance sheet. That responsibility lies with Court, or as may be delegated by Court to the Governor and the Bank's Executive. For this reason, the MPC does not have sole decision-making authority over changes to the risks on the balance sheet or the key parameters of the SMF determining those risks.[34]

Just as the Bank's executive management reached a 'concordat' with the MPC, so it also reached one with the Financial Policy Committee, which was created in 2013 to manage systemic financial stability risks. The FPC had the right to be informed about, and comment on, the design and operation of the Bank's liquidity insurance facilities, and to be consulted on liquidity insurance operations, if necessary at short notice. However, 'responsibility for the detailed design and delivery of the [liquidity insurance] is vested in the Bank's Executive'.[35]

9.3.2 Bank Liquidity Regulation and Monetary Policy

After the run on Northern Rock in September 2007 and even more after the rescue of Bear Stearns in New York in March 2008, commercial banks found it harder to attract deposits. Their liquid assets were meagre and they were obliged to curtail credit. The Bank of England provided various additional facilities to help them. Thus funds provided through extended collateral long-term repos (ELTRs, introduced in December 2007), which effectively enlarged the range of collateral eligible for the existing long-term repo facility, reached a peak of about £180 billion in January 2009.[36] The Special Liquidity Scheme (SLS),

34 Bank of England (2018a).
35 'The FPC and the Bank's liquidity insurance operations', updated June 2018.
36 Fisher (2009), Winters (2012), Bank of England (2012c, p. 18).

introduced in April 2008 on the urging of the Chancellor of the Exchequer, enabled banks to borrow Treasury bills against the collateral of existing commercial loans for up to three years. The final drawdown date was originally set at 21 October 2008, but it was extended to 30 January 2009 in the turmoil following the failure of Lehman Brothers in September 2008. The Treasury indemnified the Bank of England against any losses on the SLS, but in fact it made a profit of £2.3 billion, which was paid to the Treasury. In all, £185 billion of Treasury bills were lent. The scheme was terminated, and the loans repaid by the end of January 2012.[37]

In December 2009, the Basel Committee on Banking Supervision proposed new regulations (Basel 3), including higher minimum capital requirements and a new minimum liquidity coverage ratio (LCR) requirement. They were later adopted with little modification. The LCR requirement required commercial banks to hold enough defined high-quality liquid assets (HQLA) to enable them to survive a month in which they had no inflows and suffered maximum plausible outflows of cash. In calculating maximum plausible outflows, prescribed percentages were applied to the total of deposits from the various classes of depositors, for example, individuals, non-financial companies, financial companies, and so on. High-quality liquid assets included both balances at central banks and government securities. The proposals turned into rules with little modification. The banks were to be required to achieve a minimum LCR of 80% by 1 October 2015 and 100% by 1 January 2018.[38] Many banks began far below the regulatory minimum; moreover their access to wholesale deposits was impaired.[39]

Thereafter, financial markets experienced a recurrence, on a smaller scale, of the liquidity squeeze which had taken place during the financial crisis.[40] Commercial banks, other financial

37 Fisher (2009), Darling (2011, p. 94), Winters (2012).

38 Basel Committee on Banking Supervision (2009).

39 Lloyds Banking Group estimated its LCR at the end of 2010 at 71% (Lloyds Banking Group, 2010 results) Other domestic banks do not appear to have reported their LCRs as at that date. For UK banks as a whole, the ratio of reserve balances in the Bank of England plus government securities to deposits increased from 7.3% at the end of 2010 to 13.8% at the end of 2015 (source: Bank of England, author's calculations). This suggests that Lloyds' LCR at the end of 2010 was above average.

40 Allen and Moessner (2012).

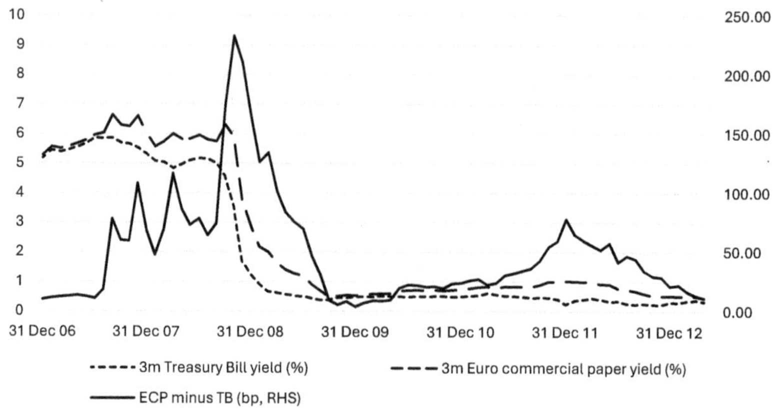

Figure 9.1 The collateral squeeze: the difference between three-month yields on sterling euro-commercial paper and UK Treasury bills, 2006–2013
Source: Bank of England. Data after 2013 are not available.

and non-financial companies, and central banks themselves all participated in a scramble for liquid assets. One indicator of the intensity of the squeeze is the yield differential between three-month sterling euro-commercial paper yields and Treasury bill yields (Figure 9.1). Both the ELTR and the SLS schemes had added to the supply of HQLA, because they provided reserve balances and Treasury bills, respectively, which were HQLA, to the banks in place of commercial debts, which were not. The squeeze was particularly intense in the latter part of 2011, on account of euro-area sovereign debt concerns and the need to repay SLS loans, the last of which fell due at the end of January 2012.[41] The availability of credit to would-be borrowers tightened considerably, as the Bank of England Credit Conditions Survey showed. Some UK banks found it difficult to refinance SLS borrowings, and Winters' review remarked that 'initially the Bank [of England] did not fully think through banks' exit from the SLS, most likely as it did not anticipate bank funding conditions remaining difficult for such an extended period'.[42] The pressure eased after large-scale provision of funds by the European Central Bank for three years against a wide range of collateral in two large operations in December 2011 and January 2012.

[41] Bank of England (2012a, p. 7). [42] Winters (2012, box 6).

Others joined in the scramble for liquid assets:

1. Many financial and non-financial companies increased their own liquid assets, partly as a precaution, and, among other reasons, because committed bank loan and back-up credit facilities had become more expensive as the commitments were subject to the banks' LCR requirements.
2. Financial companies, pressed by regulators to use clearing houses to settle market transactions, needed to hold larger reserves of HQLA to protect themselves against the risk of increases in market price volatility leading to surges in demand from the clearing houses for additional high-quality collateral against their risk positions.
3. There had been a global surge of demand for dollar-denominated liquid assets during the financial crisis, which had been relieved only by the prompt and courageous action of the Federal Reserve in extending its network of swap lines and lending large amounts of dollars to foreign central banks to enable the latter to relieve shortages of dollars in their own territories. Many of them realised that their own dollar reserves would have been insufficient to meet the demand had the Fed not ridden to the rescue, and, fearing that in a future crisis the Fed might not help them, they accumulated additional liquid reserves.[43]

The need for banks to build up their liquidity ratios helps to explain why bank credit contracted by 17.7% between the end of July 2009 and the end of March 2014 while deposits grew. The pressure on the banks eased over time: in December 2015, the Bank of England was able to say that 'Most of the largest UK firms have reported that they already meet the full end-point 100% requirement', and at the end of January 2016, the aggregate LCR of UK banks was 117.57%.[44] Thereafter, credit accelerated (Figure 9.2).

Over the period 2009–2015, when the banks were under regulatory pressure to augment their liquid assets, the amount of HQLA-augmenting credit provided by the Bank of England against privately issued debt initially fell as the £185 billion of SLS loans were repaid and the amount supplied through the ELTR fell back. Between autumn 2012 and the end of 2015, the amount provided partially recovered

[43] Allen and Moessner (2010), Allen (2013, ch. 13.4).
[44] Bank of England (2015, pp. 40–46, and 2018b, chart B5).

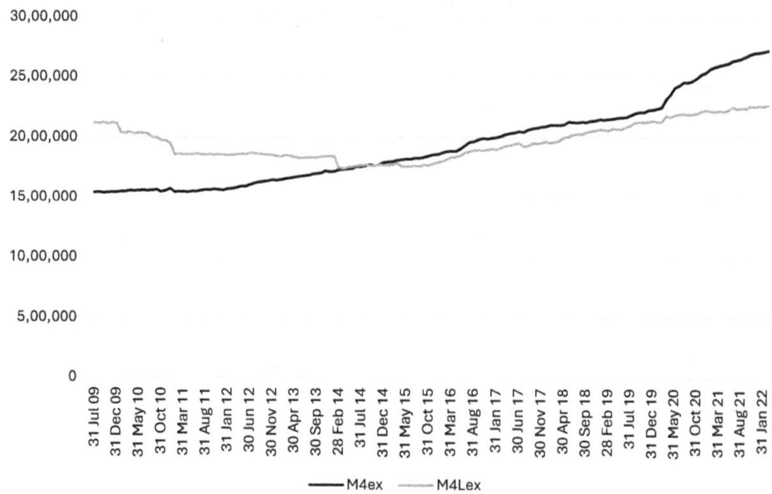

Figure 9.2 M4 excluding deposits of intermediate financial companies, and M4 lending excluding lending to intermediate financial companies (£ millions, seasonally adjusted).

Source: Bank of England. Deposits of, and lending to, intermediate financial companies are excluded from the measures of money and credit because they were thought by the Bank of England to bear little relation to developments in the economy at large.

as £69 billion was lent under the Funding for Lending scheme. The aggregate amount provided through these schemes fell on balance. Quantitative easing did not affect the supply of HQLA, since both gilts and reserve balances at the Bank of England counted as HQLA. The Bank of England thus, on balance, withdrew HQLA from the banking system in 2009–2015. A policy which had aimed at ensuring a fuller supply of HQLA in 2009–2015 would have enabled the banks to meet their LCR requirements without restraining credit so severely and made liquid assets more readily available to other parties.

At the same June 2012 meeting, some MPC members expressed concern about the effects of the LCR requirement and wished for the MPC 'to consider additional policy tools'.[45] In doing so, they implicitly

[45] Bank of England (2012b, paragraphs 28 and 31). The challenge may have been inspired by the actions of the European Central Bank, which had provided nearly €1 trillion in three-year loans to banks in the euro area in early 2012, against a wide range of collateral assets.

challenged the Bank's interpretation of their role. To judge by their public speeches at around that time, those members might have included Deputy Governor Paul Tucker, who expressed concern that liquidity regulation was over-stringent, and non-executive members Adam Posen and Martin Weale, who both expressed support for provision of credit to the private sector.[46]

At the June MPC meeting, 'the Governor informed the Committee that initial discussions were underway with the Treasury on possible measures to ease banks' funding costs and enhance their ability to lend'.[47] Shortly afterwards, the Funding For Lending scheme was announced, which enabled banks to borrow liquid Treasury bills against the security of privately issued debts, with both the price and the quantity provided linked to individual banks' performance in lending to the UK real economy. And in April 2013, the MPC was consulted about, and recorded as having 'supported', the extension of Funding for Lending.[48] While upholding the principle that the MPC had no authority over the Bank of England's asset choice, the Bank of England's executive managers perhaps allowed themselves to be influenced by MPC members' views.

After the Brexit referendum, the MPC wished to stimulate the economy and the Bank displayed greater openness to lending against private debts, in addition to rather than instead of gilt purchases. A new scheme, the Term Funding Scheme (TFS), was set up in August 2016. The peak amount lent was £127 billion, as at the end of February 2018. The minutes of the MPC meeting at which the TFS was discussed were not explicit as to which body had decided on the TFS, but called it a 'monetary policy measure', which put it into the MPC's bailiwick in the terms of the Bank of England Act 1998.[49]

9.4 Monetary Policy during and after the Covid-19 Pandemic

The first financial manifestation of the Covid-19 pandemic was a worldwide surge of offerings of government securities in March 2020, after it had become clear that the pandemic would lead to widespread lockdowns and economic dislocation, and to enlarged

[46] Posen (2012), Tucker (2012) and Weale (2012).
[47] Bank of England (2012b, paragraph 31).
[48] Bank of England (2013, paragraph 26).
[49] Bank of England (2016, paragraph 31, 2017).

government deficits.[50] In the United Kingdom, the gilt-edged market weakened sharply on 18 March, when the recorded twenty-year yield rose from 1.05% to 1.36%, and ceased to function on 19 March after a gilt auction. The DMO feared that it would be unable to sell as many gilts as it needed to without extraordinary support.[51]

The MPC held an emergency meeting that same day. The minutes record that it was convened 'to consider the response of monetary policy to the economic shock from Covid-19', but the immediate trigger was the breakdown in the gilt market.[52] The MPC resolved to buy a further £200 billion of gilts. Its stated objective was to 'improve the functioning of the gilt market and help to counteract a tightening of monetary and financial conditions that would put at risk the MPC's objectives'.[53]

In addition, the Bank introduced a new variant of the TFS with additional incentives for small and medium-sized enterprises. By March 2022, £192 billion had been lent under this scheme. Again the MPC minutes were not explicit about which authority had made the decision.[54] The Goodfriend doctrine had been put aside, but massive gilt purchases were still the main policy instrument.

The functioning of the gilt market was restored by the presence of the Bank of England as a large and regular buyer, and the DMO was able to sustain a very heavy sales programme at historically low yields. The MPC's objectives were to 'help improve the functioning of the gilt market and help to counteract a tightening of monetary and financial conditions that would put at risk the MPC's statutory objectives'.[55] The Bank later claimed to be acting as market maker of last resort, but the claim was misleading.[56] Commercial market makers facilitate trading by quoting bid and offer prices, and achieve price discovery by matching bids and offers over time. Last-resort market makers quote bid prices, or offer prices, or both, when commercial market makers are unable to do so, so as to facilitate price discovery. They buy and sell,

[50] The Bank of England described the episode as a 'dash for cash', but it is possible that the main motivation of the sellers was that the prevailing level of yields was unsustainably low.

[51] Aldrick (2020). [52] Aldrick (2020), Bank of England (2020b, paragraph 1).

[53] Bank of England (2020a, 2020b). That day, 18 March, was the third day of Andrew Bailey's term of office as Governor of the Bank of England. Truly a baptism of fire.

[54] Bank of England (2020a). [55] Bank of England (2020b).

[56] See for example Hauser (2021).

but the Bank of England bought and bought. It suppressed price discovery, rather than facilitating it.

Later, the MPC decided on two further tranches of QE amounting to another £250 billion 'in order to meet the inflation target in the medium term'.[57] The programme ended in December 2021: total bond purchases since 2009 were £895 billion: £875 billion of gilts and £20 billion of privately issued securities.

The MPC did not need to stimulate monetary growth in 2020–2021 as it had done in 2009–2012; by then commercial banks had ample liquid assets, and monetary growth accelerated sharply (Figure 9.2).[58] The MPC's actions in 2020–2021 represented a loose form of yield curve control, which suppressed the market forces that would otherwise have caused yields to rise, but did not include explicit objectives for yields.

Some commentators accused the MPC of conniving in a covert policy of inflating away government debt. It is true that inflation rose sharply after the spring of 2021. But the MPC did not foresee it: its forecasts of inflation in the year 2022 had to be progressively revised upwards (Figure 9.3). And it is inconceivable that the new Governor, during what was his first week in office, would or could have induced the other eight members of the MPC to set aside their statutory price stability objective and to pursue a different, undeclared, objective. There is no reason to doubt the MPC's integrity.

The Bank of England blamed its inflation forecast failures, particularly post-February 2022, on the Russian invasion of Ukraine and its consequences. However the MPC underestimated the risk that inflation would surge when lockdowns ended and pent-up demand was released, after a long period of ultra-expansionary monetary and fiscal policy. In doing so, it ignored the historical evidence of pent-up demand and inflation after the end of major wars, and it assumed too readily that its own credibility would

[57] This phrase was used in the minutes of the MPC meetings of June and November 2020, when further gilt purchases were decided on.

[58] The Bank of Japan has openly embraced yield curve control (Bank of Japan 2016). The Reserve Bank of Australia also embraced it in March 2020 but gave it up in November 2021 (Lucca and Wright 2022, Reserve Bank of Australia 2022). At the beginning of 2020, UK commercial banks held about 1.5 times the minimum amount of HQLA required by the LCR (Bank of England 2020c, p. 46). 'Monetary growth' relates to M4 excluding the deposits of intermediate financial companies. Source: Bank of England.

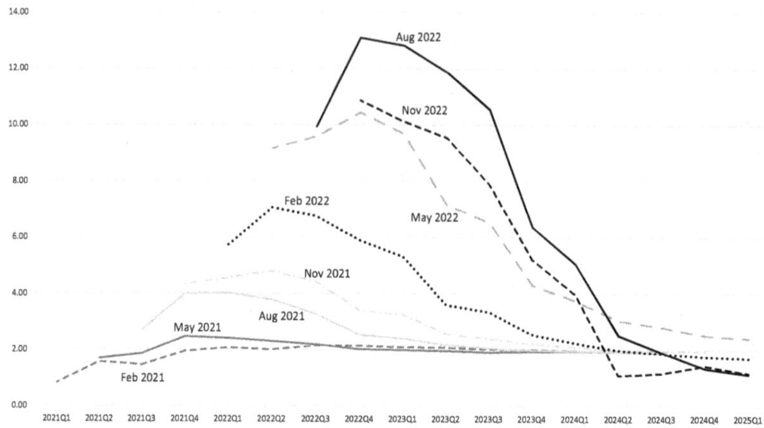

Figure 9.3 Bank of England mean inflation forecasts, February 2021–August 2022 (% p.a.).
Source: Bank of England Monetary Policy Reports, February 2021–November 2022.

keep longer-term inflationary expectations stable. The failure was not confined to the Bank of England: other leading central banks pursued similar policies and made the same mistakes. The post-pandemic inflation surge is prima facie evidence that monetary policy was too loose, and that there was too much QE.

9.5 Unwinding QE

There were several possible reasons for unwinding QE:

1. As a means of tightening monetary policy.
2. To create space to do more QE in case of need.[59]
3. To reduce the sensitivity of the public finances to fluctuations in interest rates, consistent with the risk objective of debt management policy.
4. Democratic accountability. The control of public spending depends on the Treasury, which is directly answerable to Parliament, being in a position to authorise all spending decisions. Asset purchases by the Bank of England are, in a sense, public spending decisions, because the public finances ultimately bear the risks that they

[59] This is the reason given by Ramsden (2023).

carry, but not being subject to Treasury authorisation in the same way, they are an exception to the general rule. The exception is tolerable if the Bank's balance sheet is small, but it becomes increasingly less so as the Bank's balance sheet grows.[60] The willingness of the Treasury to indemnify the Bank of England against the APF's losses gave the Bank of England extraordinary discretion to take such decisions without direct authorisation by Parliament.

The Bank of England, guided by the first two of these considerations, began QT in 2022. The APF's gilt portfolio had an average maturity of about thirteen years and a half-life of about eight years (much longer than that of the Federal Reserve). If it were concluded that the new equilibrium level of banks' reserve balances was, say, £400 billion, and if it had been decided to get reserve balances down from their peak level of £950 billion passively, by not reinvesting the proceeds of maturing assets, the process would have taken thirteen years: it would have been completed in 2035.[61]

The MPC made a very cautious statement about QT in August 2021. It said that it did not intend to use the pace of rundown of the APF's assets as a flexible instrument of monetary policy, but to announce its plans well in advance. It intended to cease reinvesting the proceeds of gilts maturing in its portfolio as soon as Bank rate reached 0.5%, and 'envisages considering beginning the process of actively selling assets only once Bank Rate has risen to at least 1%'.[62] It was implicit that the MPC considered that purely passive unwinding of QE would have taken too long.

Bank rate reached 0.5% in February 2022 and the Bank accordingly ceased reinvestments. In May 2022, when Bank rate rose to 1%, the MPC declared that it would now 'consider beginning' active sales, and in August, the Bank produced a plan, 'for implementation subject to the final approval at the MPC's September meeting'.[63] The plan was to reduce the gilt holdings in APF by about £80 billion in the first year of

60 Allen (2017). QE operations were subject to the Treasury's agreement, but the agreement seems to have been given freely on request.

61 Author's calculation. Hauser (2023) reports that the commercial banks' own estimate, as at November 2023, of their likely demand for reserve balances is in the range £335–495 bn.

62 Bank of England (2021b, box A).

63 Bank of England (2022a). The author previously proposed an operation to reduce the quantity of banks' reserve balances quickly (Allen 2021, Allen,

the programme; after deducting forthcoming redemption receipts, this would involve active sales of £10 billion per quarter.

The implementation of QE had put little strain on the infrastructure of the gilt market and required minimal co-ordination between the Bank of England and the DMO. QE absorbed part of the supply of gilts from the DMO, so that less had to be absorbed by the market. QT, by contrast, added supply from the Bank of England to the supply from the DMO, so that more had to be absorbed by the market. Thus there was more risk of gilt market dysfunction after QE had ended and QT begun.

9.6 The 'Fiscal Event' of September 2022

The inception of active QT sales was delayed by another episode of dysfunction in the gilt-edged market. Prime Minister Liz Truss, who took office on 6 September 2022, had been elected leader of the Conservative party, and thus prime minister, by advocating energy subsidies and tax cuts. These were announced by the new Chancellor of the Exchequer Kwasi Kwarteng on Friday 23 September, who spoke soon afterwards of further tax cuts to come. The DMO's gross gilt sales objective for the financial year 2022/2023 was revised upwards from £131.5 billion to £193.9 billion. Including the active sales that the Bank of England planned as part of QT, gross official sales would increase from roughly £10 billion a month in the first half of the financial year to roughly £25 billion in the second half. The announcement was not however accompanied by a new economic forecast from the Office for Budget Responsibility, which would normally have provided projections of the budget balance and the debt/GDP ratio.

The announcement led to a surge of offers of long-dated gilts, and a weakening of the exchange rate. Quoted yields for thirty-year gilts rose by well over 100 basis points between Thursday 22 and Wednesday 28 September. The offers came mainly from the pension industry. Many

Chadha and Turner 2021). Briefly, the Bank would swap a large proportion of its gilt holdings with the DMO for an equivalent portfolio of short-medium dated gilts which the commercial banks would be willing to hold in their HQLA portfolios. There would then be a very large-scale operation in which the new gilts were sold to the commercial banks in exchange for a large reduction in their reserve balances. A large amount of QT would be done in a single operation. It is not clear that it would have been open to the MPC to consider a proposal of this kind.

defined-benefit pension funds had adopted so-called liability-driven investment (LDI) strategies in order to hedge against fluctuations in the balance between the present values of their assets and liabilities. These strategies included borrowing to increase exposure to long-term gilts, as well as holding riskier and higher-yielding assets such as equities. The means used to implement LDI strategies included investment in specialised LDI funds, set up to offer LDI services to multiple pension funds. As gilt yields increased after the mini-budget, many LDI funds were presented with margin calls which exceeded their liquid asset holdings. Many of them could meet the immediate need only by selling assets: hence the offering of gilts.[64] There was positive (i.e. self-reinforcing) feedback as falls in gilt prices caused further offers.

The Bank of England Financial Policy Committee held an unscheduled meeting on 28 September at which it noted the 'risk to UK financial stability from dysfunction in the gilt market', and 'recommended that action be taken to address it and welcomed the Bank's plan for temporary and targeted purchases in the gilt market on financial stability grounds at an urgent pace'.[65] The use of the word 'dysfunction' implies that the gilt-edged market makers were unable to absorb the gilts that investors wished to sell, and Bank of England Deputy Governor Sir Jon Cunliffe noted that 'liquidity remained very poor'. The Bank was warned on the afternoon of Tuesday 27 September that if yields remained at their current quoted levels, 'multiple LDI funds were likely to fall into negative net asset value' and would need to begin winding up the following morning. The gilts that those funds had posted as collateral for derivative trades with banks were likely to be sold, 'driving a potentially self-reinforcing spiral and threatening severe disruption of core funding markets and consequent widespread financial instability'.[66]

Accordingly, on Wednesday 28 September the Bank of England announced a programme of temporary purchases of long-dated gilts, for a maximum of £5 billion a day for thirteen days beginning that day.[67] On the day of the announcement, quoted long gilt yields fell by more than 100 bp.[68] Total purchases over the thirteen days were £19 billion. They were intended to be temporary, and the Bank announced on 10 November that they would be reversed from 29 November 2022 by

[64] Cunliffe (2022) provides a fuller and very clear explanation.
[65] Bank of England (2022d). [66] Cunliffe (2022).
[67] Bank of England (2022b). [68] Cunliffe (2022).

means of sales made in response to bids from the market.[69] The unwinding was completed on 12 January 2023.

The MPC was informed of the issues in the gilt market and briefed in advance of the purchase operation: the MPC 'wanted this [the purchase operation] to be targeted and temporary so it did not appear to be monetary QE or monetary policy'.[70] Likewise the MPC was informed of the unwinding plan, and 'agreed that the sales would not affect its ability to conduct monetary policy'.[71] However, 'in line with the Bank's governance, the Bank's Executive took the necessary decisions on the planning, design and implementation of the operation'.[72] In other words, and in accordance with the terms of the concordats, the FPC and the MPC did not formally participate, even though the details of the design of operations of this kind can have very important implications for monetary policy and financial stability. And there are no published minutes of meetings of the Bank's Executive, so that the reasons for the decisions need not be disclosed. Perhaps for that reason, Cunliffe sent to the chairman of the House of Commons Treasury Committee a very clear account of what was done, and why.[73]

The temporary purchase programme was a major success, in that it prevented an episode of financial instability. Moreover, it yielded a profit of about £4 billion.[74] The Bank of England was aware of the problems that the rise in yields had caused for the pension industry and reacted to them promptly and decisively. Had it not done so, there would have been financial distress in the pension industry, arising from illiquidity rather than insolvency. Moreover, it is likely that the DMO's selling programme would have been disrupted. Because the operation was reversed fairly quickly, and because its objectives were clear – 'to restore market functioning in long-dated government bonds and reduce risks from contagion to credit conditions for UK households and businesses' – it may be regarded as an example of last-resort market making.[75]

In conducting its purchases, the Bank set reserve prices: an undisclosed 'reserve spread' was

[69] Bank of England (2022f). [70] Bank of England (2022e, Q122).
[71] Bank of England (2022b, 2022f). [72] Cunliffe (2022). [73] Cunliffe (2022).
[74] Author's calculation. [75] Cunliffe (2022).

used to calculate a yield for each bond below which the Bank will not make purchases. The reserve spread is set as a spread (in basis points) to the market mid yield at the end of each auction.[76]

Thus, over the entirety of the programme of temporary purchases, £8.4 billion of offers were rejected. The choice of the market mid yield at the end of each auction as the basis for calculating the lowest acceptable yield for the Bank's purchases was not one which would necessarily serve the Bank's objective. The purpose of last-resort market making is to maintain the liquidity of the market for issuers and investors until the commercial market makers resume normal operations.[77] The market-maker of last resort must set a price, because the market is unable to do so: the Bank of England could not, by definition, be price-neutral by following market pricing. The criterion for choosing the price at which to intervene must be the prospects of restoring two-way trading in the market at the chosen price level. The Bank's explanation of its actions does not, however, mention this criterion. Be that as it may, the Bank set, temporarily, the level of long gilt yields. The operation was an act of monetary policy, debt management, and financial stability policy.

As already noted, the temporary purchases were reversed by sales in response to bids from the market. This represented a step away from the predictability of pre-announced auctions at which all the bonds on offer were to be sold. Some such change was inevitable, in the light of limited market liquidity. Of course, the technique of responding to bids could be employed just as well in selling gilts in QT operations as in reversing the temporary purchases of September–October 2022, though it would depart from the principle of predictability that the MPC embraced in its statements about QT.[78]

9.7 Financial and Monetary Policy Risks of QE, and Governance

9.7.1 *Risks and Losses*

For much of its life, the APF made a mark-to-market profit on the interest rate risks it took; the cumulative profit peaked at the end of

[76] Bank of England (2022c), explained more fully in Anderson et al. (2023, section 5).
[77] Sibert and Buiter (2007), Mehrling (2014, p. 110), Tucker (2014, p. 31).
[78] Bank of England (2021b, box A).

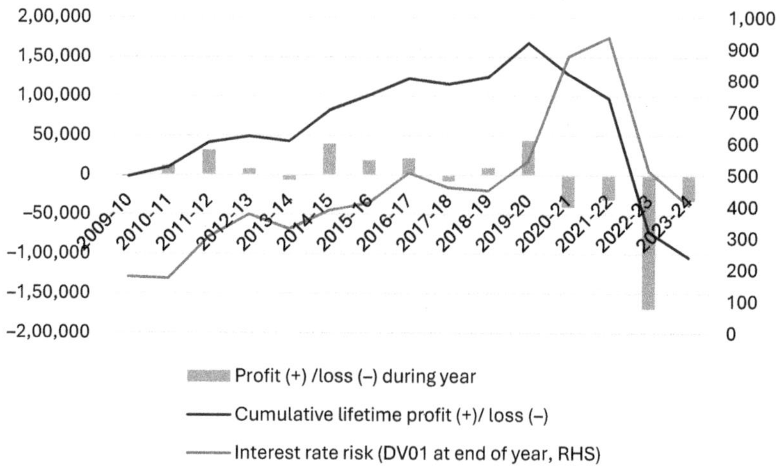

Figure 9.4 Asset purchase facility: mark-to-market profits and losses, and interest rate risk, 2009/10–2023/24 (£ millions).
Source: Bank of England Asset Purchase Facility Annual Reports. The cumulative mark-to-market profits and losses are calculated from the annual changes in the fair value of the Treasury's indemnity, reported each year in the notes to the accounts. Data are for years ending at the end of February. DV01 is the loss in value of the APF's assets in the event of a 1 basis point rise in the yield curve.

February 2020. During the Covid-19 pandemic, as the APF's assets grew and yields fell, the APF's exposure to interest rate risk soared. After the pandemic, as interest rates rose, the APF made a very heavy mark-to-market loss in 2022–2023, and its cumulative mark-to-market profit turned into a loss (Figure 9.4).

As at 29 February 2024 the cumulative mark-to-market losses were £104 billion, or about 3.5% of GDP. The final outcome will not be certain until the APF has been wound up, but it seems very likely, for example, that the £507 billion of gilts purchased in March 2020–December 2021, when even thirty-year yields never exceeded 1.5%, will show a big loss. The losses of the APF have received remarkably little public attention, even though other central banks have lost money in the same way.[79]

[79] For example, the House of Lords Economic Affairs Committee (2023) in its report on 'Making an independent Bank of England work better' discusses the risks to the public finances, but not the losses.

The scale of the mark-to-market losses reflected the long maturities of many of the gilts that the Bank purchased, which in some cases extended to nearly fifty years. At the end of the QE programme, in December 2021, the average modified duration of the APF portfolio was 11.4 years and the DV01 was about £1 billion. The average modified duration of the gilts bought during QE4 (i.e. post-March 2020) was 12.1 years. As a rough comparison, the average modified duration of US Treasury securities purchased by the Fed during QE4, as at the end of March 2022 when the Fed's QE programme had ended, was 6.2 years, and their DV01 proportionately smaller relative to the scale of their purchases. Thus the Fed's mark-to-market losses on government securities, relative to the scale of its purchases, will have been much smaller than the Bank of England's.[80]

9.7.2 Governance

It is a basic principle of financial management that someone identifiable should be responsible whenever a risk is taken or a debt incurred. However, identifying who was responsible for the QE risks and losses is not straightforward. All the operations were indemnified and authorised by the Treasury, which bears an obvious responsibility. However, in 2016 Bank of England Governor Mark Carney reassured the Chancellor of the Exchequer Philip Hammond that 'the risk management framework between the Bank and the Treasury – under which the Bank is responsible for managing the risks in the APF – will remain in place'.[81] More recently, the Bank of England Independent Evaluation Office affirmed that 'The Bank risk manages the APF on behalf of HMT [HM Treasury]'.[82] The meaning of the Bank's statements is obscure, since the indemnity issued by the Treasury is the practical expression of its acceptance of responsibility for the risks.

The Treasury further confused the issue. When asked about the loss by the House of Commons Public Accounts Committee in December 2023, its permanent secretary, James Bowler, replied:

[80] Sources: author's calculation – duration of APF assets; Levin, Lu and Nelson (2022) – duration of Fed assets; their calculation uses a discount factor of 2.5%.
[81] Carney – Hammond, 4 August 2016, www.bankofengland.co.uk/-/media/boe/files/letter/2016/governor-apf-letter-040816.pdf.
[82] Bank of England Independent Evaluation Office (2021, p. 9).

quantitative easing and quantitative tightening are part of monetary policy, so they are decided entirely and rightly by the Bank of England ... As the Monetary Policy Committee sets interest rates each month, it is looking at the interest rate – it sets the bank rate – and at what to do, periodically, in quantitative tightening ... That is entirely independent from me and the Treasury, and it is right that we leave the committee to decide on that independently.[83]

However, in a later letter to the chair of the House of Commons Treasury Committee, Bowler said that 'Each decision to increase the maximum authorized size of the APF is accompanied by an assessment of the macroeconomic and fiscal impacts, and an assessment against the framework for Managing Public Money'.[84]

As to the Bank of England, the court and executive managers, which Carney said took responsibility for managing the risks in the APF, appear to have done nothing to contain them.[85] The MPC, for its part, 'does not take into account financial profit or loss when taking monetary policy decisions, including about the APF gilt portfolio'.[86] But the MPC does not seem to have considered the risk that the financial losses of the QE programme might threaten the price stability objective of monetary policy. The condition for the public finances to remain stable is that debt/national income ratio should not rise without limit. In other words, the term Δd_t in the equation:

$$\Delta d_t = \Big((r-g)/(1-g)\Big) d_{t-1} - p_t$$

should be currently or prospectively negative, where:

d_t is the government debt/national income ratio at the end of period t;
r is the average interest rate on government debt;
g is the growth rate of nominal national income;
and p_t is the primary budget surplus (i.e. the surplus before deduction of interest payments) during period t.[87]

[83] Evidence to the Public Accounts Committee, 7 December 2003, Q43, https://committees.parliament.uk/event/19465/formal-meeting-oral-evidence-session/. Mr Bowler was not the permanent secretary of the Treasury at any time when the Treasury consented to QE.

[84] Bowler – Baldwin, 15 December 2023, https://committees.parliament.uk/work/7261/quantitative-tightening/publications/3/correspondence/.

[85] This is based on the court minutes up to October 2021. The minutes of later meetings had not been published at the time of writing.

[86] Ramsden (2023). [87] See, e.g. Blanchard (2022, ch. 4).

The drastic shortening in the maturity of the government debt, which is the essence of QE, meant that the average interest rate paid by the government (r) increased far more quickly when Bank rate was increased than it otherwise would have done.[88] It accordingly made it harder for the stability condition to be met, and more likely that the public finances would become unsustainable. If that were to happen, monetary policy would become dominated by fiscal policy, inflation would rise and monetary policy would be unable to subdue it.[89] Sustainable public finances are a necessary condition for price stability. The MPC is responsible for price stability and was wrong to ignore the profit and loss aspects of its decisions.

The National Audit Office audited the annual accounts of the APF from 2016/2017 onwards. It reported the interest rate risk exposure routinely, but if it felt any unease about it, it did not say so publicly.

All the parties directly involved seemed unconcerned about interest rate risk.[90] The Treasury subordinated the objectives of debt management to those of monetary policy without, it seems, considering whether any less financially risky monetary policy might achieve the same objective or better.

9.7.3 *Was There Any Alternative?*

Yet a combination of more lending secured by privately issued debts and fewer purchases of gilts might have produced a better macroeconomic outcome in 2009–2015 (section 3). In the period when gilt purchases were heaviest, in 2020–2021, fewer gilt purchases would almost certainly have produced a better outcome (less post-pandemic inflation).[91] And purchasing shorter maturity gilts throughout 2009–2021 would have meant smaller losses. As it is, the APF's mark-to-market losses currently exceed £100 billion, which is about 10% of gilt purchases. This is much greater than any plausible loss that might have been made on loans against the same quantity of private debts.

[88] The mark-to-market losses incurred by the QE programme consist of the present value of the additional interest costs resulting from QE and the net capital losses resulting from the differences between the purchase prices of the bonds in the APF and their redemption values.

[89] Sargent and Wallace (1981), Allen, Chadha and Turner (2021).

[90] The insouciance was not universal: see Office for Budget Responsibility (2021).

[91] House of Lords Economic Affairs Committee (2021).

As noted in Section 9.3.2, the SLS made a profit in 2008–2012. Even in 2009, the worst year of the financial crisis, UK banks' net provisions for bad and doubtful debts were lower than 0.75% of their total lending to the private sector and non-residents, and the average over 2009–2021 was 0.19%.[92] Moreover the Bank of England would have had recourse to the borrowing bank in cases where the ultimate borrower defaulted, and could have avoided interest rate risk by taking assets as collateral for short-term or floating interest rate loans.

However, loans against privately issued assets could not have cured the dysfunction of the gilt-edged market caused by the Covid-19 pandemic in March 2020. The September 2022 episode, caused by what investors regarded as a reckless easing of fiscal policy, showed how intervention by the Bank of England on a limited scale could maintain market functioning. A limited operation would have been harder to manage in the circumstances of March 2020 because the cause of the dysfunction could not be readily removed or alleviated, whereas in September 2022 the speedy reversal of the fiscal easing enabled the Bank's temporary purchases to be unwound at a profit. However, no attempt was made in 2020 or 2021 to help the market discover a level of yields at which two-way trading could be resumed without official support. It is inconceivable that official gilt purchases of anything like as much as £450 billion (the amount of gilts bought in QE operations from March 2020 onwards) would have been needed to restore two-way trading, and it is possible that a limited operation would have yielded a profit rather than a loss.

In sum, there are good reasons to think that monetary policy could have been conducted satisfactorily without running such large financial risks.

9.8 Conclusions

The model of central banking which the United Kingdom adopted in 1997 worked well until the global financial crisis. Thereafter, the lines of demarcation between monetary policy, financial stability and government debt management became blurred, and it worked less well. The statutory division of governance within the Bank of England

[92] Source: Bank of England database, author's calculations.

between monetary policy (MPC), financial stability policy (FPC), prudential supervision (Prudential Regulation Committee: PRC) and financial market operations (Bank executive) became outdated and obstructed good decision-making. Considerable efforts were made to co-ordinate the various functions, notably by means of the 'concordats', but the results were unsatisfactory, in several ways.[93] First, it was absurd for the Bank of England executives to claim that the decision about what assets to purchase was nothing to do with monetary policy, and not to allow the MPC a formal say in it. Second, the decision made by the Bank of England executives to concentrate asset purchases on gilts, which was extremely financially risky for the government, was not adequately debated or explained to the public.

Third, the way in which unexpected events are triaged – in other words assigned for attention to the MPC, the FPC or the Bank executive – is both important and opaque. In both March 2020 and September 2022, the gilt-edged market became dysfunctional, in that there was a plethora of offers and no bids, and the price discovery mechanism ceased to function. The problem was addressed in March 2020 by the MPC and in September 2022 by the FPC and the Bank executives. The assignments must have depended on some prior assessment by the Bank executives of the causes of the dysfunctions, but the assessment was not explained in either case.

The Bank of England has evidently recognised the need for some change. In September 2023 it replaced the concordats of 2017–2018 with a new statement, 'Governance of the Bank of England's balance sheet: principles of engagement'.[94] This document recognises the interests of the MPC, the FPC and the PRC in the Bank's financial operations and balance sheet, and acknowledges that they may be consulted about financial operations, but reiterates that the Court remains responsible for the risk profile of the balance sheet. In the event of a conflict that cannot be resolved by co-ordination within the Bank of England executive management, cross-membership of committees or in any other way, the Governor is to consult the chair of the Court about the process to be followed to resolve it. The new document recognises the possibility of uncertainty about the allocation of power and responsibility among the various

93 Kohn (2017) describes instances of co-ordination which are not described in this chapter.

94 Bank of England (2022a and b).

organs of the Bank. The new principles might have made a difference if they had been in force in 2008–2021, but their effectiveness depends on people who are charged with meeting particular statutory objectives being able to compromise with other people who are charged with meeting other statutory objectives. Such compromises might be elusive in an emergency.

Looking ahead, the 1997 model of central banking is likely to be further strained. Thus far, the FPC and the MPC have had the luxury of being able to plan their meeting timetables in advance: emergency meetings have been rare. Governments need to finance large deficits and refunding programmes while QT is in progress. In the future the need for market intervention is likely to recur, and more decisions will have to be made when market conditions demand it, and not necessarily when a meeting is scheduled. The Bank of England had worked on an 'financial stability asset purchase tool' and the preparations were 'at an advanced stage' by autumn 2022; nevertheless the fact that its staff had to work overnight on 27 September 2022 suggests that the plan was not ready then.[95] Any plan would require close collaboration between the Bank of England and the DMO. For example, there would need to be understandings with the DMO about which agency was to be responsible for determining the prices at which they would underwrite or cut off gilt auctions, if there were not enough bids from investors. And if market conditions suggested that it might be desirable to cancel auctions, it would obviously be necessary for the DMO and the Bank of England to make consistent decisions.[96] In the wise words of James Tobin, 'There is no neat way to separate monetary policy from debt management'.[97] Attempts to ignore this fact will not end well.

References

Aldrick, P. (2020), 'The day the financial world stood still', and 'Bank of England rode to government's rescue as gilt markets froze', interview with Sir Robert Stheeman, *The Times*, 30 April 2020.

Allen, W. A. (2013), *International liquidity and the financial crisis*, Cambridge University Press, Cambridge.

[95] Anderson et al. (2023, p. 33).

[96] The House of Lords Economic Affairs Committee (2023, p. 52) recommended that the Bank of England and the DMO draw up a memorandum of understanding.

[97] Tobin (1963, p. 148).

Allen, W. A. (2017), 'Quantitative easing and the independence of the Bank of England', National Institute Economic Review, no. 241, pp. R65–R69.

Allen, W. A. (2021), 'Managing the fiscal risk of higher interest rates', NIESR Policy Paper 25, 26 March, www.niesr.ac.uk/publications/managing-fiscal-risk-higher-interest-rates?type=policy-papers.

Allen, W. A. and R. Moessner (2010), 'Options for meeting the demand for international liquidity during financial crises', Bank for International Settlements Quarterly Review, September, pp. 51–61, www.bis.org/publ/qtrpdf/r_qt1009.htm.

Allen, W. A. and R. Moessner (2012), 'The international propagation of the financial crisis of 2008 and a comparison with 1931', *Financial History Review*, vol. 19, no. 2, pp. 123–147.

Allen, W. A., J. S. Chadha and P. Turner (2021), 'Quantitative tightening: protecting monetary policy from fiscal encroachment', NIESR policy paper 27, 28 July, www.niesr.ac.uk/publications/quantitative-tightening-protecting-monetary-policy-fiscal-encroachment?type=policy-papers.

Anderson, P., R. Fakhoury, T. Horn, W. Panjwani and M. Roberts-Sklar (2023), 'Financial stability buy/sell tools: a gilt market case study', Bank of England Quarterly Bulletin, 20 November, www.bankofengland.co.uk/quarterly-bulletin/2023/2023/financial-stability-buy-sell-tools-a-gilt-market-case-study.

Bank of England (2008), Minutes of Monetary Policy Committee meeting, May, www.bankofengland.co.uk/minutes/2008/monetary-policy-committee-may-2008.

Bank of England (2009a), Minutes of Monetary Policy Committee meeting, February, www.bankofengland.co.uk/minutes/2009/monetary-policy-committee-february-2009.

Bank of England (2009b), Minutes of meeting of Committee of non-executive directors (NEDCO), 12 February, www.bankofengland.co.uk/news/2015/january/court-minutes-2007-2009.

Bank of England (2009c), Minutes of Monetary Policy Committee meeting, March, www.bankofengland.co.uk/minutes/2009/monetary-policy-committee-march-2009.

Bank of England (2009d), 'Markets and operations', Quarterly Bulletin, Q2, pp. 68–87, www.bankofengland.co.uk/quarterly-bulletin/2009/q2/markets-and-operations-2009-q2.

Bank of England (2009e), 'Markets and operations', Quarterly Bulletin, Q3, pp. 154–175, www.bankofengland.co.uk/quarterly-bulletin/2009/q3/markets-and-operations-2009-q3.

Bank of England (2010), Bank of England Asset Purchase Facility Fund Ltd. Annual Report 2009/2010, www.bankofengland.co.uk/-/media/boe/files/asset-purchase-facility/2010/annual-report-2010.pdf.

Bank of England (2011), Minutes of Monetary Policy Committee meeting, October, www.bankofengland.co.uk/minutes/2011/monetary-policy-committee-october-2011.

Bank of England (2012a), 'Markets and operations', Bank of England Quarterly Bulletin, 2012Q1.

Bank of England (2012b), Minutes of Monetary Policy Committee meeting, June, www.bankofengland.co.uk/minutes/2012/monetary-policy-committee-june-2012.

Bank of England (2012c), Annual Report, www.bankofengland.co.uk/annual-report/2012.

Bank of England (2013), Minutes of Monetary Policy Committee meeting, May, www.bankofengland.co.uk/minutes/2013/monetary-policy-committee-may-2013.

Bank of England (2015), Financial stability report, December, www.bankofengland.co.uk/financial-stability-report/2015/december-2015.

Bank of England (2016), Minutes of Monetary Policy Committee meeting, August, www.bankofengland.co.uk/monetary-policy-summary-and-minutes/2016/mpc-august-2016.

Bank of England (2017), Bank of England Asset Purchase Facility Fund Limited Annual Report and Accounts, 1 March 2016–28 February 2017, www.bankofengland.co.uk/asset-purchase-facility/2017/2016-17.

Bank of England (2018a), 'The MPC and the Bank's Sterling Monetary Framework', updated June 2018, www.bankofengland.co.uk/-/media/boe/files/about/mpc/the-mpc-and-the-banks-sterling-monetary-framework.pdf.

Bank of England (2018b), Financial stability report, June, www.bankofengland.co.uk/financial-stability-report/2018/june-2018.

Bank of England (2020a), Minutes of Monetary Policy Committee meeting, 10 March, www.bankofengland.co.uk/monetary-policy-summary-and-minutes/2020/13march-2020.

Bank of England (2020b), Minutes of the special Bank of England Monetary Policy Committee meeting on 19 March 2020 and the Monetary Policy Committee meeting ending on 25 March 2020, www.bankofengland.co.uk/monetary-policy-summary-and-minutes/2020/march-2020.

Bank of England (2020c), Financial stability report, August, www.bankofengland.co.uk/report/2020/monetary-policy-report-financial-stability-report-august-2020.

Bank of England (2021a), Bank of England Asset Purchase Facility Fund Limited Annual Report and Accounts, 1 March 2020–28 February 2021, www.bankofengland.co.uk/asset-purchase-facility/2021/2020-21.

Bank of England (2021b), Monetary Policy report, August, www.bankofengland.co.uk/monetary-policy-report/2021/august-2021.

Bank of England (2022a), 'Asset purchase facility: gilt sales – provisional market notice 4 August 2022', www.bankofengland.co.uk/markets/market-notices/2022/august/asset-purchase-facility-gilt-sales-provisional-market-notice-4-august-2022.

Bank of England (2022b), 'Bank of England announces gilt market operation', 28 September, www.bankofengland.co.uk/news/2022/september/bank-of-england-announces-gilt-market-operation.

Bank of England (2022c), 'Gilt market operations – market notice 10 October 2022', www.bankofengland.co.uk/markets/market-notices/2022/october/gilt-market-operations-market-notice-10-october-2022.

Bank of England (2022d), 'Financial policy summary and record', 12 October, www.bankofengland.co.uk/financial-policy-summary-and-record/2022/october-2022.

Bank of England (2022e), Oral evidence to House of Commons Treasury Committee, 19 October, https://committees.parliament.uk/committee/158/treasury-committee/publications/oral-evidence/?SearchTerm=Bank+of+England&DateFrom=03%2F10%2F2022&DateTo=30%2F11%2F2022&SessionId=.

Bank of England (2022f), 'Bank of England sets out plans for a demand-led approach to unwind recent financial stability gilt purchases in a timely but orderly way', 10 November 2022, www.bankofengland.co.uk/news/2022/november/boe-demand-led-approach-to-unwind-recent-financial-stability-gilt-purchases.

Bank of England (2023a), 'Governance of the Bank of England's balance sheet: principles of engagement', www.bankofengland.co.uk/about/governance-and-funding/principles-of-engagement.

Bank of England (2023b), 'Minutes of the meeting of the Court of Directors held on 22 September 2023', www.bankofengland.co.uk/minutes/2023/september/court-september-2023.

Bank of EnglandIndependent Evaluation Office (2021), IEO evaluation of the Bank of England's approach to quantitative easing, www.bankofengland.co.uk/independent-evaluation-office/ieo-report-january-2021/ieo-evaluation-of-the-bank-of-englands-approach-to-quantitative-easing.

Bank of Japan (2016) 'New framework for strengthening monetary easing: "quantitative and qualitative monetary easing with yield curve control"', 21 September, www.boj.or.jp/en/mopo/outline/qqe.htm/.

Basel Committee on Banking Supervision (2009), 'Consultative document: International framework for liquidity risk measurement, standards and monitoring', December, www.bis.org/publ/bcbs165.htm.

Bean, C. (2009), 'Quantitative easing: an interim report', speech given at the London Society of Chartered Accountants Annual Lunch, London,

13 October, www.bankofengland.co.uk/speech/2009/quantitative-easing-and-interim-report.

Blanchard, O. (2022), *Fiscal policy under low interest rates*. MIT Press, Cambridge, MA, https://fiscal-policy-under-low-interest-rates.pubpub.org/pub/cjlwfw6d.

Breedon, F. and P. Turner (2016), 'On the transactions costs of quantitative easing', BIS working paper no. 571, www.bis.org/publ/work571.htm.

Cassar, D. (2023), 'Economics as intervention: expert struggles over quantitative easing at the Bank of England', Socio-Economic Review, mwad060. https://doi.org/10.1093/ser/mwad060.

Chrystal, K. A. (1999), *Government debt structure and monetary conditions: a conference organised by the Bank of England 18–19 June 1998*, Bank of England, London.

Churm, R., A. Radia, J. Leake, S. Srinivasan and R. Whisker (2012), 'The Funding for Lending Scheme', Bank of England Quarterly Bulletin, pp. 306–320, www.bankofengland.co.uk/quarterly-bulletin/2012/q4/the-funding-for-lending-scheme.

Cunliffe, J. (2022), letter to Mel Stride, MP, chairman of the House of Commons Treasury Committee, 5 October, https://committees.parliament.uk/committee/158/treasury-committee/publications/3/correspondence/.

Darling, A. (2009), letter to Governor of the Bank of England, 3 March, www.bankofengland.co.uk/letter/2009/apf-letter-march-2009.

Darling, A. (2011), *Back from the brink: 1,000 days at number 11*, Atlantic Books, London.

Debt Management Office (2005), Framework document, www.dmo.gov.uk/media/14536/fwork040405.pdf.

Debt Management Office (2022), 'Revision to the DMO financing remit 2022–23', www.dmo.gov.uk/responsibilities/financing-remit/full-details/.

Deutsche Bundesbank (2021), 'Government finances: central bank bond purchases increase sensitivity to interest rate changes', Monthly Review, June, www.bundesbank.de/resource/blob/869132/3334c76b68c8f8a08675f238e50f211c/mL/2021-06-staatsfinanzen-data.pdf.

Feldstein, M. (2007), 'Concluding remarks' at the Federal Reserve Bank of Kansas City Jackson Hole Economic Policy Symposium, www.kansascityfed.org/research/jackson-hole-economic-symposium/housing-housing-finance-and-monetary-policy/.

Fisher, P. (2009), 'The Bank of England's balance sheet: monetary policy and liquidity provision during the financial crisis', 19 November, www.bankofengland.co.uk/speech/2009/the-bank-of-englands-balance-sheet.

Goodfriend, M. (2011), 'Central banking in the credit turmoil: an assessment of Federal Reserve practice', *Journal of Monetary Economics*, vol. 58, no. 1, pp. 1–12.

Goodhart, C. A. E. and R. M. Lastra (2020), 'Equity finance: matching liability to power', *Journal of Financial Regulation*, vol. 6, pp. 1–40.

Hauser, A. (2021), 'From lender of last resort to market maker of last resort via the dash for cash: why central banks need new tools for dealing with market dysfunction', speech at Reuters, London, 7 January, www.bankofengland.co.uk/speech/2021/january/andrew-hauser-speech-at-thomson-reuters-newsmaker.

Hauser, A. (2023), '"Less is more" or "less is a bore"? Re-calibrating the role of central bank reserves', speech to Kings College London's Bank of England Watchers' Conference, 3 November 2023, www.bankofengland.co.uk/speech/2023/november/andrew-hauser-keynote-speech-bank-of-england-watchers-conference.

HM Treasury, Bank of England and Financial Services Authority (2007), 'News release: liquidity support facility for Northern Rock plc', 14 September, www.bankofengland.co.uk/news/2007/september/liquidity-support-facility-for-northern-rock-plc.

House of Commons Treasury Committee (2012), 'Bank of England November 2011 Inflation Report: oral and written evidence', HC 1675, https://publications.parliament.uk/pa/cm201012/cmselect/cmtreasy/1675/1675.pdf.

House of Commons Treasury Committee (2024), Quantitative tightening, 5th report of session 2023–2024, https://committees.parliament.uk/committee/158/treasury-committee/publications/.

House of Lords Economic Affairs Committee (2021), Quantitative easing: a dangerous addiction?, 1st report of Session 2021–22, https://committees.parliament.uk/publications/6725/documents/71894/default/.

House of Lords Economic Affairs Committee (2023), Making an independent Bank of England work better, 1st report of Session 2023–24, https://committees.parliament.uk/publications/42289/documents/210238/default/.

James, H. (2020), *Making a modern central bank: the Bank of England 1979–2003*, Cambridge University Press, Cambridge.

John, S., M. Roberts and O. Weeken (2012), 'The Bank of England's Special Liquidity Scheme', Bank of England Quarterly Bulletin, www.bankofengland.co.uk/quarterly-bulletin/2012/q1/the-bank-of-englands-special-liquidity-scheme.

King, M. A. (2011), speech to the Institute of Directors, St George's Hall, Liverpool, 18 October, www.bankofengland.co.uk/speech/2011/speech-by-mervyn-king-to-the-institute-of-directors-st-georges-hall-liverpool.

Kohn, D. L. (2017), 'Co-operation and co-ordination across policy domains', speech at joint Financial Stability Institute and Bank for International Settlements conference on supervisory policy implementation in the current macro-financial environment, Basel, 19 September, www.bankofengland.co.uk/speech/2017/cooperation-and-coordination-across-policy-domains.

Levin, A., B. Lu and W. Nelson, (2022), 'Quantifying the costs and benefits of quantitative easing', NBER working paper 30749.

Lucca, D. O. and J. H. Wright, (2022), 'The narrow channel of quantitative easing: evidence from YCC down under', Federal Reserve Bank of New York Staff Reports no. 1013, April, www.newyorkfed.org/research/staff_reports/sr1013.

McLaren, N., R. Banerjee and D. Latto (2014), 'Using changes in auction maturity sectors to help identify the impact of QE on gilt yields', *Economic Journal*, vol. 124, pp. 453–479.

Mehrling, P. (2014), 'Why central banking should be reimagined' in Bank for International Settlements, Rethinking the lender of last resort, BIS papers no. 79, pp. 108–118, www.bis.org/publ/bppdf/bispap79.pdf.

National Audit Office (2023), Managing government borrowing, Value for money reports, www.nao.org.uk/reports/managing-government-borrowing/#downloads.

Office for Budget Responsibility (2021), *Fiscal Risks Report*, Office for Budget Responsibility, London, https://obr.uk/frr/fiscal-risks-report-july-2021/.

Plenderleith, I. (2012), 'Review of the Bank of England's provision of emergency liquidity assistance in 2008–09', presented to the Court of the Bank of England, October, www.bankofengland.co.uk/-/media/boe/files/news/2012/november/the-provision-of-emergency-liquidity-assistance-in-2008-9.

Posen, A. (2009), 'Getting credit flowing: a non-monetarist approach to quantitative easing', speech given at the Dean's lecture series, Cass Business School, London, 26 October, www.bankofengland.co.uk/speech/2009/getting-credit-flowing-a-non-monetarist-approach-to-quantitative-easing.

Posen, A. (2012), 'Making the most of doing more', speech to the Barclays 'Short end rates seminar', London, 11 June, www.bankofengland.co.uk/speech/2012/making-the-most-of-doing-more.

Ramsden, D. (2023), 'Quantitative tightening: the story so far', speech given at the Bank of England, 19 July, www.bankofengland.co.uk/speech/2023/july/dave-ramsden-speech-on-quantitative-tightening-chaired-by-money-macro-and-finance-society.

Reserve Bank of Australia (2022), Review of the yield target, www.rba.gov.au/monetary-policy/reviews/yield-target/index.html.

Sargent, T. J. and N. Wallace (1981), 'Some unpleasant monetarist arithmetic', Federal Reserve Bank of Minneapolis Quarterly Review, Fall.

Sibert, A. and W. Buiter (2007), 'The central bank as the market maker of last resort: from lender of last resort to market maker of last resort', CEPR VoxEu column, 13 August, https://cepr.org/voxeu/columns/central-bank-market-maker-last-resort-lender-last-resort-market-maker-last-resort.

Tobin, J. (1963), 'An essay on principles of debt management' in *Commission on money and credit: Fiscal and debt management policies*, Prentice-Hall, Englewood Cliffs, NJ.

Tucker, P. (2012), 'Property booms, stability and policy', speech at the Investment Property Forum's Alastair Ross Goobey Memorial Lecture, 12 June, www.bankofengland.co.uk/speech/2012/property-booms-stability-and-policy.

Tucker, P. (2014), 'The lender of last resort and modern central banking' in Bank for International Settlements, Rethinking the lender of last resort, BIS papers no. 79, pp. 10–42, www.bis.org/publ/bppdf/bispap79.pdf.

Weale, M. (2012), 'Monetary policy: navigating rough waters', speech at the Hart Brown 8th Annual Economic Forum, University of Surrey, Guildford, 21 June, www.bankofengland.co.uk/speech/2012/monetary-policy-navigating-rough-waters.

Winters, B. (2012), 'Review of the Bank of England's framework for providing liquidity to the banking system', Bank of England, https://elischolar.library.yale.edu/ypfs-documents/8404/.

Index

For EU product safety concerns, contact us at Calle de José Abascal, 56–1°, 28003 Madrid, Spain or eugpsr@cambridge.org.

www.ingramcontent.com/pod-product-compliance
Ingram Content Group UK Ltd.
Pitfield, Milton Keynes, MK11 3LW, UK
UKHW010902150626
472204UK00010BC/465

* 9 7 8 1 0 0 9 7 4 2 2 9 0 *